Thrown Away Children: Billy's Story

Thrown Away Children: Billy's Story

By Louise Allen
with Theresa McEvoy

WELBECK

Published by Welbeck
An imprint of Welbeck Non-Fiction Limited,
part of Welbeck Publishing Group.
Based in London and Sydney
www.welbeckpublishing.com

First published by Welbeck in 2022

A CIP catalogue record for this book is available from the British Library

ISBN
Paperback – 978-1-80279-118-1

Typeset by Roger Walker
Printed in Great Britain by CPI Books, Chatham, Kent

10 9 8 7 6 5 4 3 2 1

Every reasonable effort has been made to trace copyright holders of material
produced in this book, but if any have been inadvertently overlooked the
publishers would be glad to hear from them.

Foreword

Thank you for reading about a thrown away child. *Another* thrown away child. There are so many of them, but these are important stories that need to be told. Billy is one more marginalised child in my long foster care history who deserves to be loaned a voice and listened to. I am privileged to work with children, and I learn something from every child I encounter. I learned a great deal from Billy's story. Perhaps you will, too.

This was a tough story to write. I feel as though I say that every time, that I repeat myself over and over with each story in the series, but this was one of the hardest. Even after all I have experienced in the world of foster care, I can still be shocked by the grotesqueness of human nature, and the warped adult behaviour that is exhibited towards children in particular. Perhaps this is the worst I have written about so far.

Billy Blackthorn, as you are about to discover, was born into a family that existed, somehow, outside the law. Not in the American Wild West in the 1800s, but in suburban Britain in the 2000s. Their lawlessness was allowed to flourish. One family name – Blackthorn – became synonymous with an entire housing estate. A whole network of streets became a 'no go' area for the rest of the community. Families who weren't connected to them but moved onto the Blackthorn estate soon found a way to move out again, anxious not to become tainted by proximity. A cycle, lasting many years, was started. Within that context, multiple crimes were committed – including crimes against children.

The anarchy exhibited by the Blackthorns went unchallenged for years. Perhaps it was thought to be best for everyone if it was left that way.

Everyone except the children.

Did key individuals make themselves complicit in the abuse and neglect of our children by doing nothing?

You be the judge.

The cases I reveal in my books are all based on true experiences, but I have changed names and some details to protect their identities as they go on to build new lives and families of their own.

PART ONE:
Before

I. Jade

'Ketchup?'

Bobby is much closer to the ketchup bottle than Jade is, but it is Jade who heaves herself up from the sofa in response to the summons. Standing, she arches her back, rubbing her hands up and down in the hollow. Next she circles her shoulders and breathes out a deep sigh as she tries to loosen the cramped muscles there.

'Did you hear me?'

'Coming.' Jade moves past Bobby towards the cupboard, finds the ketchup bottle and places it on the table in front of him.

There is a grunt of acknowledgement.

Instead of sitting straight back down, she decides that she might as well 'go' now she's up. Jade feels the urge to wee almost constantly these days. The end of the final trimester is always tough. She squeezes past the table, intending to head down the hallway to the loo.

This time round she is the size of a walrus – or at least that's what it feels like. And there are still a couple of weeks to go until the due date, supposedly. It's as if her body, so familiar with the stretching and distortion required to house a baby for nine months, has assumed the dimensions in advance of needing to. She slides her hands around to the front of her bump where, although she can't feel them through her kitten-patterned pyjamas, she knows that the stretch marks are. She got away with it after the first baby, Jazz, left her flesh intact, but the little silvery slithers appeared across her stomach when Silver was born, and they've only gotten worse with number three growing inside.

Bobby, sitting at the table with a copy of *Sporting Life*, lets out a belch as she passes. He has finished up his full English and pushes the plate away from him. There is nothing left on the plate except patches of grease and a slither of fatty bacon rind.

'Better out than in,' he says, winking at Jade.

He applies the phrase indiscriminately, to babies as well as belches and farts.

Jade isn't so sure. The little man she carries inside is safe. For now.

But she knows that she won't be able to protect him once he's outside the womb. In some ways it's probably for the best that the foetus has already been assigned a social worker. The official line with the authorities is that the social worker is necessary because of Jade's age, but that's ridiculous. She's 16 and knows exactly what to do: the first two births were straightforward. Women have been doing this for centuries. Probably longer. Anyway, the social worker, whoever it is, won't hang around long. They never do. No, the real reason she feels anxious, Jade knows, is because of the world she is bringing the baby into, and the nature of her own family: the Blackthorns. There is nothing she can do about that. Like everyone else around her, she is powerless.

Jade stands up from the toilet and reaches to flush the chain. 'Chain' is the word she uses in her mind, but it's a generous description when no such thing hangs down to pull on. The mechanism has been broken for as long as she can remember, so you have to stand on the paint tin next to the toilet bowl, push it down with your hands and then hook it up with a screwdriver to make the cistern refill. As she performs the familiar action, she feels the first of the tell-tale tightening pains around her belly and senses that today is going to be the day, early or not.

She sighs hopelessly.

What will be, will be, and there is nothing whatsoever she can do to change that. She wouldn't even know where to begin. Jade is so very tired, and the tiredness resigns her to the inevitability of it all. What little fight she might have once had has been well and truly knocked out of her, for good.

In the bathroom she stuffs a few things into a carrier bag: deodorant and toothbrush. It's a toothbrush that has seen better days, but it's the sort of thing that you only notice when someone else is going to see it. Perhaps they'll give her a new one in the hospital. They've probably got some toothpaste in the hospital, too. She hopes so.

She selects a couple of the least grubby t-shirts from the pile on the floor in the bedroom she shares with two sisters. Patti, smoking out of the bedroom window, turns and raises a knowing eyebrow as Jade stands back up and lets out a little groan when another stab of pain comes.

'It's 'appenin' then?'

Jade nods. 'I think so. Soon anyway.'

'Ah, just as well. Can't stay in there forever.'

Jade nods again. Patti hesitates for a moment and then goes over to give her sister a hug. Jade is surprised by the gesture. They aren't usually a demonstrative family. Not in that way. She nestles her head into Patti's shoulder. It feels nice, if a bit weird. She's always admired her older sister's deep red hair. Patti has the true Blackthorn colouring, while Jade's is more of a strawberry blonde shade, but for a moment the two colours are intertwined, as if the hair could all be from a single head.

Patti breaks away first. 'Bobby takin' ya there?'

A shake of the head. 'Nah.'

'Why not?'

'Cos I ha'n't asked 'im.'

She pauses for a moment and looks at her sister. 'I don't want him to. I mean, I don't *need* him too.'

That sounds a bit like a betrayal, so she adds, 'I mean, it's only just started so I'll be alright on the bus.'

'Oh for fuck's sake, Jade. He can drop you off. You just need droppin', don't ya? You don't need anyone wiv you in there. You know what you're doin'?'

Jade nods once more.

Patti nods and blows out a ring of smoke. 'Good girl.'

She is a year older than Jade and knows the drill just as well, if not better, than her little sister does.

'Well, I hope it comes quick this time. The little man, I mean. I hope he don't give you no trouble comin' out.'

Jade isn't worried about that part. Her body knows what it's doing. Giving birth's the easy bit.

It's after that there will be trouble.

II. Joseph

Joseph reaches for his car keys on the edge of the shiny granite top of the newly installed breakfast bar. He takes a moment to run his hand along the smooth edge of the worktop. He's pleased with the finish, and takes pride in all the little details of his flat. In the narrow hallway he takes a moment to straighten the mirror.

'It's a very difficult job, and the only way to get through it is if we all work together as a team. And that means you do everything I say.'

He twists his soft Cornish burr into a hackneyed impression of Michael Caine, grinning at his reflection. *The Italian Job* is his favourite film, just as it was his father's, and all references to it evoke treasured childhood memories of staying up late with his dad to watch it.

It's a cliché, he knows, but the gleaming Fiat 500 parked outside his flat really is his pride and joy. He's happy to tell people that, and even uses those words. 'There she is: my pride and joy.'

Izzy, his girlfriend, argues that *she* should really be his pride and joy, but he retaliates that the car is more reliable. He doesn't mean it, and Izzy doesn't mind. And she likes the car, too. While not quite the Mini Cooper of the film, his model is based on the 1950s Nuova, so has a classic feel and manages to celebrate the Turin setting of the heist. He had to pay extra for the chequered sports side-stripes, but it was worth it. Against the Passione Red exterior it looks like a racing machine despite being a practical small car, perfect for the mileage he does. It was touch and go whether he would get the finance for it on top of the mortgage for the flat, but the demanding work hours mean that he doesn't have a chance to spend much money on anything else.

Things are tight, but he is pulling it off.

The car is not the only link to his father. Joseph chose his degree in applied social work to follow directly in his dad's footsteps: 30 years in social services. It sounded like a prison sentence rather than a profession, when you put it like that. Joseph had taken his current job on the advice of his father, too. Better pay as a locum. Shorter placements. Greater variety. More opportunity to gain experience working for different local authorities. The chance to pick and choose the teams he worked with. It also means that he doesn't have to become embroiled with the local office politics, a pursuit that doesn't interest him in the slightest. He sees office politics as a dull provincial outlet for middle-aged, bored (and boring) women. Mediocrity is not for him. So the apparent freedom of locum work suits him. For the time being, at least: until the car is paid off.

Joseph leaves in plenty of time to enjoy the drive to work without any pressure. The half-hour journey takes him first through open countryside, then onto a dual carriageway, where he can open the Fiat up, and finally into town, where he takes several side streets that make his journey a little longer but avoid the waste of life that is traffic lights.

He arrives at the office early enough to secure a good little parking spot, on the street directly outside, where the sports checks and stripes at the car's rear are in good view of his desk. He enjoys the peace of mind that comes with being able to see that his little car is safe. The view also acts as a continual reminder of the rewards for doing his job.

There is a perceptible spring in his step as he carries his coffee to his desk, ready to start the day. It will begin with an hour of tidying up some of his online administration. Joseph feels utterly in control of things, unlike the two Sarahs who sit at the desks either side of him. Both of them annoy him for different reasons, although one thing that unites them is their ability to complain incessantly about their workload.

'Someone's pleased with himself,' observes Sarah One.

Joseph isn't particularly close to his colleagues, but he knows that this one is married, with a wild teenage son who always seems to be in trouble at school. This means Sarah One regularly has to leave the office to intervene in some way. Joseph is surprised she gets away with it as much as she does. It doesn't seem fair on the rest of them, but such is life. It's one of a list of things that he holds against her.

'Merely enjoying the joys of a spring morning,' he smiles. He nearly adds, 'Anything wrong with that?' but then stops himself, remembering that he is trying not to allow himself to be aggravated by her patronising tone.

'Paperwork all up to date, then?' Sarah Two asks. She is younger than Sarah One, by at least 10 years, closer in age to Joseph. She is also far savvier and more ambitious than her colleague. This makes her more of a threat, though he wouldn't use that word out loud. It means that she is competitive, more likely to try to get one up on him, even though they are ostensibly working on the same team. Joseph has to watch himself around her to make sure that he isn't caught out. Sarah Two has a model campervan attached to the top of her computer. Whether it is representation or aspiration, Joseph isn't sure. He's never bothered to ask.

He knows that she is engaged, though. It would be hard to miss that piece of information. A picture of her fiancé sits in an Ikea novelty photo frame next to the campervan. It is no accident that Sarah Two has selected an image of him in full naval officer uniform; she manages to include the fact in conversation as often as she can and in the unlikeliest of ways. By contrast, Joseph tries his best to keep the details of his long-term girlfriend out of office conversation. Some things are better left private, and Izzy wouldn't appreciate being discussed with his work colleagues.

Joseph generally tries his best to get along with the two Sarahs, but the truth is that he finds both of them overbearing. They also go about social work entirely the wrong way, as far as he is concerned, with undue zealousness about keeping children with their birth families, seemingly at all costs. Joseph thinks this is probably because Sarah One is a mother herself and sees it as being some sort of sacred bond. Or perhaps it's because she has so clearly made a mess of bringing up her own son. He isn't sure what Sarah Two's motivation is, but given the way she goes on about her forthcoming marriage and sings the praises of James and what a great father he'll make, motherhood can't be far off for her either.

His ideas about social care are, like his taste in films and cars, mostly inherited from his father. They are both firm believers that often families need strategic support – not the blues-and-twos approach beloved of some social workers and authorities, flying in heavy-handedly. But each to their own. His dad repeatedly warns him to not get caught up with 'other' social workers' practice unless it is worth officially complaining about. Joseph and his father share a strong belief in the significance of the individual: that one good social worker with the right mentality, and a good heart, can make the difference to children's lives.

'Yep. Paperwork pretty much in order,' Joseph says. 'Now, if you'll excuse me, I just need to finish something off.'

He doesn't want to be rude, but he also doesn't want to get caught up in pointless chat. Life's too short.

Sarah Two evidently realises that she has been dismissed, and he sees them share a look. Let them. He has things to do.

Not long after, Amber, the department manager, appears suddenly at Joseph's desk. He likes her even less than the two Sarahs. She is another insufferable type, like the Sarahs, in Joseph's opinion. Her 'special' hobby is making organic beauty products. She is older still, in her fifties perhaps, with a rotund figure. Honestly, why can't people just look after themselves? She also sports what Joseph has come to think of as the 'social worker's bob', so ubiquitous is it amongst women of a certain age in the various offices he has worked in. She wears far too much of the colour purple, which she teams with chunky silver jewellery that, in Joseph's opinion, just emphasises her size rather than turning attention away from it. She looks like she probably has more than two cats. Her rapid appearance means that he has to quickly switch tabs away from the news website where he has been reading about a water pollution issue just along the coast from where his parents live.

Luckily there is always a little waft of perfume before Amber arrives, a little scented alarm bell going off, so Joseph is able to flick back to a report that he is working on and appear engrossed in its completion. Joseph had, originally, wanted to study Environmental Sciences, but after his A-level grades didn't turn out quite as he had hoped, or been led to believe, by his school, he ended up switching to a social work degree. His decision was taken mostly on the advice of his father. Hearing about environmental damage on the scale that this water company has just caused always upsets him, though. Joseph was raised to be caring, to be aware of others and the environment, and to always try and do the right thing, however difficult that might seem to be.

Because Amber is a heavy smoker – another thing Joseph can't abide – she smells of mints and cigarettes, on top of whatever organic nonsense she has concocted. Joseph resists the impulse to put his hand to his face and block out the smell.

Amber clears her throat, and Joseph isn't quite sure if that means he's been 'caught out.' Still, his paperwork is meticulous, much more so than anyone else's in the room, in spite of his high caseload, so she can't have too much to complain about, even if she has seen him momentarily off-task.

'Morning,' he says cheerfully, deciding that he will front it out.

As she turns more fully towards Joseph, he sees that in Amber's hand is a heavy-looking doorstop of a file. It makes Joseph wince even before he has seen what it contains.

'Morning,' she says. When she talks she sounds a little breathless. Probably to do with the cigarettes. Her round moon face, wrinkled like old paper, offers him up a wide, fake-looking smile to go with the minty exhalation.

Just get on with asking me to take the case, whatever it is, Joseph thinks, willing her to move on and get the pungent tobacco-mint compound away from his desk. He sometimes thinks that managers target locums for more cases than they should, vindictively, because the locums earn more per hour than local-authority-employed social workers. He already has more than his fair share. He knows that he is only meant to have 18 cases at any one time; the authority guidelines are clear that a social worker should not have more than that number. He has more than 20 already, but he won't complain.

The two Sarahs pretend to be busy, but Joseph knows that their ears are flapping, ready to see what they are not being asked to do.

Amber places the black box file next to Joseph. On the front is a sticker bearing the name 'Blackthorn'. She lifts the lid. Inside are several brown paper folders, stuffed to bursting. A musty smell reaches Joseph, who isn't sure if it's something to do with Amber's perfume or the file.

The two Sarahs, Joseph notices, puff out their cheeks and suddenly look impossibly interested in their own computer screens.

A shaft of sunlight pierces the office suddenly, falls across Joseph's desk, and catches Amber's face. The light hardens her features, and she looks far older, homemade organic beauty products aside. A waxing gibbous moon, Joseph now decides.

From the box, Amber selects a thin brown folder with the name 'Billy' written across the top in heavy black marker. She looks around and then pulls up a chair from a nearby empty desk.

'Not an extra case, despite how it might look. Straightforward job, in fact. It won't take much out of your day. Can you collect a young mum from the maternity unit this morning and take her home?' Her voice is light, jovial even.

Joseph wonders, momentarily, why she feels the need to draw up a chair in order to make this request. As she says, it seems like an easy enough job, so why the out-of-character behaviour from his manager?

As if to confirm the strangeness, she stands up quickly, straightens her skirt, and then sits straight back down again, inching her chair a little closer to his, so that he feels the full force of eau de Amber.

'When I say *young*, she's actually only sixteen.'

'Ah.'

'Her name's Jade. And it's not her first child. She's had two others.'

'Three children by the age of 16? Wow.'

'Quite. But that was all taken care of at the time, and not a factor here.' Joseph can't quite see how that isn't a factor, but Amber moves on quickly. 'Once you get to Jade's home, just quickly drop off Mum and baby.' She clears her throat. 'Bobby will sign the paperwork, and then we'll see you back here.'

'Who's Bobby?'

Collective keyboard clacking from the Sarahs stops at the same moment, so that the office is suddenly quiet.

'The—,' she breaks off before finding the right word, '– the leader.'

'The *leader*? O–kay.' Joseph draws out the syllables but manages to keep a straight face, even though her words have made him picture himself as the hero of a sci-fi comedy adventure, uttering the immortal words, *take me to your leader*.

'The dad, I mean,' Amber corrects herself.

'The baby's father?'

The two Sarahs pop up from behind their screens in unison. He senses a thickening of the air.

'Um, well, he's Jade's father.'

'Right.' Joseph is even more confused. Something is going on here. There is some information that he isn't party to, something that everyone else in the room seems to know about. He feels decidedly uncomfortable. His boss is behaving decidely oddly.

'On this occasion it'll be best if you don't engage in any conversation with him. Just drop off and leave.'

She pauses for a moment, and then, perhaps to make sure that he has understood, adds to her instruction, 'You'll probably need to get going in about ten minutes. Make sure that you don't stay any longer than that. Get yourself out of there.'

Now he feels like he has accidentally strayed into a Bond movie. Something is definitely up. He looks over at the Sarahs, but they have disappeared back behind their screens and remain quiet and occupied.

'Ten minutes. Right you are. Anything else I should know?'

'That's it, I think,' she smiles brightly. 'Nothing else you need to know.'

Joseph isn't so sure.

III. Jade

Jade stands outside the hospital sliding doors. She is still wearing the kitten pyjamas, but now they are partly covered by a slightly grubby pink velour dressing gown. She grinds out her roll-up against the bricks of the wall before dropping the stub to the ground and working her way slowly back inside to the hospital reception.

She turns and glances back outside, looking up to the skies. It is not a hopeful look, more resigned. Like a patient who has accepted a terminal diagnosis, rather than one who has just brought new life into the world. Whatever will be, will be.

She nods politely to the woman on reception as she passes. Jade knows the people here. She knows her way around the place well, too; knows that if she cuts through radiography she can get back to the maternity ward far more quickly than the way the signs tell you. Not that she can read very well, anyway. You find other ways of working things out.

It was almost exactly this time a year ago that she gave birth to a baby girl here. Her firstborn came into the world in this hospital, and her second, too. She still sees plenty of Jazz and Silver around the place, though she doesn't have much of a say in anything to do with what happens to them. The raising of a child in the Blackthorn clan is a shared responsibility. Jade has plenty of cousins and siblings on the estate. Childcare is shared between them. It wasn't so hard to give up her first baby, though; she was so young and didn't really understand what was happening. Harder the second time, when she understood more about what it meant to carry a child around inside for nine months. She thinks about Silver each time she sees those little stretch marks on her tummy. It's as if there is still a part of Silver connected to her. She wonders if she will feel the same way about this baby.

She'd like to hang around at the hospital for as long as she can. It's quite nice having meals brought to you, not having too much to do. Though a bit boring.

Back on the ward, she lies down on her bed. She is the youngest new mum in the room, without a doubt, but there are other differences, too. Jade's 'room' (she thinks of it as a room, because you can draw the curtains around and shut everyone else out, a luxury she has had little experience of) is the only one that isn't festooned with flowers and cards. There is no celebration balloon bobbing up near her pillow, no giant teddy bear with a big blue bow, no gift-wrapped bundle of baby clothes sitting on her bedside table, no stream of relatives to visit: none of the normal trimmings of a new mother. But she didn't have them with the previous births either. Not even the first time.

Not that she really cares about that sort of thing. Besides which, there is nothing to celebrate. Jade feels no joy at having brought a new life into the world. Quite the opposite, in fact. There is acceptance. There is resignation. But, aside from being utterly worn out, there is another, stranger, feeling eating at her.

A feeling of guilt.

Guilt at having inflicted her own fate on another. At least it's a boy; that is something, she supposes.

This exhaustion. It is more than the usual marathon of giving birth. She is physically tired, of course. But weary, too, of the world itself and the restrictive choices it seems to have offered her so far. There are supposed to be hormones that make you feel good after giving birth. That's what one of the midwives said. They evidently haven't kicked in yet. They could do with bloody well hurrying up.

She looks down at the baby through the clear plastic of the cot. He has a little wrinkled face. She should probably think of a name so that she can stop thinking of him as 'boy'. Billy sounds nice. Billy the Kid. He was a fighter, she thinks. An outlaw. It seems like a strong name. And he'll need to be, God knows. Sometimes she thinks that their estate is a little bit like a cowboy film. Not quite with sheriffs and cowboys, though there are plenty of guns. More like an unruly county, where the police and other figures of authority are too scared to tread for fear of reprisal. Jade has no fear of the authorities. Bobby and her uncles have seen off enough police, headteachers, health visitors, social workers and security guards for Jade to understand that they hold no jurisdiction on the estate. She could, for example, shoplift with impunity, knowing that even if she was stupid enough to get caught, nothing would ever come of it once she gave out her address. But there is a heavy price to be paid for enjoying that level of power in the community. Easier to just accept it and not question too much.

She leans over and gives the boy a kiss on the end of his tiny nose, in spite of herself, and smiles as his little mouth opens and closes, though his eyes remain closed. He looks like a little baby bird waiting for the worm to drop into its mouth. He'll need feeding again soon. It's annoying that the midwives bang on about breastfeeding so much. She's had it nonstop since he arrived: Why doesn't she just give it a little try? Mother's milk is best for baby. All that malarkey. Well, maybe it is best for baby, but it isn't really best for mother. Jade doesn't really have that option. It just slows you down from getting your body back into shape and being able to get on. It isn't worth getting too attached to the kid. Billy the Kid. She learned that lesson the hard way the first time, but she thought it would be different with Silver. It wasn't.

She won't be so foolish again.

IV. Joseph

Joseph gathers his keys and stands up, placing the slim paper file into his designer satchel, and leaving behind the Blackthorn box file which, frankly, looks like it needs a good sort out, stuffed full of dog-eared envelopes, spreadsheets and handwritten notes. He tries to whistle as he strolls over to his car, but the tune won't come and the notes fall on the air. He glances back at the window just before he opens the car door, and sees that Amber and the Sarahs are standing up and looking at him. This morning really has taken a turn for the weird.

He throws his satchel onto the passenger seat, but then has a quick second thought before he drives off. He gets back out of the car, opens up its tiny boot and pulls out a tartan blanket. He places that on the passenger seat under his satchel.

He parks easily in the new hospital car park. He has heard several colleagues complain about it. Sarah One regularly moans about the fact that she doesn't understand it. She has been a regular visitor over the years on account of the wayward son who apparently spends a great deal of time visiting A&E with various sprained and broken limbs and near-misses. Sarah Two agrees that it is a terrible car park.

For Joseph, this just confirms his beliefs about his colleagues: they are unduly resistant to change. The car park couldn't be simpler. A digital picture of your number plate is taken on entry, and lets you out the other side once you have paid, without the fuss of having to locate a paper ticket, or worry about overstaying your time. Joseph smiles at their ineptitude. He agrees with his girlfriend Izzy on this one. The world is separated into those who struggle with car parks and those who don't, and he is firmly in the latter category. Those who struggle with car parks belong to an ever-growing group of sensitive snowflakes.

Izzy is a chef, and therefore her working life doesn't neatly align with Joseph's. Far from causing a problem, in fact, this arrangement suits Joseph just fine. It means that their dates are generally confined to weeknights, leaving his weekend evenings free.

He glances back at his car as he presses the remote lock. He likes to think that the car is winking at him as he walks away from it. The maternity unit shares the entrance with A&E, and is busier than he expects. Just as airports are split into happy people (reunions and adventures) and sad (departures and goodbyes), he notices a mix of frightened and relieved people dotted about the reception.

Joseph doesn't know about the radiography cut-through, and takes the long route around the corridors. When he reaches maternity, he checks that he is wearing his lanyard before he, a male, enters this predominantly female enclave.

Sanitising his hands with the proffered gel, he walks into the corridor of the maternity unit. Joseph likes to feel at ease, and this is not his natural comfort zone. He hears women scream and shout, and finds it alarming. He would like to think that he will make a sensitive birthing partner when the time eventually comes, but this is not an area of life that he knows a great deal about. Perhaps it's wrong that men seem to be kept away from all this sort of thing until it's their partner's turn.

He walks uneasily to the desk where three female nurses are sitting. One is on the phone, one is looking at the computer. The other, a woman in her forties, stares right at him. He doesn't get as far as making his enquiry because the lanyard gives him away.

'You're here for Jade?'

The nurse stands up before Joseph has a chance to give his reply. She leads him along the corridor, and says, 'She'll be back next year.' The sigh that accompanies this statement suggests that she is sympathetic rather than critical, and Joseph has no answer other than to nod.

The nurse shows Joseph to a side waiting room and Joseph is greeted by his first view of Jade.

She is sitting in a chair flicking through her phone. On her lap is a mauve bag that looks as if it could do with a good wash. Next to her, but far enough away for her to seem quite disconnected from it, is a cot.

'Did you bring a car seat?' the nurse asks.

'No,' Joseph swallows, and is unable to stop the horrified expression from taking over his features. Why didn't bloody Amber mention that if it was going to be an issue?

'They can't leave the hospital without a car seat, I'm afraid.'

But Joseph hasn't got this far without thinking on his feet. He remembers that there was a Halfords sign at the business park on the way to the hospital.

He smiles winningly at the nurse. 'No problem. I just need to make a quick call.' He winks, in what he hopes is a reassuring but not patronising way at Jade. 'I won't be a moment.' Of course he needs a car seat. He steps outside the side room and a few paces along the corridor so that his conversation isn't overheard.

Amber answers her phone immediately. Joseph explains the car seat situation.

'Shit,' is her less than helpful response.

So Amber hadn't thought of it either. That's something.

'I can't approve expenses for more than £25, so I'll have to get permission from my line manager before I can authorise it.'

While she is wittering on with her explanations, Joseph looks up the Halfords website on his phone. He sees the cheapest baby car seat is £124.

Amber sounds stressed when he delivers this information.

'Look, my manager won't be able to approve expenditure for anything over £80. I'll have to go above him.'

It feels like one of those moments that you could not possibly make up. A baby, a young mum, a social worker and his manager all have to wait whilst approval is sought from the two managers above for the buying of an essential bit of kit to get this baby home safely. It's the sort of in-house procedural 'bollitics' that drives Joseph mad.

He decides to use the time that it will take for him to get an answer from the powers that be as productively as he can. He will endeavour to get to know Jade. The nurse sits on the arm of Jade's chair while Joseph sits to Jade's left and begins by asking her how she is, and then how the birth went. If anyone looked through the little window in the door to the room, it would seem the most bizarre of family portraits. Jade is nothing if not consistent in her replies to Joseph, though the response is more like a repeated sound than an actual word.

'Alwite.'

'Alwite.'

'Alwite.'

It doesn't matter what he asks: about the hospital food, how she feels about going home, how the baby is doing, the answer is the same. Conversation is made more awkward by the fact that Jade has a habit of not looking at him when she replies. She directs her gaze to one side of him and tilts her face downwards towards the floor. It's most disconcerting.

'So what have you decided to call him?' he asks. Although 'Billy' is written on the front of that slim file, it wouldn't surprise him if the child were to be christened 'Alwite'. In fact, the more he hears her say it, the more it starts to sound normal and he begins to think it might, in fact, be a good name for a baby.

But no, Jade confirms that this is 'Billy'. It is something of a relief to Joseph to hear syllables that don't involve 'all' and 'wite'.

Jade gives nothing else away.

'He's—' Joseph breaks off, peering down into the cot. How does one describe a baby when they all look a bit the same anyway? 'He's, er, beautiful.' Beautiful isn't the word to describe this wrinkly pink thing, but there is something namelessly lovely about a newborn. All that pink plumpness signalling unsullied perfection and promise. 'Yes, beautiful,' Joseph repeats. He isn't very good at babies. He hasn't really encountered them very much in his personal life. There are no young nieces and nephews to contend with, and his friends are too young to be thinking about settling down and starting families. He realises with a start that he and most of his friends are more than a decade older than Jade, and this is her *third* child. Why the hell aren't social services crawling all over this case? Jade is just a child herself, though you'd never know it from her careworn face and downcast eyes, which have probably seen plenty of things that they shouldn't.

But nothing he says gets through to her. All Joseph's previous training and experience appear to be redundant against this 16-year-old and her nonchalant ability to shrug him off. He manages not to coax a single piece of useful information from her in the 15 minutes it takes before he deems it time enough to check whether there has been any notification on his phone.

'Nothing yet,' he explains. 'So, have you got everything ready at home? How's the set-up for the baby there?'

'Alwite.'

Of course it is.

When he eventually runs out of questions and Jade deems that perhaps enough is enough of this decidedly awkward conversation, she announces that she needs the toilet.

With Jade out of the room, Joseph leans across to take his first proper look at baby Billy. He is fast asleep in that baby swastika pose of arms bent up and legs bent down. The nurse looks towards the door and then repeats a variation of her earlier prophecy.

'She'll be back in a year.'

According to her badge, the nurse's name is Rosie. Joseph leans back. 'Do you know who the dad is, Rosie?'

Rosie's face fills with concern. 'It could be any of them.'

Joseph is horrified and would like to seek further clarification, but it is at that moment, finally, that his phone alert goes off.

'Yep, go for it. You can get the car seat on expenses,' Amber confirms.

Joseph mentally calculates that because it is early enough in the month, he still has adequate funds in his account. He wonders what they would do if that weren't the case, and he didn't have the means to purchase the car seat. A question for another day.

Rosie signals a welcome back to Jade, but when the girl sits back down she seems to slump more than before and looks a little defeated.

'Good news,' says Joseph, in an effort to cheer her up. 'I'm off to Halfords for the car seat; it's all been approved by my manager. I'll be straight back and then we can get you out of here.'

Jade doesn't seem to register much of what he is saying, engrossed in the business of texting. She doesn't look up as she gives the predictable, 'Alwite.'

The assistant in the store attempts to show him how the car seat straps into the car, but Joseph is impatient and doesn't really listen. How hard can it be if someone like Jade is expected to operate one?

After making his purchase, Joseph returns to the hospital car park. A little sign is now showing it as 'full', even though he can see, quite clearly, an empty space on the left-hand side. Still, for some reason the technology doesn't register it, and he has to wait another six minutes for a further car to leave before the barrier will allow him entry.

'Stupid bloody car park,' he mutters.

This whole 'quick trip to the hospital' has now taken most of the morning, and Joseph is beginning to feel that his entire day is rather sliding out of his control.

Back at the maternity ward, the kind nurse Rosie helps strap baby Billy into his new throne. She now looks as unhappy as Jade does, with something more in her expression that Joseph can't quite work out. He can't help thinking that this is all wrong. Welcoming a new life should be a joyful occasion.

'Right then. Shall we get this show on the road?'

He walks with Jade to the car park, holding Billy's car seat under one arm. He expects to have to navigate the way back out of the hospital, but actually, she seems to know some shortcuts, so he spends the time marvelling at her insider knowledge of the hospital layout, and also at how heavy a baby and a car seat are. Just as he is trying to actually get the show on the road, there is another call from Amber.

'Are you ready to take Jade and the baby home?'

'We're just trying to work out how to get the car seat strapped in properly and we'll be on our way.'

'Good, because the family is getting impatient that they've been waiting so long.'

Are they, indeed? thinks Joseph. *Well, I'm getting impatient too.* He keeps his voice level and attempts to hide his own frustration.

'No worries. We won't be long.'

'Don't forget: once you have the paperwork, just leave.'

'As per your previous instruction, yes. I *was* listening.'

Then she says something that Joseph registers as rather odd. 'Do not make eye contact.'

He dismisses it as a rare joke from Amber.

'Bingo.' The seatbelt clicks in behind the seat and seems secure. There is only a sad smile from Jade in reply. It must be tough on her. He briefly tries to imagine what it must be like being a 16-year-old girl having her third baby. He realises that his empathy has some limitations.

V. Jade

Jade looks at the blanket, carefully positioned on the front seat of the car, and hesitates. It must be there for a reason, and must therefore mean that he doesn't want her to sit there. She moves to open the back door and climb in there instead. Perhaps he spilled something earlier and it's drying out.

She should probably sit in the back with the baby any-how. It's probably more the done thing, to sit with it. (Though she has picked the name Billy, 'the baby' comes to her mind more readily.) More to the point, if she sits in the back then this bloke might stop asking her all the bloody questions. She'd like to tell him to put a sock in it, but given that he's bought her a car seat and all, that would probably be rude.

She doesn't really understand quite what all that car seat fuss was about anyway. A waste of time and money, really. She could quite easily have held the baby in her arms for the journey home. It all seems a bit unnecessary, however much they insisted it was for the baby's safety. Plus, all the car seat protection in the world isn't going to help the kid once he gets home.

'Alright?' Joseph asks her before he pulls away.

He must really like that word. He uses it a lot.

'Yep, I'm alwite. Thanks,' she remembers to add. He is, after all, giving her a ride home, which is much better than having to get the bus, even if it does mean that she'll get there quicker.

'Good. Now, what's your postcode?' he asks, fingers poised over his mobile.

For a moment she has the horrors that he is somehow going to ring her postcode and speak to Bobby, but then she realises that it must be an app with a street map or something. She wants to be helpful, she really does. But honest to God, she has no idea what the postcode is. She's never actually needed to know before.

'Um, I'm not sure,' she mutters, blood rising to her face. It's embarrassing, that. She makes a mental note to look up her postcode and learn it when she gets back, but then realises she wouldn't know where to look it up. Perhaps it's written on the street sign for the estate. She must remember to notice next time she passes it. 'It's number sixteen though. I know the way. I can tell you which roads to take from 'ere.'

He pulls away like an old man – and yet he looks like a boy racer in these wheels. She wonders if it's the baby making him drive so slowly. Men are funny sometimes. She pulls at a loose thread in the ripped knees of her jeans. She is glad to be able to get back into her jeans, but they aren't comfortable and cut in at the waist with all the loose baby flesh hanging over the top. Most of it is covered up by her grey hoodie for now. She'll be back to normal in no time, though. Bobby won't give her very long.

This Joseph character seems nervous. He keeps glancing back over his shoulder or catching sight of her in the rearview mirror and smiling. Harmless enough, but utterly hopeless, she thinks. He doesn't stand a chance against Bobby. Perhaps she should warn him. But what would she say? Where would she begin?

'Left at the end,' she says instead.

She toys with the idea of giving false directions. She saw a film once where two women in a car just drive over the edge of a cliff. A helicopter and police cars are after them, but instead of giving up they look at each other and decide to keep on going. It's a beautiful moment. That must feel good, in the air, taking control. But there are no cliffs or canyons nearby, and this bloke cares too much about his car to want it to soar through the clouds in a moment of madness.

Before long they are turning into the estate, and it is too late to think about movie endings.

All too soon, they arrive at the house.

VI. Joseph

Joseph parks where Jade has indicated and gets out of the car. Out of habit, he stretches, even though the journey hasn't been a long one. He stops awkwardly, mid-stretch, as he has the strangest sensation of being watched. He straightens his shoulders and shrugs off the feeling, going round to the rear on Billy's side of the car to unclip the car seat. He wonders whether the car seat is now a gift, or remains the property of social services. He'll cross that bridge later.

'That one, over there.' Jade points to a house across the road, behind a little patch of green that, inexplicably, has a caravan and a Range Rover sitting in the middle of it.

From this short distance it looks, as far as Joseph can see, like a typical council house, just without the pride in appearance that Joseph remembers from his grandparents' council house. Theirs was all clipped privet hedge with coiffured shrubs and colourful seasonal bulbs under the sitting-room window. Though the plots are similar (even the open door is in the same place), Jade's looks more dystopian than chocolate-box. It's not untidy as such, just bleak. No flowers, no colour, not even any curtains hanging in the windows. Nothing to say 'home'. It is as if it has somehow been bleached of all comfort. Through the windows of his grandparents' place he always noticed the very clean, off-white linings of the pale blue and rose-patterned curtains. The windows there shone clean (his grandmother was a great believer in the miraculous cleansing power of vinegar and baking soda), but here the panes are grimy and dark, with no sense of anything enticing beyond.

He nods, and walks towards the open door carrying the car seat with Billy still strapped in, sleeping soundly. As he gets nearer he realises that it isn't, in fact, open: there is no door. It is missing. There is just a hole in the house where a door should be.

Joseph politely signals for Jade to walk in front of him as he carries the new tiny pink baby through. As he crosses the threshold he senses a change in atmosphere. The hallway is lined with men, who stop talking and stare. Always ready with a film analogy, he feels as if he's just walked into the Slaughtered Lamb in *An American Werewolf in London*. They walk silently past man after man, each seemingly more thuggish than the last. Jade walks with her head down and hoodie right up, leading him past the bizarre guard of honour. Some of the men stand upright with their arms folded, one leans menacingly against a door frame; another draws deeply on a roll-up cigarette.

All their gazes feel fiercely threatening. It's worse than the Slaughtered Lamb. It's Clarice walking down the prison corridor to meet Hannibal Lecter for the first time.

Though the hallway is short, it seems to go on and on, until eventually Joseph enters a small and shabby kitchen. Another man is standing in this room. When they make eye contact, Joseph almost expects to see Hannibal Lecter's iconic restraining mask. Instead, he sees an older man with a very worn, lined face, from which peer very bright blue eyes. The man is large; he seems to take up most of the available space in the room. He stands tall and stares directly at Joseph. Even the smell of this man feels threatening, as if the testosterone is oozing from every pore, along with sweat and tobacco. The whole house, in fact, smells of this very pungent male odour. Joseph wonders where all the women are. Didn't Jade mention a sister?

Joseph has the same feeling of absolute inadequacy that he once had when he accidentally spilt the pint of one of the rugby jocks in the student union bar, and looks away immediately.

Another man, who seems to have appeared from nowhere, lifts the baby seat from Joseph and swings it up onto the kitchen table. His upper half is covered only by a vest, and tattoos snake round his wide arms.

Any thoughts Joseph harbours about negotiating the return of the car seat evaporate immediately. Whatever challenge to his manhood or weird superiority battle is going on here, Joseph has already lost. Amber's advice about not making eye contact is totally unnecessary; Joseph has no intention of doing such a foolhardy thing. In fact, he borrows Jade's technique and finds himself looking to the side and slightly down, away from the older man in front of him – who must be Bobby, the senior Blackthorn. Anything to avoid those too-blue eyes. There is no doubt about who is the alpha male in the room, and Joseph certainly isn't going to offer any challenge to that status. He kind of understands why Amber had used the term 'leader' this morning.

Jade moves to the back of the kitchen and leans against the grubby backdoor window. She takes out her phone, but says nothing. Neither does anyone acknowledge her return.

The older man waves the paperwork into Joseph's face and then shoves it into his chest with force enough to make Joseph stagger backwards.

'There.' The single syllable seems to contain the growl and gravel of a thousand cigarettes, and the menace of a thousand knives.

'Thank you,' Joseph swallows, wondering if everyone else in the house can hear the 'please don't hurt me' entreaty that the words contain.

He begins to back away, clutching the papers as if they are a shield while acknowledging that something is very, very wrong. There is something almost ritualistic in the air. God knows what will happen to the baby once he is gone. There he is, placed in the centre of that table as if it were an altar, and trussed up like the sacrificial lamb. Whatever is going to happen next, Joseph is powerless to stop it.

He offers a tight smile to Jade, but it is an empty gesture. The young mother doesn't acknowledge him at all, just carries on staring at her phone screen through the chaotic curtain of hair that has escaped from her hoodie. The feeling of helplessness intensifies, and Joseph can do nothing more than turn on his heels towards escape. In the narrow hallway one of the men grabs his arm and growls in his ear, 'Any unnecessary interest from social services and there will be trouble, got it?' Joseph makes no response, anxious to just get the hell out. He is grateful for the lack of front door, which speeds his exit once the grip on his arm is released. He hears some more words from one of the men, but he chooses to try and unhear them. Convinces himself that nothing more was said. Outside, he almost breaks into a run, and is utterly relieved to reach the safety of his car.

Turning on the engine and putting it straight into gear, Joseph drives off. He winces at the high-pitched squeal of tyres on tarmac as he tries to pull away too quickly. He is off the estate before he realises quite how hard he is breathing, and halfway back to the office before he realises that he doesn't have his seatbelt on.

He knows that he has to write up his report of the morning's events, but there are no words to describe the scene he has just experienced or to communicate the level of unease he felt. Still feels.

He has a horrible sensation of having just thrown Jade and Billy to the wolves.

VII. Joseph

It is long after lunch by the time Joseph gets back to the office building, but his appetite has deserted him. He takes the lift instead of the stairs, and has to think for a moment before he can call to mind the office security code and key it in. The Blackthorn encounter has unsettled him deeply.

In an effort to regain a sense of normality, he composes a text to Izzy:

Weird day, I'll bring wine and a takeaway, fancy sweet and sour?

He slumps down into his office chair and stares at the screen.

Neither Sarah is anywhere to be seen, but various colleagues are dotted around the office. He needs to get a grip. Pulling his chair tight to the desk forces Joseph to sit up straighter. He accesses the reporting file and girds himself to complete it.

When Amber approaches, Joseph smells the tell-tale waft of mint and tobacco before she actually appears. Usually he finds it too overpowering, but this afternoon it signals a kind of normality and acts as a welcome relief after the pungent Blackthorn stench. He wonders, briefly, if children would find the scent off-putting, and then reflects that in her managerial role Amber is highly unlikely to actually encounter children, unless it was a very serious matter. That gets him thinking about the hierarchy in children's social care, and as Amber's moon face comes into view a few seconds after her perfume, he decides that he never wants to rise to the heady heights of management. After all, his father has never had a good word to say about a manager either.

'Hi, Joseph. Good to see you,' Amber says.

Good to see him? Since when has she cared that much? Joseph manages not to give her a questioning frown in response.

'How did it go then?' Amber asks. She tilts her head to one side and peers at him sympathetically, mustering a tone and body angle that must be taken directly from the managers' handbook, but all her earnestness feels totally insincere to Joseph.

'Well. It was quite a—' Joseph isn't sure of the word he is looking for. 'An experience,' he decides, realising how utterly inadequate that is to describe what happened earlier. As he gives his account and adds a few details about the household, he's aware of the way that his voice shakes occasionally and knows that he sounds tense and upset. He is, but he would rather that his manager didn't know it.

'I had to leave the car seat there,' he finishes lamely.

Amber holds out her hand for the receipt. 'Don't worry, it's no problem at all. I'll sort that.'

She is being unusually helpful and supportive, and while Joseph is grateful, he is also a little wrong-footed. Why is she being so nice?

'Well done, you survived the Blackthorns.'

He nods. He does feel as though he has survived something.

'I didn't like it. I feel as though—'

But Amber cuts him off. 'When you've finished drafting your report, send it over. I'd like to have a look.'

This request is also unusual. Like most managers, Amber rarely has time to read or comment on the day-to-day reporting of social workers' business.

He parks whatever he might have been about to share. 'No worries.'

'Good-oh. Great stuff.' She beams at him before departing back to her glass cubby-hole of an office. Again, weird, but then Joseph is finding everything weird about today.

Eventually, Joseph finds some words to write, but they are words that say none of the things that he wants to say: that the Blackthorns and everything about them is wrong. That he was utterly terrified inside that household and felt that anything might have happened. That he felt terrorised by the air of lawlessness they seemed to give off. That their little enclave might as well be a different planet for all the jurisdiction he had over it. That Billy and Jade were in some terrible, nameless danger. He tries to work out what he can actually write, what counts as quantifiable. *There were too many men and they all looked like thugs*. No. That sort of value judgement wasn't encouraged. *There were no signs of any women* might sound sexist. Men should be just as capable of looking after a baby as women. And anyway, Jade had mentioned a sister and aunts when they were at the hospital. Perhaps they were just out shopping somewhere. And that explanation was also sexist. But it was odd that there were no female family members there to welcome Jade home, wasn't it? He settles on: *There were a number of male family members present when we arrived.*

But how to explain it? *I didn't like the main Mr Blackthorn's eyes. They were too blue, and too far apart.* Not exactly a crime. *They all stood in the hallway and looked at me when I got there.* It sounded pathetic. Schoolboy stuff. Yet Mr Blackthorn's behaviour *was* threatening, there was no doubt about it. But what had he done exactly? *He handed me the signed paperwork too roughly*.

Not having a front door probably wasn't a crime either. Anywhere else in the world it might be considered a safeguarding issue, but not on the Blackthorn estate. No one unconnected with that family would willingly set foot in that place. And you'd have to be foolhardy to do so uninvited.

He eventually settles on: *There didn't seem to be a secure front door*. It is legitimate to list concerns one might have following a home visit, but he can hardly write that the black hole in the centre of the house brought to mind the gaping mouth of hell.

No, it is all fanciful. And if Billy and Jade were in any kind of danger, then his manager would have briefed him more fully with specifics of what to look for, surely. Or the baby wouldn't have been allowed home with Jade. He fills a page and a half that communicates none of his fears, and emails it over.

Amber waves at him and smiles again to show that she has received it, then gives him a thumbs up. She really is behaving oddly.

A few moments later she wanders back over to him in her mint cloud.

'Why don't you finish up early today?' Amber says.

Joseph doesn't need to be asked twice.

He drives back to the flat and showers again, even though he showered this morning, as if he can somehow scrub the Blackthorn experience out of his skin. Freshly changed, he heads back out to Waitrose for his wine of choice, a Saint-Émilion that is also a favourite of his father's. The purchase makes him think of his dad, and he gives him a call.

'Hi, Dad, you okay?'

'Good, son, how about you?'

'Alright.' As he says the word, he hears an echo of Jade, and endeavours to be a little more eloquent.

'No, actually, I'm not alright. It was a bit of an odd one today, if I'm honest.' Joseph goes on to give a more nuanced account of what has happened, knowing that his dad is a good listener and needing to get the 'real' version off his chest after the sanitised report that he emailed to his boss.

At the end of Joseph's tale, his father says nothing, leaving a long pause down the phone line. Joseph allows the pause to open up. This is his dad's way, and though it used to irritate Joseph, he has grown used to it: a tactic applied indiscriminately to children, adults, or foster carers to make them say more, usually the important stuff. Today he is grateful for it.

'I was really scared,' he admits, in the void of the pause.

Joseph hears his father take a deep breath. 'Sometimes there are cases that are wrong on every level. You know in your bones that it's all bad, but there's nothing you can do. Sometimes the system cannot catch them, families like these Blackthorns. Either they're too clever or the system is too corrupt, or perhaps a bit of both. You did what you had to do, and it sounds to me as though you couldn't do any more.'

'But it was so wrong. And I know this is going to sound ridiculous, but it felt like a ritualistic killing was just about to take place. Like a sacrifice.'

'What's your manager's take on it all?'

'Well that's just it. She behaved really weirdly. She was nice. Too nice. Uncharacteristically nice.'

'She's protecting you. She's protecting you, but she's also protecting herself and her bosses.'

Joseph hears his father's voice soften. 'This stuff happens. It shouldn't, but it does. A case like this tests you more than you think possible, but that's the nature of the beast.'

At Izzy's house normality resumes. Izzy has prepared the table, placing a scented candle in the middle.

'Can we lose the scent? Do you mind? I've inhaled enough smells today. I'm only interested in the smell of the takeaway and wine.'

Izzy laughs and they tuck in. With a few glasses of wine he manages to push thoughts of Jade and Billy and the Blackthorn clan away.

Early the next morning he stares at the fridge magnets on the side of Izzy's fridge while he sips his coffee at her kitchen table. One comes from a trip they had early on to the Science Museum in London. There is a picture of Albert Einstein with a quotation split above and below his portrait: *The important thing is not to stop questioning. Curiosity has its own reason for existing.* Joseph's dad frequently talked about 'professional curiosity.' Joseph takes a final slurp of the liquid before heading back to his own flat to shower and change before work.

He sends an email to Amber. He outlines some of his concerns, much more honestly than he did in the report. He demands to know why Jade has been allowed to have a third baby, why social services didn't intervene more directly after the first one, when she was clearly underage. The talk with his father has fired him up.

He knows that he is not finished with the Blackthorns. He will pursue this.

VIII. Joseph

The office is buzzing when he arrives, slightly put out because he has had to use the staff multi-storey car park today instead of finding a nice on-street spot. Colleagues and some employees he doesn't recognise are moving with varying degrees of purpose around the room. People move chairs, sit on tables and appear to be assembling. What did he miss with his early departure the day before? Joseph boots up his computer and logs into his email. A three-line-whip-style memo from the head of the operations team has been sitting there since 4.45pm the previous day. There is no other information than 'Staff Meeting 9am'. It is almost 8.30am and the room is nearly full.

He busies himself helping to move chairs and tables before the two Sarahs arrive. They seem unfazed by the level of office activity and hang their coats on the back of chairs, smiling and greeting colleagues. Coffee and snacks are placed on desks around the room, and the enticing aroma of warm sausage roll travels past his nose.

A man in a good-quality wide pinstriped suit walks through the double doors shortly before 9am. He is clearly in no doubt as to his own level of importance, and is flanked by two women.

Joseph looks at the first Sarah with an inquisitive, lumpy brow.

Sarah One mouths, 'Andrew Maynard-Brown,' back at him along with a knowing look.

Joseph, none the wiser, gives a questioning shrug. Sarah scribbles *Director of Children's Services* on a post-it and hands it to him discreetly, like they are passing notes in class.

Good, thinks Joseph. His instant point of reference is the Blackthorns, especially since his email to Amber. He feels a shiver of anticipation, but one that is tinged with excitement that the family are going to be taken on. He feels proud to be a social worker. This is why they do the job.

Amber leans back, half-sitting, half-standing against a desk to his left. In today's outfit choice she has surpassed herself. She is dressed in hues of purple and green, head to toe, complemented by bright turquoise nail polish. The word that springs to Joseph's mind is 'peacock'. It makes him think of his grandmother, who refused to allow peacock feathers in the house, claiming that they were bad luck.

He tries to push thoughts of his own family from his head and settle down to listen to whatever is about to be said in this meeting. Amber's hands are clasped in front of her, displaying the nail varnish in all its glory, and her rapt expression suggests that she is something of a fan of this Andrew Maynard-Brown character. She gives a little clap before clearing her throat and standing up to make the introductions.

'Welcome, everyone,' she begins, which feels to Joseph just a little off, given that they have all been summoned here in no uncertain terms – not to mention that most were required to be present in the room as their place of work.

'We are extremely privileged to have Andrew here this morning—'

Interesting that his celebrity is such that he doesn't even need a surname, thinks Joseph, but Amber's admiration is genuine.

'Also here with us are the Head of Comms Kitty Sykes, and Head of Public Relations Sue Smith. Over to you, Andrew,' she gushes, as though presenting some ghastly breakfast television item.

As though there are subtitles or the scene is being dubbed, Joseph can hear his father's voice playing over the top, his cynicism a constant reality check. *There she is, paving the way to her own promotion. Andrew Maynard-Brown. Who the hell does he think he is with his flashy little suit and his double-barrelled surname?* … or perhaps it is his own voice he hears. It's difficult to tell. He seems to be becoming more like his father every day, he realises.

Andrew moves with practised ease to centre stage and opens his arms to welcome everyone into his own circle. Amber seems almost to pull out of a little curtsy towards him as she steps back.

'Good morning, folks. I want to start by thanking you all for the excellent work you do.'

There are smiles and nods of sheepish acceptance around the room. *How are they falling for this?* Joseph thinks, deliberately making himself stay still and not outwardly respond to Andrew Maynard-Brown and his smooth patter.

'Nationally, social workers are receiving a pretty bad press right now.'

When weren't they? That was standard Sunday lunch fare in Joseph's household growing up. The way that not only social workers, but their clients were viewed negatively within society. No one could see the good that they were doing.

'It looks like the media have it in for you.'

Again Joseph does not move while he takes in what Andrew says. Interesting choice of pronoun: 'you' rather than 'us'. That speaks volumes about his management style.

With his semi-grey curls cut into a memory of longer hair, he looks more like a banker than the Head of Children's Social Care. He is clearly the top of the tree – no relaxed off-the-peg plain suits and t-shirts for him. That won't do at all for the king. Nevertheless this is, surely, a build up to the big announcement about how all that narrative will change once they collectively take on the Blackthorns and rid the community of this menace once and for all.

Andrew continues his spiel about social workers' reputations within the media and society more generally. The two corporate women must be there to help with risk assessment and data protection when the news about the Blackthorn family comes to light, Joseph thinks. In spite of his initial animosity towards Andrew Maynard-Brown, he is keen to hear exactly what form their direct action will take, and listens intently to what comes next.

'We are facing a serious threat to our sector—'

Yes, yes we are, thinks Joseph eagerly.

'– because not enough people are stepping up to take the courses on offer, and not enough social workers are going on to work within local authorities when they have graduated.'

Oh.

'A significant number are leaving the sector before they have even begun, and, as I'm sure you are aware, there are significant numbers of our local authority social workers moving to the independent sector or becoming locums.'

Joseph's mounting support for the man evaporates in an instant. Since Joseph has been a locum since graduation, he is uncomfortable with being directly and publicly criticised. The thought crosses his mind that perhaps this speech has been crafted by the Comms and PR people as a technique to create tension among them all. He quickly dismisses the idea. He doubts that any of the people in this room are quite that clever.

Andrew moves to one side and Kitty steps into the space he has just vacated. Like him, she is dressed in a smart, corporate suit, a world away from the more relaxed attire of most social workers. Joseph guesses that she is in her early thirties. Her calves are thick and her ankles skinny, which makes her look a little bit like a goat. As she opens her mouth to speak and performs a little cough, he notices that her teeth are a shade too white. A level of vanity that Joseph despises.

'You are by far the best people to recruit more social workers. You are the best placed to help us drive up the numbers of people coming into this wonderful sector.'

Sarah Two moves her hand to attract Joseph's attention. She is displaying a middle finger. Now it is Joseph's turn to do a pretend cough, to cover up his laugh.

There is another 45 minutes of this recruitment drive, alternating between Kitty, Andrew and Sue – older, near retirement, there for additional gravitas – before Amber rises back into the position next to Andrew. Once again she oozes subservience. To accompany her, Sarah Two is bending down to her bag at the side of her chair and is miming being sick. Joseph, who has never seen Sarah behave like this before, is almost beside himself.

'So, if you recommend someone to become a social worker, and they graduate and work for the LA, you will receive a £500 finder's fee!'

With that punchline delivered – of shunting recruitment and retention problems onto the shoulders of the overworked and underpaid social workers – the stars of the show gather themselves to leave. It suddenly dawns on

Joseph that throughout the artful performance, nothing has been said about the Blackthorns.

The room empties, and staff move back to their own offices to gossip and raise eyebrows.

Joseph sets about accessing the Blackthorns file.

Online, there is a lock on the file requiring a password to access it. Having not encountered anything like this before, Joseph puzzles over it for a moment. He leans over to Sarah Two.

'What does it mean if there's a lock on a file?'

She looks up from her screen and fixes eyes on him. 'Someone doesn't want you to see it.'

'Right.'

Under normal circumstances, Joseph would just march up and ask his manager what's going on, but these don't feel like normal circumstances. Something isn't sitting right about this whole thing.

He tries again, just to make sure. Still locked.

'So how can I access the children's files?'

This time Sarah Two speaks without looking away from her screen. 'You have to get permission from Amber or her manager.'

'But *why* would a child's file be locked?'

Sarah One looks up sharply. 'You heard her. Because they don't want you to see it.'

Joseph suspects that she knows exactly whose files he is trying to access.

He returns to his screen and tries one more time, hoping that a magical dropbox will appear and grant him access.

Instead it is Amber who appears. She is upon him before he twigs from the aroma-alert. The moonbeam face isn't as smiley and friendly as before.

'Joseph, would you mind just popping to my office?'

Office is a grand name for her little pod, but Joseph nods obediently. 'Sure, Amber.'

He follows behind her, glancing backwards at Sarah Two, who gives him a raised eyebrow.

Back in her pod, Amber sits down in front of her computer and peers up at Joseph. If he is getting the schoolboy treatment, then it is somewhat negated by the pixies and fairies she has stuck to the top of her PC. Next to her keyboard is a small bowl of mauve and brown crystals. Joseph can't quite take her seriously as a result. She is a hard woman to figure out, he thinks. Everything about her suggests a free-spirited weekend in Glastonbury, so how and why did she end up in this constrained machine of a system?

She says nothing, so Joseph makes the decision to sit without invitation. She has just asked him there, after all. Amber's eyes follow his movements, but she still doesn't speak.

Emboldened, he asks, 'Is there something I can do, Amber?'

'Yes. Yes, there is. I got your email. You're to leave the Blackthorns case well alone.'

Joseph squints quizzically.

'It's no longer your business, I'm telling you. So stay away.'

She stands up to indicate that the conversation is over and there will be no explanation and no discussion.

He nods. Inside, however, his system switches to red alert. This is not going to go away, whatever she thinks. He will not be defeated, he won't be put off that easily. Not Joseph. He has a friend in the Child Protection department two floors down.

It is time to call in a favour.

IX. Joseph

They meet in the park near the office, which only reinforces Joseph's feeling of being in a movie of some sort.

Matthew shares Joseph's opinion that there is a dark side to data protection. It hides a great deal. As well as protecting people's identity, it also protects lies. He takes his mobile phone out from his coat pocket. He is clean-cut, smartly dressed. Everything about him screams 'efficient'.

'I've screenshotted some pages of the Blackthorn file that you asked for. You're right. It makes for very interesting reading. It's a weird one. A whole family, baby after baby, born to very young mums. But no intervention from us. No follow up. Nothing. They all go back home.'

'If you can call that home,' Joseph mutters.

'I'll send you the photos. There's too much to sift through on a phone. It would take us all afternoon.'

It isn't a night where he was planning to see Izzy anyway; she's working at the restaurant, so he will have plenty of time to focus this evening.

'I owe you.'

'I'll be interested to hear how this pans out.'

'Don't worry. You will.'

Joseph stays up until 2am scrolling through page after page of Matthew's screenshots. Matthew is right. It is a story of baby after baby returning home, even when they are born to very young, and in some cases underage, mothers. The

Blackthorn children do not seem to attend school regularly, but are not pursued by the welfare officers. There are some references to home-schooling, but no inspection or checks on the quality of home-schooling being given. Jade herself appears in the file as one of those being home-schooled. There are reports of suspected abuse from hospital workers, from teachers, and from health professionals over the years, but there is no evidence of serious case notes for any of them.

Nothing is ever followed up.

Just a few lines here and there from social workers appear in the notes. Different social workers each time. No one seems to do the task twice. He double checks. Yes, each entry has been made by a different social worker. There is no continuity at all.

He spots Amber's name in the file. When she was a beat social worker she took a baby back to the Blackthorn home. That was how long ago? He does a double take: 14 years.

What on earth is going on?

Although he doesn't get a great many hours of sleep overnight, the adrenaline means that he feels wide awake in the morning. The office is back to normal this morning, though only one of the Sarahs is at her desk when he arrives.

'Morning, Sarah.' He stops himself from adding 'One' out loud. 'How are you today?'

She moves her head in a nod while chomping on a croissant. There is a bakery a few doors down, but Joseph has resisted its enticing smells this morning. Not everyone is capable of his level of restraint, though.

'I'm well, thanks, and how are you?'

He thinks for a minute. 'I am well, Sarah. I am very well indeed. Thank you for asking.'

He has quite a to-do list. He needs to catch up with a couple of other social workers, the police and a school. Boxes need to be ticked and files need to be closed. It will be another day stuck at his desk dealing with the greedy monster that is children's social care bureaucracy.

He types away with purpose, pulling down case notes for the children he is due to see later this week. There is never a moment when he isn't busy. Court paperwork takes up a great deal of his time. At one point he catches a glimpse of Amber sitting in her cubby hole, staring at him. He decides not to wave. That's the sort of thing his dad would do, but he will play this differently. Instead, he stares back at the screen.

At lunch time he decides to go to the park to eat his meal deal from the Tesco Express on the corner. He texts Matthew to see if he fancies joining him. No response there. Unsurprising – Matthew's always busy. Instead he passes the time on his own and takes only a short break before finding himself back at the office.

The afternoon feels long, and he welcomes the arrival of 5pm on the office clock. Tonight is an Izzy night, and Joseph can almost taste the wine he is just about to get from Waitrose, along with some ingredients to make a lasagne at her house. If he is honest, he sometimes prefers being at Izzy's. Her little house is warm and welcoming, much more so than his stark flat. Izzy has the ability to make the place feel homely, but it's also not without style. He stands up, pulling the coat off the back of his chair. Amber is still in her office, talking to a colleague. He walks out of the door and down the 1950s concrete staircase, his fingers sliding down the banister next to the large blue square tiles as he heads towards the staff car park.

He pulls out his keys from his pocket, but stops in his tracks at the sight that greets him. The keys fall to the floor with a clatter that he doesn't hear. He feels quite sick. Ahead he can see only carnage, the remains of his beloved car.

It has been completely vandalised.

X. Joseph

Joseph knows that the damage to his car originates with the Blackthorns. Or rather, he *feels* it. He'd have trouble proving it, but Bobby, or, more likely, one of his henchmen, has to be responsible. There's no other explanation that makes sense for such a violent, wilful act. All the way through, he has sensed that he is being warned off. Yet Amber is fearfully dismissive of any such accusation being levelled against the Blackthorns. Somehow the CCTV in the staff car park 'wasn't working', so there is no record of how his car was damaged. There is no question that it was deliberate, malicious, and will cost thousands of pounds to put right.

He's also received an email from Amber suggesting that he should brace himself for a safeguarding investigation. He knows there has been nothing wrong with his conduct. It's a spurious claim. Perhaps another way of warning him off the Blackthorns. He takes the day off work and spends it cleaning his already immaculate flat, as if to distance himself even further from the grime of the Blackthorns.

That night he has a visitor. Two visitors, in fact. They may or may not be men from the Blackthorn house. It's difficult to tell in the dark. He wouldn't be able to pick them out of a lineup but they have the same, thuggish look. One of the men has a gun. It isn't pointed at him directly, but the man angles it in such a way that the security light from the porch leaves him in no doubt. He growls at Joseph that his career in social work is over 'if he doesn't drop it.'

He closes the door behind him, and double locks both front and back doors. He should tell the police, but he doesn't. He doesn't even tell Izzy.

He doesn't return to the office, but hands in his notice the next day. It feels good. He walks taller, a weight off his shoulders. This world is not for him. The world needs good social workers, but society doesn't support them. He can't fight the world's battles singlehandedly.

Though he isn't a quitter, he knows when to bail out. Perhaps social work never really was for him. Perhaps he was simply becoming what his father wanted him to become. He swerves a work leaving do, sensing that he won't be much missed anyway. He will be a conversation piece between Sarah One and Sarah Two for a few days; then they will all move on with their lives, and he'll only be remembered as a signature on a file here and there.

Within the week he has moved in with Izzy and put his own flat on the market. Being the perfect starter home for a young professional living and working in the city, it sells absurdly quickly. He hasn't really had it for that long, but makes an easy £20,000 on the sale, even after the solicitor and estate agent have each had their cut. Not quite a year's salary, but not far off.

Every cloud has a silver lining, he decides, putting the Blackthorns and his colleagues far behind him. He tells himself that he dreamt the visitors with a gun.

Izzy has wanted to own her own café for several years, and that is what they will do. They will move on and sell her house, too. Use the proceeds from their combined sales to buy a place together and invest in a small café. They can live out

Izzy's dream. Joseph's dad will get over the disappointment, eventually.

It takes a good few months to find the right rental premises, and it is a little way away. Even better for a fresh start. At the same time they buy a home off-plan on a new development just out of town. Life is filled with the busyness of choosing furnishings for a house. He discovers he has opinions on all sorts of things: fabric for curtains, handles on the kitchen cupboards, the design of cornices, the style of taps. Joseph has final say on decisions in the house, Izzy at the café. They work well as a team. It's hard work physically at times, especially at the beginning when he finds himself flitting between accountant, waiter, washer-upper, interior designer and cleaner, but none of it has the emotional drain that social work did. But Jade, and Billy, still pop into his head at random moments. When he is stacking the dishwasher or chopping salad for a busy lunchtime, there they are, lurking in shadowy corners of his mind. He wonders why they, of all the children he has worked with, refuse to budge. But really, he knows why: it is the nameless horror of that Blackthorn estate; the lawlessness, the acceptance, the covering-up. And on the worst days: his own complicity, his own cowardice.

None of it sits comfortably.

It takes another 20 months after they are properly settled in for the café to turn a profit, but the day they go into the black again is a good one. Another year more and Joseph is able to step back from the day-to-day running of things a little. He has an idea that he may pick up his environmental studies at some sort of evening class, even gets hold of some prospectuses to begin looking at courses. By Christmas he is putting an application together for the following September.

The world keeps on turning. Jade and Billy visit less frequently, only on the nights when he's had too much wine (now bought wholesale and not from Waitrose).

It's nearly the end of lunchtime, and he's busy tallying up the previous day's orders out the back, when Izzy shouts to him, 'Someone to see you, Joseph!'

He barely recognises Matthew, his old work colleague from Child Protection.

'Wow! Good to see you. You look different. Good-different, I mean.'

The most obvious change is that Matthew has grown his hair. The neat short back and sides he used to sport has been allowed to grow down in long dark waves. He holds a hand out to shake Joseph's and Joseph notes, with some surprise, the friendship bracelets on his wrist.

'It's been a while. I forgive you for walking out on me and not saying goodbye.'

Joseph feels momentarily alarmed. It's true, he walked out of that office and left everything. He didn't stop to say goodbye, even to his friend. This probably does require an apology.

'Listen mate, things were tricky back then,' he starts to explain, before he realises that Matthew is joking.

'Four and a bit years ago, now.'

'Is it that long?'

Life is so busy at the café. Joseph has barely noticed the time passing.

'Anyway, even if I had stopped to share my fond farewells, you wouldn't have been there. You were always busy, always out on a case.'

'Still am,' says Matthew. 'Busy, that is. But not too busy for a spot of lunch.'

He takes off his jacket and Joseph is surprised to see a Radiohead t-shirt beneath. He gestures to an empty table and the two old friends sit down to lunch.

Seeing Matthew brings that final business with Jade and Billy flooding back. All the impotence at not being able to intervene. The terrifying sensation of being sucked into the Blackthorn vortex, briefly, and the relief at having been spat back out again. The horrible feeling of having walked away and done nothing. The certainty of conspiracy in circles of silence.

Izzy brings over two paninis with today's special filling: camembert and redcurrant. 'So, are you going to introduce me?'

'Yes, of course. I'm sorry.' Joseph makes the requisite introductions. 'A real blast from the past.'

'Well, I hope you're not going to drag him back into that murky past,' Izzy smiles as she puts the plates down and walks back to the kitchen.

'So, what brings you all this way?'

'Oh, I heard how good the paninis were,' Matthew deadpans, biting into his.

'Seriously, mate. How did you manage to track me down?'

Matthew laughs. 'A doddle. Don't forget, I worked in Child Protection. On a par with MI5.'

'Fair enough.'

'No, it was actually a deep, undercover operation, called Facebook.'

Now it's Joseph's turn to laugh. It makes him recall the funnier days with old colleagues, the shared gallows humour. He realises with a little jolt that he misses that camaraderie.

'Well, I'm glad you did.'

'And I did genuinely see the café reviews, and the menu,

and thought it probably was worth the drive. And it is,' Matthew says, with another bite of his sandwich.

'Do you still work there?'

'No, no, I left not long after you did.'

'Why?'

Matthew leans back into the curved wooden chair (bought by Izzy at an auction, as a job lot with 12 other random wooden chairs and small tables, to give the café a French Bistro feel). He takes his time, as though it is a huge effort to get the words out. 'I left because of the Blackthorns, actually. After I opened their file, you remember I screenshotted the pages.'

Joseph most certainly does remember.

'It really sickened me. No sooner had we taken a child into care, they were back home. No children in school, but no follow-up from the education welfare officer. It was a mess. It didn't make any sense. And then I discovered something really interesting, something that wasn't in the file.'

'Go on.'

'Nearly twenty years ago now, when all of this started, there was a Terry Blackthorn on the council.'

'What? You're joking.'

'I'm not. He died a few years ago now, but it looks as though old Granddaddy Blackthorn got interested in politics and went and got himself elected.'

'But how? If he's connected with that family, who'd vote for someone like him?'

'Well, not many people. But there was no opposition to his seat. My guess is that they were all scared off. And that would have helped to make the whole family untouchable. But it gets worse.'

'Worse than a corrupt councillor who chooses not to send his kids and grandkids to school?'

'Wait till you hear how corrupt. It's all part of a bigger pattern. In the early eighties there was a housing act that gave five million council house tenants the right to buy their homes from their local authority. Well, once Terry Blackthorn arrived on the council, houses in the vicinity of his home quietly went on the market without any explanation, and they weren't sold to their tenants. Suddenly the name "Blackthorn" begins to appear on every deed in that row. Land next to the estate was sold for development. Farmers sold hundreds of acres which somehow the Blackthorns capitalised on, even though the land was not theirs. The Blackthorns didn't move into bigger, more luxurious properties with their new wealth. Instead, they stayed put in their kingdom. They began to creep out to take over most of the council estate. A few pensioners stayed put, refusing to be intimidated by the Blackthorns. But when they died their houses were taken over. They've got their claws into the bloody lot. It was the last straw, really, when I discovered that. It kind of destroyed my faith in the system, I suppose. And I'd never have even looked into it if you hadn't brought it all to my attention by getting me to unlock that file. So in a roundabout way, I can blame you for my departure!'

'If it's any consolation, I left because of them, too. Someone destroyed my car, the day after I got those screenshots. My car was vandalised, I suspect by a Blackthorn. It was a write-off and I suppose—' he pauses for a moment. 'I suppose I didn't feel safe anymore. Sorry, that sounds weird.'

'No, it doesn't. I heard about your car. Bad business.'

Joseph still can't bear to think about his run-in with the Blackthorns, even after all this time. He changes the subject. 'So, what are you doing now?'

'Good things. Me and a friend set up a youth club.'

'Ah, that explains your attire. A bit more down with the kids these days.'

Matthew smiles. 'Yeah, well, we wanted to help with the increasing numbers of exclusions from schools.'

This is familiar territory: Joseph and Matthew have discussed this at length in the past. Both shared the view that the secondary education system is set up to create trauma, disobedience and defiance, and is the last place that some children need to be.

'You know, for the young people who need a bit more attention. The ones who have been failed by school. The ones who struggle to have their needs met. Square pegs in round holes.'

Joseph does know. They remember a teenage girl who was raped most mornings by her mum's boyfriend before she went to school. A girl who was then excluded after she threw a chair at her angry shouty male maths teacher, and then sent to a secure unit to complete her 'education'. Both men recall the outrage they felt at this outcome.

'A punishment for what happened to her.' Matthew shakes his head. 'Ridiculous. No wonder she threw a chair. Not good at all.'

'Education is a battle through adults' biases, poor kid. Too many of the teachers are biased against these children.'

'Too right.'

This reflection sparks the ex-social workers to remember some of their original passion for working and supporting children. Joseph launches into an old diatribe about social justice. Four years evaporate in an instant, and Joseph finds himself fired up about all the things that café culture has made him forget.

Matthew nods in agreement. 'Take those Blackthorns. It feels to me that something was totally wrong there. No way should those children have been sent back. They should have been in full-on therapeutic centres. Not thrown back to the wolves.'

Joseph shudders, remembering having that very same thought about throwing Jade and Billy to the wolves. He has carried some of that guilt with him since that day, he realises now.

'Listen. I've been tipped off by an old colleague that on Wednesday there will be a raid on the Blackthorns. The whole lot. Their houses and caravans. It's going to be a big operation. Police, social services, the lot. Most of the children there have never been registered. Who knows what they'll find?'

Matthew pauses in his narrative, letting all that sink in.

'But why now?' Joseph asks, puzzled. 'Why can they put a stop to it all now when they couldn't before? What's changed?'

'Bobby's dead, that's why.'

Hearing his name brings that intense moment inside the house right back to Joseph. Those cold blue eyes staring him down.

'Not just him. Bobby and three other men. I think one was a brother, the other a son, not sure about the last one.'

The thugs standing in the hallway watching as he walked past, carrying Billy, appear in Joseph's mind's eye. The ones standing outside his home. The flash of a revolver in the dark. A tension that he didn't know he still felt is suddenly released.

Matthew continues, 'They were in Ireland. They were big on boxing, apparently, and had gone over to watch some fights. While travelling to County Cork they got involved in an accident with two lorries. All four were killed outright. The papers say that Bobby was decapitated when his Mondeo went under one of the lorries. Quite the Shakespearean ending.'

'I don't remember *The Tragedy of the Ford Mondeo*.'

'You know what I mean. Now they're not around, I suppose the police feel that they can conduct a raid and dismantle their hierarchy.'

'It shouldn't have to come to that before the police are involved.'

'No, but—' he breaks off. 'I thought you might want to know. I thought you might even like to be walking past there at 7 o'clock on Wednesday morning. To see it end.'

He doesn't have to think for very long before he gives a quick nod. 'Yes, I think I would like that. I think I probably *need* that.'

It will be closure for something that has haunted Joseph for too long.

XI. Joseph

Wednesday comes around fast, too fast for Joseph. Izzy is sympathetic when he explains his plans.

'I remember. I remember it all. How could I forget what you were like after the car?' She pauses for a moment. 'Can I come?'

Joseph is surprised, but grateful for the support, as ever.

In the blue-black light before dawn, they put a sign up announcing that the café is closed for the day. It's frosty, and he has to de-ice the car for a few minutes before reversing the Citroen Picasso out of the driveway. Driving is never now quite the joy that it once was for him, but the Picasso does at least have an effective HVAC system to clear the windshield, he'll give it that.

Along the way they chat about the café, plan a new menu, and Izzy broaches the subject of a 'them' Saturday.

'What exactly is a "them" Saturday?'

'Well, "them" is just a community platform that operates through the lens of the LGBTQ community. We can afford to have a "them" day, and more than that, we should.'

Joseph is sceptical, but Izzy is enthusiastic and insistent.

'Our market is mainly middle-class vegans and vegetarians. We can't just be against transphobia, we've got to make a stand. We have to do more. It's a good way to show our support, I think. Trust me.'

Joseph doesn't really see the point, but he gives in. Izzy has been right on most things to do with the café, and she's probably right on this, too.

'Pick a date then.' By the time they have agreed when it should be and how it should be marketed, they are arriving in the familiar environs of their old hometown.

As they enter from the south side, it seems impossible that at the other end is a lawless community. They drive past a grey-fronted stylish-looking bar-restaurant that they eye up for lunch.

'That's new.'

Even though things have changed in the last few years, and the High Street has a different complexion, Joseph remembers exactly where the Blackthorns live.

It's still early. They are in plenty of time to scout out a good spot. The estate is even worse than he remembers. The sprawl of former council houses now resembles a scene from a dystopian movie. There are vehicles everywhere, parked haphazardly across the meadowland in front of the houses, some without wheels, standing on bricks. Many look as if they haven't moved in a long time. Trees are also growing on the meadowland in front of the houses, trees that Joseph doesn't remember. At least it covers some of the eyesore.

'I think we'll park back up near the High Street and walk back. Then we can find a space on the other side of these trees where we can see the action from a safe distance.'

Joseph holds Izzy's arm as they quietly stumble into a tree and shrubbery. They duck down, hearts racing, waiting to see the action. Izzy is trying to work out how the police vehicles might enter the site. They watch out for the glimpses of large white vehicles through the trees lining the sloping lane down from the village to the site. They wait.

They are waiting a long time. The couple have not anticipated that the police might have a plan that is not based on a prime-time Scandinavian murder drama. There are no vehicles anywhere nearby. Rows of white vans and cars are actually at the outer rendezvous point, more than a mile away, but they are not to know that. The police are on foot, and silently swarm in from all angles, unseen by Joseph and Izzy. Suddenly the couple spot the action and are shocked by the speed, silence and scale of the operation.

There are dozens of officers outside three houses. Joseph remembers going into the middle one of them that day with the baby. He takes in again the scale of what is going on here this morning, and inhales deeply. Everything he felt that day comes washing back over him: the humiliation and impotence that he felt. How he knew none of it was right, but couldn't do anything. The way he gave into his fears. He criticises himself again for his own weakness.

Watching the numbers of police, he knows that whatever went on here was bad – really bad. He berates himself for putting his own fears above the needs of the children who live here. He feels sick. This is all coming five years too late.

Izzy is excited by the drama. She reminds him of a scene from a film, where the camera focuses on a beautiful woman cheering her horse on to win a race. But it doesn't feel like that for Joseph.

Outside the doors, police stand ready, one on each door-step holding a red metal enforcer. The police behind carry extendable auto-lock batons. There are firearms officers in wait. There is a signal, and the main action begins. Dogs barking is the first thing Joseph notices. The Blackthorn dogs, there to protect whatever darkness has been happening on this land for years.

Izzy is buzzing, and, just as two children are brought out by three police officers, Izzy lifts her phone. Joseph sees Izzy lift her arm. Without thinking, he grabs her arm and pulls it down. She drops the phone.

'Fucking hell, Joe.' Izzy's face is red, her hair falling back across her eyes.

Joseph, though, is in a fury, shaking. He looks at Izzy, 'For fuck's sake, they are children.'

Now that the first forays have been made, the scene changes. Police vans now begin to appear on the site, and other people emerge. Men, mostly men, but some women, are handcuffed and put into the backs of the vans. Computers and hard drives are carried out by the police. Crime scene investigators with large cameras take images of everything and everyone as they are removed. Cameras and lighting equipment are set up. Two more cars empty of more uniformed police. Where are the social workers? Joseph looks hard to see if he can see Amber or the Sarahs, then realises that they probably do everything they could to avoid being on site in such a dangerous location.

He hasn't thought about them in such a long time, but this is a big operation: the Child Protection team will have had to pull in more personnel from other departments. They will be on standby for what's happening, and have their work cut out today in strategy meetings for all the children. Imagine trying to find placements for all of them. Joseph counts at least a dozen, but they keep coming. The children are met by social workers and police officers. From his distant vantage point, Joseph finds himself crying. Kind professionals wrap blankets around each scared child. One of them will be Billy. It should have been him placing them. And it should have happened a long time ago.

'I'm sorry,' Joseph whispers to the air.

Izzy takes his hand. 'We've seen enough. Let's go.'

XII. Joseph

Matthew and Joseph sit up late into the night, demolishing a decent bottle of whisky between them. It's not the usual tipple for either of them, but the day's events have taken their toll.

'How did it ever get like that? I know you mentioned a Blackthorn on the council. Terry, was it? But that doesn't explain the whole set up. Why the caravans and all those vehicles, and the horses, for God's sake? I mean they're not travellers, are they, in the true sense of the word?'

Matthew becomes increasingly loquacious in correlation with his whisky consumption. He's done his homework on the Blackthorns. 'Well, yes and no. You can have the full history lesson, if you like.'

'Try me.'

'Strap in. The Blackthorns were originally descendants of the Scottish traveller community. They settled in the area after the Second World War.'

'Blimey, it is a history lesson. I thought you were joking.'

'I just got interested in the whole thing. My degree was in Anthropology, so it's sort of my area.'

'Mine should have been Environmental Science.'

There is a detour into reminiscing about student days, before Matthew takes up the story once more.

'Originally they were offered council housing back in the 1950s. It was a way of integrating travellers and gypsies within the community. They manufactured communities by creating purpose-built council estates on the edge of villages and small towns. But what the local parish and town councils hadn't known at the time was the hostility that already existed between the Roma and the traveller communities. They were all lumped together without any awareness or interest in the historic and ethical and cultural wars that existed between them.'

'Sounds like a recipe for disaster.'

'Yep. After many fights and crimes, the Roma moved on. That left the opportunity for the Blackthorns to muscle in properly. Terry Blackthorn seems to have used his council influence to somehow arrange for larger groups of his extended families to join them on the council estate at the edges of the quiet community. They soon dominated the housing and ruled over the surrounding land. Unsuspecting farmers didn't do much to oppose the land takeovers from the Blackthorns. Soon the Blackthorn name was known throughout the region and beyond. I mean, you'd heard of them, hadn't you?' Matthew pushes the whisky bottle back towards Joseph, who refills both their glasses.

'Actually no, I hadn't. Not before that file landed on my desk. But then my family were from miles away. I grew up in Cornwall and then my folks moved to Wales, don't forget.'

'Well, for years they lived their lives in and out of the council houses, tethering their horses to the metal porch posts of the council homes. Though homes is a bit of a misnomer, because they were never used in a conventional domestic homely way. One house became the equivalent of the community centre, where children and teenagers would run riot. Another house became the kitchen and area for raising the babies and children. Another house became the

Blackthorn headquarters. It was never entirely clear who lived in which house or caravan, and the children and adults seemed to move fluidly between them all. The Blackthorn community lived like this for years, but something changed in the eighties when Terry Blackthorn got himself elected and shored up their status by making it all legal, if not legit.'

'It's a hell of a story.'

'And it's not finished. We probably don't know half of what went on there.'

'What happens to those kids?'

'I think there are tough roads ahead.'

PART TWO:
Louise

Chapter One

The water finally runs clear.

I've been washing up my watercolour mixing pots in my downstairs loo-cum-brush-cleaning room, opposite my studio. I like to clear the decks when I've finished an illustration. I'm some way through the maddest art project I have done for some time. The idea grew from being fed up with children's mental health services. I wanted to find a way to communicate to children a simple life message: we can't feel happy all the time. Stuff happens. There are good days and bad days. Life is like the Circle Line on the London underground: it goes round and round, and sometimes we want to get off, but miss our stop. I have listened to *A Kiss in the Dream House* by Siouxsie and the Banshees three times in a row today. It's an album from my post-punk days that's full of melodrama and dark imagery, but it's nostalgic and cathartic for me. I *think* it's helping the art.

I return the pots and brushes to their homes and smell good things coming from the kitchen as I cross the hallway. My thoughts turn to dinner and the evening ahead. This is the joy that comes from the double whammy of working from home and being married to a man who likes cooking. I'm almost at the studio door to shut up for the day, when I change my mind and have a quick check of my emails. In particular, I'm looking out for foster care referrals. Generally, the local authority send out dozens of referrals each week looking for suitable foster homes for vulnerable children locally, and I've been hearing that recently there seem to have been even more than usual. I have space at the moment. My nest is filled only with my birth children, Jackson and Vincent, and my long-term foster child, Lily. All three are at secondary school now. I'm used to having four, and sometimes five, children in the house. It never seems to stay at three for very long.

Nothing doing though, still no referrals for me. This is strange, but I have a bit of an inkling.

I send a brief message to a fellow foster carer on WhatsApp. Like us, following the relentless wet weather, Lisa's home has recently been flooded. The horrible brown water has been coming into our hallway for years. During the wettest times I find myself out in the road until all hours of the morning in a high-vis jacket, sweeping it away from the door. The cars going by just wash it in more. It's hellish and dangerous, but sort of manageable. Then we had three larger-than-usual floods in one year. I can't describe how horrible the flood water was – full of sewage. I had to scrape off the poo that stuck to our walls. The hall floor rattles because it was lifted by the water. The June flood was so bad it appeared in an ITV documentary as well as being splashed all over the news.

It's horrid, and this time round it is taking months for the smell to go.

Because Lisa and I were flooded, we are both now 'at risk' of further flooding, so placements for new foster children are temporarily suspended. I suspect it's something to do with the local authority's insurance. But they are quite happy to leave Lily here, which shows how barmy it all is. I narrow my eyes and try not to feel too wound up. This is hard, as I'm now harbouring the knowledge that it might well be the same local authority who are effectively responsible for flooding us.

The world seems to have gone bonkers. Or perhaps it's just my age. But I hear it from people in their twenties and thirties too, so perhaps there's something in it. Jackson and Lily discuss the world a great deal, particularly on days when they've had a religious education lesson at school. I loved RE when I was at secondary school. It was the most philosophical of all the subjects, and teenagers love to be invited to really think about things. The children blame the flooding on the Boomers and Generation X. Well, that's me. I have to agree, too, because I watched *Blue Planet* and found myself crying my way through each episode. I had to force myself to watch them, because after the first 20 minutes of the first one I was already heartbroken and it would have been easier not to watch. But watch I did. So, for days since, I have been in mourning for the planet. I am guilt-ridden by every can of Boots Strong Hold hairspray that I ever used in the eighties (necessary at the time for recreating those Siouxsie Sioux hairdos). Then there are the countless aeroplane journeys, the mountains of ugly-looking plastic toys I have bought children over the years, the multiple times I have eaten in fast-food restaurants for convenience.

It's easy to hate myself.

But yesterday at dinner time, the WhatsApp Flood Group kept pinging with news that a report had revealed the flooding is actually caused by the run-off from the over-growing of maize. This causes soil erosion which, in turn, creates compacted fields. I've had a chance to do a bit more research today, and I think there's something in it.

Lloyd is stirring the curry when I enter the kitchen, and I receive a reproving look because I'm yet to put the rice on.

Apparently no one can boil up basmati rice like I can. I'm not flattered, or convinced (come on, really?), but busy myself getting the rice pan onto the hob to humour him. There's a ping on the phone from Lisa, replying to my text. She still seems to be off the referrals list, too, so it isn't personal, but she adds fuel to the flooding fire when she remarks:

Guess what? The run-off from the fields rushed over blocked drains and into our town.

There are links to a couple of reports. The County Council hasn't cleared or repaired the drains for years, even though they said that they had. The drains are blocked, with tree roots growing inside them, or they are collapsed and broken. The ditches are blocked, too. This combination of environmental factors and poor management is creating a local dystopia.

I feel strangely happier, and bizarrely relieved. I share the good news with Lloyd. Our floods are the fault of blocked drains and farmers. There's still the matter of the hole I created in the ozone layer with my hairspray, but I'm not singlehandedly to blame for the flooding. It feels weirdly comforting.

As Lloyd chops a red onion and cucumber into thin slices for the raita, I salivate for what's coming. I love curry. My favourite dish is tarka dhal. I love lentils. But I'm undiscerning. I happily eat curry of all descriptions. I love the smell of onion, garlic, cumin and garam masala. It's a combination that makes me feel inexplicably happy.

I rinse the rice in the sieve under the tap. The next stage is crucial. I remember years ago Levi Roots said on a cookery show to 'rinse the starch off the rice'. Well, if it's good enough for him ... I boil a kettle and heat some olive oil, and throw the wet rice in. It makes a great sound. Then I pour boiling water over the rice. I enjoy the whooshing business of the steam of the oil, rice and boiling water. When the rice is ready I put it back in the sieve and wash all the remaining starch off. Then I tip it into the dish and microwave it for three minutes. Lloyd might make fantastic curry, but perhaps he's right, I *am* the rice queen. Yes, I'll take that title.

Just when I feel as if I'm really nailing being 'in the moment', the phone pings. And pings again. And keeps pinging. Surely not the Flood Group again?

But it's not my fellow floodees: it's a different group, a local foster carers' network (some, like Lisa, are in both groups.) Five of the 38 WhatsApp group members have messaged simultaneously. First is Ali, who I love for her 'effing' this and 'effing' that, although I can't be in her company too long or I start going all dockyard too. She is such fun, and I adore her – but typically, her message on this occasion simply says 'WTF?' which leaves me none the wiser.

I scroll down. Debbie is a little more demure: *Why are there so many children all of a sudden?* Lisa sends me another message: *Have you had a referral? Check your email.*

I crease my eyebrows. 'Lisa's got a referral, so why haven't we?'

'Huh?' says Lloyd, but I'm halfway out of the door and heading along the corridor back to my studio. A decent foster carer in their prime *expects* to have a foster placement, flooding or not. I lift the lid of my laptop and, sure enough, in red text and capital letters, 'REFERRAL'.

I click into the email attachment and there is a picture and a name: Billy Blackthorn. Fostering services don't normally attach a picture of a child in the first instance; they usually prefer to do that in Adoption. Perhaps they think that foster carers will select and reject children according to how they look. I have never heard of such nonsense. Generally, foster carers' criteria is much more about age and needs. Far more useful in making a decision to see if the child in question will fit in with the other people in the home and with their commitment of time. Most foster carers have to work these days. The 1970s value allowance just doesn't cut it in today's terms. The reality is that most of us are actually paying to *be* foster carers, when you factor in school holidays and afterschool arrangements. No wonder they are struggling to recruit new carers. I scan down the page and then return to the wording of the email. I'm more interested in reading about the child and the circumstances than hearing from a social worker.

Yes, I'm being asked to consider taking Billy Blackthorn. So it looks like they may now be doing a U-turn. No mention of flood risk here. My phone keeps pinging. It's Ben, another one of our little carers' network. He's delightful. Sadly, his husband left him last year. As a single foster parent, Ben has managed to keep on the sibling group of three who he and the 'one we never mention' had looked after for five years before that. That's commitment for you. It can't be easy being a single foster parent; it's hard enough when there are two of you. But he is brilliant. He was a successful chef working in Mayfair until he and the OWNM decided to nest together and raise children. His message reflects my own thoughts: *Cripes, what's going on?*

More and more pings from different foster carers follow, all basically wondering what the hell is happening. We've all received referrals for different children. Our little group is being 'flooded', but with this group it's children rather than water.

By the time I return, Lloyd has placed the feast on the table. And it really is a feast, especially given that it's only Tuesday night. I walk around the kitchen with the phone in my hand.

'Really, Louise? You look remarkably like one of the older children.'

I realise, alas, that this isn't a reference to my youthful good looks, but to the fact that my eyes are fixed on the screen, which means that I'm not looking at what I'm doing.

'Hmmm.' They talk in that distracted way, too. I pull out one plate at a time from the rack, pile them up and with my strong hand take them to the table to distribute while reading more messages.

'Seriously . . . ' Lloyd is about to huff and puff and be cross that I'm only half present in the room when Vincent arrives. He's wearing his onesie and asks, 'When's dinner ready?' (or something like that). I'm not really listening, and too busy looking at the messages to make a comment like, 'When do you think, Vincent?', given that Lloyd has already placed the big pan of curry loveliness onto the stripey-coloured table runner in the middle.

Lloyd, already frustrated with me, can't resist.

'Vincent, what does it look like I'm doing?'

Vincent has reached that teenage growing stage where his nose has grown but the rest of the face is still to follow. Other bits of his body are doing the same: limbs too long for his height. It makes him look all gangly and not quite in proportion. The blue tartan fluff of his onesie is also at odds with the usual teenage attire, too. The whole effect is adorable.

Lloyd's comment goes straight over his head, and his answer is to grab a poppadom from a plate and sit down.

They must have a sixth sense, because Lily comes in next. Her version of hello these days is restricted to, 'What have *I* got?' Having Lily as our only vegetarian can be a challenge given that she still doesn't like a single vegetable. Chips and crisps count as vegetables to her, and a baked potato during a full moon. We buy her many expensive pies and patties, tofu, quorn: you name it, we've tried. Lloyd gets more frustrated than me, and I suspect that's because his family was more middle-class than mine. We had 'tea', his family had 'dinner, darling'. He expects more of the meal, and more of us in response to it, than I would. I have learnt to keep a few cans of tomato or winter vegetable soup in the cupboard. Sometimes I will make mashed potato mountain. Lily loves it. I put a mound of mash in a bowl and pour soup around it like a castle with a moat. It's guaranteed to annoy Lloyd, who prefers a 'proper' meal. I wonder if this goes on in other households. I imagine it does.

The phone keeps pinging but it's not acceptable at the dining table, so I put it in the sitting room, out of temptation's way, and return to the table. I can still hear it, though. I feel about 14 and I know Lloyd is not impressed. Oh well, we'll get dinner over with and then I'll get back on it.

Jackson isn't joining us yet. He's still out at rugby training. I serve up his portion on a plate and cover it with tin foil until he returns. I'm rather humouring the rugby thing. Jackson *looks* like he's built for rugby. When rugby players see him, they want him in their team, but I know he will never pursue it. I've stood on the sidelines with the other parents, cheering and chatting. I've seen him run for the ball, knock into another boy, and then stop mid-play to ask if he is alright. Jackson is not aggressive in the least.

It's good that he's trying it out, but I'm sure it will be short-lived.

The feast is devoured and the table cleared. I rinse the dishes before I stack them into the dishwasher. Recently I was listening to a science programme on Radio 4 where various experts were discussing the findings that using a dishwasher, even half a load, is actually more ecological and cheaper than using a washing-up bowl. I close the doors and press the on switch. *Rhmmm.* The water surges behind the closed door, and I'm satisfied that I'm doing at least a little bit to offset those hairspray cans. I dry my hands on the tea towel, throwing it on the floor in front of the washing machine, and put on the next load.

Even though I'm itching to get back to my phone, I make sure all of this is done properly. If any of my kitchen appliances break down, it alters my life immeasurably. Therefore I keep them all oiled, limescale-free, and with clear filters. I have learnt the necessity of looking after my domestic infrastructure. I need my home to run smoothly.

I pick up the phone. Unsurprisingly, there are a few more WhatsApp messages from the flood group. Brian, who is a retired planning officer, is hilarious. His favourite epithet for those in charge is 'liars and cheats', and he often sends messages questioning their tax rates and payments. Like me, he believes in the importance of 'following the money'. I got that phrase from a professor emeritus called Eric. He was an economist, whose professional opinion was always sought after in the wake of a disaster such as a bombing, or an influx of refugees, and particularly so around election time. He would always advise people to 'follow the money'. I thought he was a genius, until I realised he had nicked it from the 1976 documentary-style film *All the President's Men*. Whatever its origins, I have found it a useful adage.

My focus switches to the other big chat of the evening, the foster carers' WhatsApp group. I have 11 new messages. There is one from Sylvia, whose husband is a policeman. He is very nice; I like them both very much. I enjoy their resistance to not joining in a moan about the system. They usually rise above it. But occasionally something rattles them, and then you can't get them to shut up. Sylvia's comment is quite out of character.

Howdy partners, it looks like all these children come from the famous Blackthorn family home. They're bad news, the whole family. There are a lot of children.

There is a second message from her below the first: *This is not going to be easy. None of what went on in that family was good.*

There is a third message from her, which reads as both a warning and a call to arms: *Look after yourselves, this is going to be interesting so let's do it together.*

The plot thickens. I move to the sitting room to find Lloyd, who is now lying on the floor with a cushion under his head, watching something unfathomable called *The 100*. It's an American sci-fi drama of some sort, not my thing.

'Have a look at this.' I show him the picture of Billy and the rest of the referral. There is hardly any information to go with it, which means either they have none, or it's terrible so they've redacted it. I don't share Sylvia's pearls of wisdom.

Lloyd is tired and says, 'Yes, if you want to. I'll leave it to you.'

Bad move. He knows I'm likely to say yes. Ordinarily I would leap in straight away. We've been waiting for a foster child since Floodgate, after all. And I can't help but be intrigued by the notion that suddenly a whole raft of children are looking for homes at the same time, and they've all come from the same place. There would be great support from within our local carers' group if we were all to invite children into our homes simultaneously. But Sylvia's words have sounded the warning note they intended.

I decide to sleep on it.

Chapter Two

The next day, Lloyd is up at 5am. He is ready for his business trip to Germany, where a group of designers, engineers and marketing people will meet to plan campaigns for the year ahead. Lloyd is part of the graphic design team and likes going to these things. Who can blame him? It's as close as he gets to peace and quiet. I remember hearing that during their marriage, Paul and Linda McCartney were never apart. Blimey. I can't say that would suit me – I think I'd scream. But not everyone's the same, thankfully. I am still heavy-lidded and full of sleep when he makes his departure. Though a relatively early riser myself, this is just a little bit too much before dawn for my liking.

Once the children are up I ask them if they could give me five minutes of their attention to look at the referral for Billy Blackthorn. They are experienced foster siblings, they know their stuff, and they're old enough for their voices to be important in the decisions that we make as a family.

I show them the picture and the blurb that has come with it.

'Is that all there is?' Lily asks, incredulous.

Vincent shakes his head. 'Never a good sign when there isn't much info.'

I smile. They sound like seasoned foster carers themselves.

And I agree. It never *is* a good sign. Perhaps way back in the beginning when I was a shiny brand new foster carer, I might have toyed with the idea that there was a mystery, or perhaps an opportune moment for a clean slate. But now, years in, I see that limited amount of information and the alarm bells ring. Experience has made me suspicious.

The phone pings, as Lily makes an observation. 'Hmmm. He's got weird eyes.'

I think she's referring to a kind of unevenness between them. I noticed it too and suspect astigmatism or something, but, unlike Lily, would be too polite to draw attention to it.

It's a fairly inconclusive exchange before they all rush away from the kitchen and back to their various rooms and activities. There are unsubtle attempts to nick a bag of crisps or a KitKat to eat on the way. Honestly, I just cooked them a good breakfast. Hollow legs!

I scoot around the house, gathering laundry, opening windows. My birth children always sleep with a little gap of air. Like me, they like the fresh air and a room that doesn't smell. Foster children, on the other hand, are often not taught the joy of an aired room, fresh bedding and clean sleepwear. Lily's room looks like she was burgled by a poltergeist, and can often smell like an open grave. Okay, that's a little harsh, but no matter how often I tell them not to take food to their rooms, they all do. Lily is particularly guilty, and hasn't joined up her thinking on the laws of crockery: what plates and bowls go up, must come down.

The phone pings again, reminding me that I didn't check the last notification. It's my fellow flood foster carer, Lisa. She's agreed to take one of the Blackthorn children. I thought she might. She's a single mum and depends on every penny. When foster carers are without a placement, they are without their living too. I have always thought this was the wrong way to reward long-term foster carers. But, of course, according to the government, and national and local authorities, we're below the basement in the house of parenting. Her next message wants to know if I'm going to take one.

Oh God, I don't know.

I think part of my reluctance is because I'm a bit cross with the local authority and their capacity to change the goalposts so often, and always to suit themselves. In our guest room above the dedicated children's rooms, we have an antique Breton bed. It's a small double bed, probably four feet wide. We slept in it together once. Lloyd fell out. No, I didn't push him. There just wasn't as much room as we're used to. At our last annual review, we were told by the fostering approval panel that because of the spare room, we could only do emergency respite. (There is a bit of the 'blues and twos' excitement and drama about emergency placements.) But rather than say, *Yes, great, that's another bed. Thanks for offering*, one of the panel decided that foster children would be, and I quote, 'traumatised' if they slept in a double bed.

Give me strength.

We missed out on helping several children because of that weird mentality. That is, until one night, when we were asked to take a 13-year-old girl as an emergency placement. I suppose they must have been desperate to resort to our outrageous offer. We put her in the guest room and she loved it. In fact, she loved it so much she told her best friend and fellow foster child to come too. That child kicked up a stink with the social workers, because she wanted to stay as well. We ended up having both girls sleeping in the Breton bed for a weekend – totally untraumatised, I might add, and a bit like the actual normal behaviour of two teenage besties.

I send a holding message back to Lisa. *I don't know yet, I'll have a think.* It's true: I really am undecided on this one.

Next, I open up my email inbox to find 10 red-flagged emails. I am popular all of a sudden. All are from the placements team. *Have you had time to decide?* Blimey, they're desperate. It is laughable the way that suddenly being in the foster carers' flood risk chart doesn't seem to matter anymore.

Oh Louise, get over yourself! I annoy myself sometimes with the over-analysis. Thankfully, another text has arrived to prevent me hurtling down an alleyway of rant. Dara, our most brilliant supervising social worker, wants to come over. That'll be nice. She has been with us for quite some time now, and we get on very well. But why is she coming over when she could talk to me on the phone? I feel a bit on the back foot today and need to get on. There seems to be a lot of work to do. Foster carers' days are often like liquid: we end up moving and flowing according to what's pushing or pulling us. I would like to say 'ebbs and flows', but that's too gentle for how the life of a foster carer sometimes feels. Still water one minute, hurricanes the next.

I say yes to Dara popping round, and also add a question in my text. *Have you seen the referral?* She comes straight back in the affirmative.

I decide to wait until I have seen her, and not to respond just yet to the now very desperate-sounding placements team. Another red flag email from them has popped up in the time it has taken me to read and reply to Dara. I'm feeling a bit bombarded, even though nothing's actually happening. I think I'll take the dogs for a walk and clear my head. Dealing with the flooding has made me physically tired, and the constant threat of more bad weather is keeping me anxious. I've been made to feel guilty for 'neglecting' my house and carelessly allowing it to flood, in spite of raising my fears with the appropriate bodies over the years. Then I've been penalised for it as a foster carer. The whole thing makes me more than a little angry.

It's not dissimilar to children entering the care system. In many cases, neighbours, friends and family will have gone through the process of lodging their concerns, only to feel as though those concerns have been ignored. I read recently about a little girl who was beaten and killed by her mother and mother's partner. The grandparents and some of their own friends repeatedly expressed their anxiety about the situation, but nothing happened until it was too late. There seems to be a 'cross your fingers that it goes away' mentality. The child died. Now they *are* doing something. But it won't bring the child back.

The flooding is destroying lives and livelihoods, but again I suspect nothing will be done until something serious happens – perhaps until someone dies. It must take a special kind of mentality to operate in local or national government.

I've got my wellies, two coats, a pair of gloves and two dogs, and will feel better for a blowy walk up on the hills.

Back at home, with my head now a little clearer, I dry Dotty and Douglas off with Vincent's old beach towel, kept by the back door for this purpose. The Jackawawas (Jack Russell-Chihuahua crosses) have run their little legs off, and my cheeks are rosy with the exertion. There is something about going for a walk that is inexplicably good. Now I'm feeling less explosive, and ready to begin the day properly.

Time to take another look at Billy's referral. But straight away I see another red flag email from the placements team. I realise that I don't like their attitude – that's what's wrong. It feels intrusive, rude and pushy. I don't want to wind myself up again, so I delete those follow-up red flags to make sure that they aren't shouting at me from the inbox, and concentrate on Billy. I look closely at his picture, because there isn't much else to go on. As Lily said, there is something wrong with his eyes. Astigmatism in one eye can cause a lazy eye, where the vision doesn't develop properly. It's important that it's caught early so it can be treated, but of course, that's unlikely to be the case when a child has come into care as a result of neglect. The window of time to strengthen the weak eye and correct the vision with glasses may have passed by the time they come into care. It's difficult to treat a lazy eye after the age of six. It's one of the first things I do with a new child: eyes, teeth, and doctor's check. I then do my own observations of their mental health. Lloyd always says that children should have a complete mental and physical health check as they come into care. Then they are more likely to stay in placements, because foster carers can plan better and engage with the issues much earlier on, rather than feeling bombarded and unsupported. It's always the 'bleeding obvious' when it comes to problem-solving with children's social care. I just think the system has grown beyond all reasonable thinking because it's one great big decrepit piece of machinery itself: the basics are missed because there's always a crisis to focus on.

Normally I love looking at pictures of children's faces, but I'm having a different experience looking at Billy's picture. In the absence of words, a picture tells its own story. Billy's face is, for want of a better word, flat. It's nondescript. There are none of the usual quirks in expression, a curl of the corner of a mouth, a glint in the eye, to give anything away. Billy looks empty, despite the difficulties that he has been through. I wonder if I am just making excuses, procrastinating with my decision to accept his referral. Something is holding me back, though. Normally I would love the challenge of being able to help make a child smile, to hear laughter, to be part of the process of making things better. I don't know why, but for some reason I'm not getting this buzz from Billy.

I read the referral in full again. It doesn't take long:

Billy is 5 years old. He has experienced neglect and other suspected abuse. Billy and his siblings came into care together after some concern from the community.

I normally read several pages, and have got quite good at reading between the lines, but this is it. They either know nothing or are, as my children so astutely pointed out, hiding something. Which is it? The plethora of those red-flag emails testifies to how desperate the authorities are. I keep looking at his face. He has thick brown curly hair, arched eyebrows, but those eyes, is it just the stigma? I don't know. He has hazel-green eyes, but the eyelids are large and heavy, like hoods, or blinds half-closed. He has a sweet little nose, his face is heart shaped, he has a soft cleft chin that will grow into one like Clint Eastwood's. They can look very attractive. I notice another red flag email has arrived. *Leave me alone!* The authority's pushiness has the opposite effect of that intended, only increasing my determination not to reply straight away.

I carry on with some work, or try to, fully aware that I'm distracted. I have an illustration on the go, inspired by a seahorse. I choose to do a bit of the work that feels like colouring in – nothing too taxing on my brain. I half-listen to *Woman's Hour* as I drift off into thoughts about colours at the bottom of the sea and how beautiful and graceful seahorses are. I've almost pushed the Billy question out of my mind when a notification arrives from the foster carers'

WhatsApp group. It's Sandra. She is a retired nurse who has, to use her own phrase, 'seen it all.' I believe her and the stories she comes out with. Her message is an update for those of us still considering referrals.

Her ward was delivered an hour ago. So far, the 11-year-old boy has sat in the corner of her kitchen, head down, not a peep. Sandra is a legend: if anyone is able to coax a child out of their shell and away from their fears, it's her – especially when her homemade brownies are on offer. She adds vanilla ice cream while they're warm. I know this because I popped over for coffee a few months ago and nearly moved in because her baking is so amazing.

Just as *Woman's Hour* signs off, Dara knocks at the front door.

I can tell immediately that something's up. I've known Dara longer than most of our supervising social workers. In the past (I refrain from saying 'normally'), they have often lasted only a few months. I don't take it personally. I know it's the system pushing them away because they've had enough. Initially I think she's come to tell me about Billy, to persuade me to take him, or to warn me off, but no, she shakes her head. It's not about Billy.

'Or not directly,' she adds, in her clipped, efficient and well-enunciated Slavic accent, with its tell-tale rolled 'r' sounds.

I lead her into the kitchen, the first port of call for anyone arriving at our house, but I detect a heaviness in the air. I switch on the coffee machine and turn to face her. She doesn't say anything, but her eyes begin to well up.

'You're leaving, aren't you?' My tone is more accusatory than I intend.

Her brow creases. 'Yes, I am.'

Oh dear, this calls for posh chocolate cookies. I bypass the biscuit tin and plonk the box down on the table. If it were dinner time I'd bring out the wine and kettle crisps. I feel so deflated, but Dara looks crushed. Our relationship, no, our *friendship*, is such that I can say:

'Dara, please don't bullshit me. What's going on?'

She looks sad. It's been a while since I've seen her, actually. Our last supervision meeting was a month ago. I got a feeling then that her sparkle wasn't quite as bright as it had been, but we all have off days. I thought she was tired.

I'm right. She is tired, and it all comes pouring out. She's tired of feeling like it's coming at her from all directions, tired that she is not being listened to, tired of the negative attitude some social workers and their managers have towards the children and the foster carers.

I let her vent. I've been here before with social workers when they've resigned. I know how liberating it can feel to get thoughts like this off your chest.

'But Louise, let me tell you about the final straw that broke the camel's back.'

I love her oh-so-precise English, even when she's using an idiom like this.

'Five weeks ago I had a very busy day visiting all my foster carers and trying to help create some traction in their requests for support from the system. Then I went back to the office to write up my reports. I was sitting at my desk and I heard two colleagues talking. They were so full of mockery.'

I misunderstand. 'Mocking you?'

'No, mocking the taste of one of their foster carers. They mocked her curtains, her carpets, her choice of furniture. Everything. They criticised her clothes and her hair.'

She puffs up with anger as she recounts the story. 'And do you know, Louise, they did not once talk about her work.'

'Did you know the foster carer they were mocking?' I ask.

'Yes, of course. I knew her well. She was one of mine until I complained about my workload. They swept several of mine from one postcode over to a new supervising social worker, then I lost touch.'

'Is she a good foster carer?' I ask, knowing damn well that we aren't allowed to talk like this, really, but she isn't revealing names. We're not supposed to talk about anything that isn't directly related to the fostering situation – or at least that's the impression that's given, but that's not how human relationships work. It's not how friendships are built.

'Yes, Louise,' Dara nods, sadly. 'She and her husband are lovely, kind people. They are very experienced. They have been fostering for over twenty years, and this is how we treat them? It is not cricket. I just couldn't stand it any longer.'

It most certainly isn't cricket, and at any other time, I'd be amused by the way she uses another colloquial phrase (does she even know what cricket is?), but she is too distraught for jokes now.

'What will you do instead?'

'I'm going to have a break first of all. I think I'm entitled to that. Then I think I may do something different. I don't really know.' She smiles.

'You're *definitely* entitled to a break,' I tell her.

That smile is why I liked Dara the moment I met her. Wide-eyed and utterly open, it's a 'whole face' smile. They're rarer than you might think.

'Who knows? I may help a certain foster carer with her work,' she adds.

We say no more. I don't *think* the local authority have

taken to putting spy technology into my kitchen (though it can feel like that at times), but we know we are trespassing further into dangerous territory.

The conversation moves onto Billy Blackthorn. I run down the corridor into my studio and grab my laptop. Surprise, surprise, another red flag email from placements.

I open it with a raised eyebrow and watch Dara's expression. She is not amused either.

She tuts. 'I *told* them that I would talk to you first, and that you had a flood risk warning on your file.'

'Looks like it's no risk at all now that they're in dire need,' I laugh.

'It isn't right.'

'No, well, never mind the rightness or wrongness of it. What do you know about the Blackthorns? What's going on with all of this? I know that there are suddenly a lot of children.'

'A *lot* of children. It is a little bit weird. Normally we would catch wind of a case like this, but all I know is that two days ago there was a raid somewhere—' she breaks off to gesture vaguely in the direction of the garden, 'in the northeast of the county, and there are over twenty children now needing emergency placements.'

'A raid to remove twenty children. That's high drama.'

'Yes, but I don't know much more than that.'

'Where's Billy staying right now?' I ask.

Dara shrugs her shoulders. 'He could be staying with a social worker. That's happened before when we can't find a placement.'

'That's definitely called taking your work home with you. Tell me, Dara, I'm really in two minds on this one, and I need your honest opinion. Should we take this child?'

I trust Dara totally. We've been through so much together. She, like me, knows that sometimes we just have to take a punt.

'Why not, Louise? You're itching to be involved. I can tell.'

While Dara munches on a consoling cookie, I text Lloyd in Germany to see if he's happy about us having Billy. Amazing that he's travelled to central Europe in the time it has taken me to get everyone out to school, do the morning chores, and get cross about some emails.

Within a few minutes, two emojis appear: a smiling face followed by a thumbs up. Good enough. I lean towards my laptop.

'Here we go then.'

I compose my short response to the Placements Team, resisting the urge to thank them for all 12 of their emails, or to point out that they should have contacted Dara first. Sometimes the Placements Team will circumnavigate a protective supervising social worker to get a child parked as soon as possible. They will also have noticed that we were on hold, pending a further flood-risk assessment, and perhaps they assumed that we might be in need of the money. They will know as well as I do that foster carers can end up living a hand-to-mouth existence because of the poor allowances, exacerbated if they haven't had a placement for a while. Perhaps they have bombarded my inbox because they suspect that I will take any child just to get the finances working again.

We are interested in fostering Billy. Can you ask his social worker to contact me, please? I leave my number below.

Dara and I chat about other things. About Lily and her homework. She is as bright as a pin, but lazy. We chat about how perhaps that laziness is actually more to do with avoidance. Avoidance that is perhaps triggered by her fear of failure, in turn created by her low self-esteem. Around five minutes later, my phone goes. I don't recognise the number.

A female voice responds when I pick up. 'Hello, is that Louise?'

'Hello, yes, that's me.'

'My name is Jessica Smyth. I'm Billy's social worker and I wanted to talk about him with you, if that's okay?'

I signal a thumbs up to Dara while I say to Jessica, 'I'm with my supervising social worker right now. Are you happy for me to put you on speaker phone?'

Before Dara had handed in her notice she would have been keen to work with Jessica, to establish a relationship with her (she is one of those protective supervising social workers, after all), but it doesn't matter now. Still, I'd like her to hear the conversation.

I mouth, 'Do you know her?'

She shakes her head and shrugs her shoulders.

'So, Billy and his siblings were brought into care two days ago,' Jessica explains once I have switched the speaker on.

I ask the question we all ask about sibling groups: 'Why are the siblings being separated?'

'There's rather a lot of them. There are twenty-six in total.'

'Twenty-six *siblings*,' I repeat, to confirm that I've heard her correctly, while Dara and I look at each other, our eyes like saucers.

'That's right,' she gives a little, strangled laugh.

I sit up a little straighter. 'Woah, that's a lot of siblings.'

'We're not quite sure what any of them are like, and it's pretty chaotic if I'm honest.'

I like Jessica's honesty, already.

'We're going to have to do the assessments once they are in placement,' she continues.

'Where's Billy now?'

'He's with one of the Child Protection team's social workers. I mean, you can imagine, with this number of children so suddenly, the situation required a different approach.'

'I'll bet.'

'I mean, I've taken a little girl myself for two nights, while Placements try to find somewhere, ideally in-house.'

We all know that it's much cheaper to foster children using 'in-house' carers like us, on the books of the local authority. We also know that most teenagers will do the rounds of the IFAs (independent fostering agencies) at much greater expense, because generally most foster carers want easier children and see teenagers as more of a challenge.

I personally disagree with this philosophy. I've looked after plenty of younger children who have run me ragged, while teenagers, who of course have their issues to manage, have on the whole been wonderful to work with.

I ask about the basic, practical stuff next. 'What's he like? What does he like to do?'

Jessica won't know it, but me asking the question means that I'm no longer merely 'interested' in Billy; inside I've said 'yes' to having him.

'Not the answer you want, but so far, we haven't been able to ascertain any information about any of them beyond names and rough ages. It would, ah, appear that most of their births are unregistered.'

'Most of their births are not registered?' I repeat, incredulous. This is an enormous act of neglect and cruelty, as far as I can see. It makes me sick to the core, because it means that their parents or whoever was looking after them did not want them *officially* in the world. If that is the case, you have to ask, *why?* There isn't usually a 'good' answer to that question, in my experience.

I agree to be in at lunchtime, because Jessica would like to drop him off.

That's it. It's as quick and easy as that. After no placement for a while, I will welcome young Billy Blackthorn into our home today.

Chapter Three

Dara goes into a weird professional mode.

Because I know her quite well, I recognise this demeanour, and try not to smile too much when she transforms suddenly from the relaxed, shared intimacy of a few moments earlier into what appears to be an impersonation of someone 'doing' a social worker. Her compassionate face is firmly fixed in place, and she is full of helpful advice, all the while modelling a calm and helpful demeanour.

Meanwhile, Jessica doesn't hang about.

Within minutes an email arrives, confirming that she and Billy Blackthorn will be arriving at 1pm.

'The eagle is landing at one o'clock,' I say to Dara.

'Right,' she says, looking at her watch and evidently doing some calculations. 'I've got a supervision on the other side of town to fit in first, but I will be back here with you before 1pm.'

Another reason I adore Dara. No de-mob sensibility here. She just makes things happen. She's truly a good human. I'm always grateful for the chance to work with caring human beings. I find that with that deep empathy, there's usually a good sense of humour. I'm not sure how I would have coped in the corporate world. I might have been sacked for laughing too much and not taking 'strategy' seriously enough.

My strategy for today is simply to cross my fingers and hope it all goes okay. The pace of the day is so fast that I didn't even ask Jessica what food Billy liked. Not that she would have known the answer, I suspect. I think I've got all bases covered in the freezer, and if all else fails I've still got packets of Fox's Christmas biscuits selection in a cupboard. Nobody's going to starve.

I look around at the house, trying to imagine someone seeing it for the first time. It's in pretty good shape, all things considered. The children haven't broken the sofa or pulled the curtains down lately, so that's a good start. I whizzed the vacuum round yesterday, and mopped the floor. That's why I have lower back pain. I knew housework was a health hazard.

I have an hour until Billy and Jessica arrive.

My tummy is rumbling, but I'm in a two and eight so can't eat until the little fella is in and the social worker has gone. I've worked with a social worker called Jessica before, and it wasn't that great. It's funny how you make certain associations with certain names. Years ago, an old boyfriend's mum, who was a teacher, told me that she dreaded Christophers in her class. She said that they were always a bit cocky and sure of themselves. I don't know about that, but I suppose being a teacher must give you a bit of insight. I know that a lot of my friends are called 'Kate' or 'Sarah' since I moved to the West Country. When I lived in Portsmouth my friends' names seemed to be much more diverse.

I chastise myself for going off on another little thought-tangent. I'm literally driving myself crazy. I hate these weird little pockets of time, when there's not quite enough to achieve anything, but it's not short enough to justify *not* achieving anything. I go upstairs and check the bathrooms, then take one last look at the room that has been available but inhabited for weeks thanks to the flooding.

I hope Billy likes it.

By 12.45pm, Dara is back. She dashes in and hangs up her coat and hat without invitation, as though she is at home. I'm delighted that she can do that. I eye up the hat, a rather lovely fawn wool with the softest fur bobble sprouting from the top. She didn't get that from New Look. Standing in my kitchen, she places herself in front of me and rubs my arms up and down with both hands.

'I'm going to miss you, Louise. And your family. There has never been a dull moment.'

'Oh, shut up, and get on with life,' I say, but only because I'm feeling emotional. I'm going to miss her, too.

She hands me an envelope. Inside is a card. It is a thick, expensive card from the Victoria and Albert Museum. I recognise the image, 'Strawberry Thief,' one of William Morris's famous repeating designs. It's based on the thrushes that he discovered stealing fruit in his kitchen garden. I have the background design curtains in my middle room. This is a room in my house where children and pets are not allowed to go without permission. The vinyl and turntable are in there, along with our precious books. The books are all carefully arranged according to Lloyd logic, so I haven't a clue where anything is, but it looks good. Dara knows it is a special place for me. Inside the card is a long and lovely message that includes her private number and email. Good old Dara. I will find a way to let her know how much I think of her, too.

At last, the sound of the door.

I am released from the frustrating anticipation and endless mind-chatter. I know my role: I am a foster carer. I have purpose. Here we go. Let's meet Billy Blackthorn.

I can only see the silhouette through the glass panel of the front door. A tall lady, with lots of hair. And, just above the lowest bit of patterned glass, a head moving up and down. Deep breath.

I open the door. 'Hi Jessica, and you must be Billy.'

Jessica smiles at me and says, 'I'm Emma.'

Right, okay then. Who knows what happened to Jessica?

'Hi Emma,' I try again. We smile at each other and then I'm straight back to Billy. He is about the right size for a five-year-old boy, a bit on the thin side, but he looks nourished. Though 'looking nourished' can really mean anything. His hair is curly and looks reasonably well cut, though my eagle eye, acutely trained in headlice spotting, is activated. There is definitely some jumping activity.

I make my quick mental list of things to target over the next few days. I'm used to it now, and can make all this happen in a matter of seconds. If you're familiar with the *Terminator* films then you'll know about the machine's motion tracking, search modes and facial identification capabilities. I have the foster carer's version of that. I scan Billy quickly so he doesn't feel uncomfortable, and Emma doesn't think I'm a weirdo.

I wave them in joyfully. I'm always genuinely excited by a new arrival in our home. I notice that Emma gently places a few fingers very lightly on his upper back to encourage him in.

Billy crouches, bent-kneed, leaning forward, like a skier at the top of the slalom, and launches himself over the threshold step. Then begins laughing. I guide them towards the direction of the kitchen, where Dara is evidently 'negotiating' with Dotty. Dotty is much more than a little dog. It would be more accurate to say that she is one of my foster caring assistants. Right now, she is as excited as I am, and while it would be difficult to prove, I'd say she knows exactly what's going on here, knows that there will be work to do. Dara is trying to get her to stop barking, in case Billy is not comfortable around dogs. It can be a bit hectic with doorbells and dog chaos if you aren't used to it. Dotty is just letting us know that she is here should her services be required.

Billy hears the bark and darts through the hall towards the sound. He shoots a quick look at me, releases an enormous smile and begins pulling at my arm.

'Dog, dog, dog,' he shouts, excitedly. Then he begins to bark.

Dara gives up and releases Douglas and Dotty into the hall. Emma backs away. I'm sure that if you are a social worker, whose job it is to go into people's homes, then you probably have some experience of man's best friend, especially in areas like this where everyone has at least one dog. She seems scared. They are a bit loud, but being half Jack Russell and half Chihuahua, they only come up as far as most Labradors' knees.

Billy thinks the dogs are hilarious. He runs along the hall calling out, 'dog, dog, dog' again, in between the intermittent barking. 'Come on!' he calls, I'm not sure to whom, and then confidently turns left and heads along the corridor towards my studio. I rush ahead of him, closing all the doors. I don't want this little whirlwind in the middle room, and definitely not in my studio, where I have all sorts of stuff in progress. Big jars of water are lined up against the wall board, with soaked water colour paper taped onto them.

I suddenly feel self-conscious. It's having a new social worker in my midst. You never know if they may take umbrage to, well, anything really. We're trained not to raise our voices. That might well work if you only have one child and plenty of calming, scented candles. In my house, raising one's voice is sometimes the only way we can be heard, or head off danger. But for now, I must be the lovely therapeutic foster carer who lives and breathes the messages from the training sessions. Training sessions, incidentally, which are often run by people who have never fostered children.

I manage to shut my studio door and usher Billy and the dogs back to the hall, where Dara is talking to Emma. I know that she will be doing much more than talking, she'll be checking her out.

We all move towards the kitchen and pull out chairs, apart from Billy, who is looking in the larder cupboard by the fridge. That was skilful. I'm impressed. I genuinely did not see him flit over to that part of the kitchen. He's like a ninja.

Emma pulls out some paperwork from her bag. I've got the same one from H&M, and I use mine when I go to meetings in London. Big enough to carry my laptop, water bottle, makeup, plus my little travel medical bag and sweets. It has the artful knack of looking more expensive than it was: at £15.99, a bargain. She seems a little new at this, a little stagey in her approach. I can see from the way Dara is behaving towards her, more like a kindly aunt now rather than a fellow professional, that she has drawn the same conclusion.

I put the dogs in the garden while watching Billy out of the corner of my eye. He moves around my kitchen as if he is casing the joint, but I know he isn't. I've seen this with some of the other children I have looked after. I think of Abby and Stella, in particular. They were like cats on hot tin roofs when they arrived. Dark pasts create future fears, and a new place is suspect. When you have been badly treated, the fear is that it will happen again.

I let Dara and Emma talk while I walk, very gently, nearer to Billy. He moves towards my cupboard of doom, the one I really would prefer the social workers not to see. It's full of games, badly stacked by the children, and there's one nestling in there that I'd rather didn't come under the close scrutiny of the social workers.

Billy's got it. Great! With some kind of sixth sense, he has reached for Cards Against Humanity. The older children (my stepchildren from Lloyd's previous partner) have moved out now, but they brought it round for Christmas. They sat at the kitchen table, drank cider, played the game and laughed raucously while I watched *Call the Midwife* and munched on Twiglets in the sitting room. Sometimes you feel that social workers will be freaked out if foster carers show any signs of behaving just like normal people do. I'm cross with myself for being so keen to put up a front in this way. I think it's just that I know what silly things have been pounced on by social workers in the past.

I manage to remove the cards from him without drawing too much attention to them.

'Would you like a biscuit?' I ask.

Billy is impressed with this idea, and follows me over to the other side of the kitchen to the coffee and tea zone. Cups line the cupboard and biscuits fill the tin. What five-year-old wouldn't like the biscuit tin? I open the lid and tilt the tin to show Billy just what delights he can try. His eyes are huge, the smile is wide. I realise he is literally salivating when dribble begins to spill out of the corners of his mouth onto his top. His top and entire outfit have all the signs of emergency. The jumper is the wrong size, as are his trousers. His shoes are clearly out of date: blue and red Spiderman-themed Velcro plastic trainers. I think Jackson had the same ones years ago. I didn't notice a suitcase or a bag with his stuff in, and he wasn't holding a teddy bear, which many do as they come to the door, even the teenagers.

'Emma, has Billy got a bag?' I pipe up.

She reaches down into her bag and pulls out a semi-filled Sainsbury's plastic shopping bag. She holds out her arm indicating for me to take it while she stays locked in conversation with her short-term mentor, Dara. I hold the biscuit tin towards Billy for a second time and he happily takes another. I put the tin down and look inside his bag.

I don't really like disturbing the mentoring session that is taking place, but there are practical things to consider here. 'Emma, sorry, is there more stuff coming?' I pipe up again.

She moves her eyes away from Dara the Sage for a moment. 'No, that's it.'

A little, 'Wow', spills quietly from my lips before I can help it. I reach for the biscuit tin to offer Billy another. I want the social workers, even my lovely Dara, to hurry up and go. I want to get on and help this child, whose whole life can be contained in half a carrier bag. Just a few sweatshirts. No keepsakes; not even a cuddly toy, it seems.

Eventually they get up and I make all the right noises: that everything will be fine, I will check in again in the morning, let them know how he settles, yes, yes of course. Politely, I open the front door and wave goodbye.

Billy is by my side. Or at least he was a second ago. Where's he gone now?

He has transported himself upstairs. I can hear him and the dogs running along the landing. I head upstairs after them, foster carer's caring but firm smile drawn onto my face, ready to head off any resistance to coming back downstairs. Just as I approach the three musketeers, Billy, Douglas and Dotty, the door goes.

'Stay there, I'll be straight back,' I say. The dogs might understand, but Billy doesn't. I watch him head into Jackson's bedroom as I run back downstairs.

It is Emma, holding a set of teddy bears. *There* they are, I think. I smile and thank her, and quickly run upstairs with them. Two were clearly old friends of Billy, that could both do with a wash, but not yet: too soon. The other teddy is new. Billy sees the teddies and grabs all three.

Normally, a social worker would have had a quick look at the child's bedroom. I guess Emma, Jessica, and actually every social worker in the local land, is up to their eyes with the Blackthorns; they must feel like it's coming at them from every direction. Today is all about speed, and Billy certainly has some speed, I can tell you. Each time I take my eyes off him for a fraction of a second, he's gone. I can find him easily because he's got the dogs following him everywhere. They are ruthless. I know they're eyeing him up as someone who might potentially provide them with titbits. They won't let him out of their sight.

I have another déjà vu moment. Right now he reminds me again of Abby, a little girl who had been sexually abused. It's the hyper-hurtling around at breakneck speed that triggers the memory. Let's hope he has a happier history than she did.

Chapter Four

'Hey Billy, do you want to come and see *your* new room?'

I avoid starting his stay with a lecture about privacy, and use my happy voice to lure Billy away from the other children's bedrooms, switching the focus to show him his. He comes bounding towards me like an eager puppy.

I open his door with a 'ta-da' fling.

'Is this my bed?' he asks, looking up at me.

Excellent. Barking is not his only method of communication. That's a relief. 'Yes, Billy. This is your bed and your room. This is where you will sleep.'

Normally my next move would be to invite a child to unpack their bags – or on a bad day, bin bag. But there is nothing for this little boy except half a Sainsbury's bag.

I watch him put his two old teddies on his bed. He puts the new teddy, his best teddy, in pride of place on the windowsill, as though he wants to admire him. It's an ugly-looking teddy, I have to say, but there's no accounting for what appeals to different people.

I spend a bit of time with Billy. He definitely seems to like his room. He keeps looking out of the window. I wonder what he can see from his height. Only his head is above the windowsill. I crouch down next to him to get closer to his perspective. The garden disappears, leaving only the tops of the trees and the sky. It's quite freeing, seeing all that space. I'm used to a more closed-in view of the garden and surroundings.

Billy is hyper-alert. He reminds me of an anxious meerkat. His head is constantly moving, looking this way and that, but his eyes swivel back to me the whole time. I wonder what to do next. This boy needs some new clothes, but the other children will be home soon, so we can't go shopping today. There's not enough time. I decide that a temporary solution will be to rummage in the storage bags that I stow in the guest room, by that double bed of fostering doom. Maybe there are some socks, pants and pyjamas in there.

First, I plonk myself down on Billy's bed to give my aching back a rest. Billy walks backwards away to the other side of the room, keeping his eyes on me the whole time. Uh oh. That is not a good sign. It is a feeling all too familiar.

I get straight back up and tell him a little bit about the room and where we will keep his new clothes when we get them tomorrow. I don't think I should be too far into the room with him. I make a mental note to let him into the room in future, and to make sure that I hang back by the door as much as I can. I recognise these signs, the way he backed away from me then. Coupled with that hyper-edginess, I am almost certain that someone has sexually abused this child, as well as neglect and likely emotional abuse. After a few years, sadly, you get a nose for it.

I do a massive yawn which takes me by surprise, because I certainly don't feel tired. I'm not sure where it comes from. I must be feeling stressed, or overwhelmed by what might lie ahead. I have been here before, and it's part of the role of a foster carer to take all the issues on board and make it work in the present for the child.

I know that the round-up of Blackthorn children was a high number. Billy's life has been utterly transformed from everything that he knows, in the space of a short few hours and days. We are dealing with many factors and emotions here, my own as well as his. I have to be strong and not fold. This is about the children and making things right.

I remember one child we looked after who had some interesting behaviours. So interesting we managed to get on the CYPMHS (Children's and Young Person's Mental Health Services) list. The poor therapist had to take three days off work after working with the child for an hour. If it was so traumatic for the therapist, what must it have been like for that child?

A therapist has to take care of their own emotional and mental health. But so do the foster carers and their families who live with the child and experience everything they do. All the time. Unfortunately, the children's social care system hasn't quite reached the stage of acknowledging that we're not actually robots, nor are our families. I brace myself as I watch this young fella. I brace myself to help him, and to wade through the bonkers treacle of 'support'.

I look at my watch. It's 2.30pm, an hour until the other children will be back from school. The scene is so well rehearsed, and I can picture it. They will throw their bags on the floor and sweep the kitchen for food – especially Vincent, who is having another growth spurt. Until then, I don't really know how to fill the time. I walk Billy around upstairs, giving him the full tour. I show him the bathroom, and each child's room from the doorway. In my best Mary Poppins voice, I explain that he mustn't go into others' rooms. I have a rush of panic as I remember Abby again. She destroyed some of Lily's and the boys' most precious possessions. I really don't want that to happen again. The dogs know that they're not allowed upstairs, but I have to explain this to Billy. All I can do is set the boundaries and hope for the best.

I blink and he's gone. Where is he now? I walk past the big window on the stairs landing overlooking the back garden. I catch a glimpse of something moving. The dogs are here, so it must be a cat.

'Bi-lly?' I call out his name in a sing-song voice. Nothing. Down the stairs, I find Billy's Spiderman shoes on the floor by the kitchen. Hmmm. He can't have gone far, and he won't be outside. I'll humour him for a moment. I go into the kitchen, remembering that I haven't yet fed the dogs today. This explains why they are stuck to my ankles. And I thought it was affection. I open the fridge and pull the dog food from the shelf. I say dog food – it's actually dog *and* cat food. A while ago I realised that the dogs were eating the cat's food and vice versa. So now I give both species the same and, so far, they look fine.

I gather the bowls up from the floor, and as I come back up to a standing position, I glance out of the kitchen window. I see a small boy sitting on the garden bench. There he is. No shoes on. It's cold outside. I open the back door and call Billy's name. He looks at me, offers me one of the wide smiles, and shoots back inside under my arm. He's like Dash in *The Incredibles*, whose superpower is superhuman speed – enabling him to run on water without sinking.

In an attempt to slow him down for a second, I ask Billy what food he likes. He doesn't reply.

'Go on. What's your favourite thing to eat?'

Again, no answer. When I offer him a biscuit again, he snatches two and laughs. It's the sort of cheeky thing a child you know well would do because they know they would get away with it. But right now, it just feels like he's hungry.

I tell Billy about the other children, so he knows who to expect.

He makes a face a bit like the 'wow' emoji.

'They will all be home soon from school,' I explain.

He nods and smiles, but I can see that it's not really going in. His eyes continue to dart around the place, looking for the next adventure, or the next threat.

Dotty barks at me. *Get on with it, Louise. Make my dinner.* (I have become fluent in dogspeak.) I begin to load the bowls up with dog-or-cat biscuits and dog-or-cat food.

Suddenly Pablo, my black tomcat, throws himself in through the cat flap. He doesn't miss a trick. I put the dog bowls on the floor in the same spot they have eaten from for the last eight years. I turn to ask Billy if he would like a sandwich or something, and guess what? He's gone again.

But not very far this time. I lower my gaze and find him on the floor, scooping food out of Doug's bowl with his hand and putting it in his mouth. He must be quite smart, because he chose the nicer dog to take from. If he'd done that to Dotty, chances are she would have growled and chased him off.

'Don't eat the dog food, Billy,' I say, gently.

'Fuck off.'

Ah. Right. I think for a moment and decide that this behaviour is going to have to be called out at every stage. But for all my talk, I am strangely afraid of him. There is something a little scary about him. I try to work out what it is, why I feel that way. He's scary because I feel that I have very little influence.

I remind myself that he hasn't been here for two hours yet and I'm going to need to be patient. He has said a few words to me since he's been here, but mainly I'm getting grunts, barking, and strange random snorts.

I try again. 'Billy, sweetheart, please don't eat the animals' food. It's not very nice and it's just for the pets, not us humans.'

He looks at me and, as if an internal switch has been flicked, he gives me his wide, slightly soggy smile.

I turn around and hold the bread out to show him what we're going to eat.

He tilts his head back slightly and then spits aggressively at my feet. Then he's back to smiles again, and I'm a little confused.

I take a deep breath and ask him not to spit. He spits again, laughs, and runs out of the kitchen into the sitting room. He's at the TV and looks as if he's just about to throw the remote control at it, when I say, 'ice cream.'

I don't know what it is about those two little words, but it always works. He drops the controller onto the rug and skips into the kitchen. I get a bowl out and find the scoop from the drawer, by which time he's gone. He's back on the floor trying to eat Doug's dinner. Poor Doug looks at me with a forlorn face.

'Come on, no dog food. Would you like some ice cream?'

He's standing right next to me in a flash. I ask him firmly not to touch the dogs' bowls again. I warn him that they may bite him if they think he's trying to take their food. It still seems unfair that a foster dog will be destroyed if they bite a foster child. Sometimes *I've* wanted to bite a foster child because their behaviour has been so awful. I have looked after some children who I know have hurt my dogs. They have tended to target Dotty; maybe Doug has a better hiding place. I must watch this and try to keep him away from them at their mealtimes.

Billy likes the ice cream, and for a minute or two he sits nicely at the table.

First home and through the door is Jackson. He's got his own key to let himself in. Working from home, I'm usually here anyway in the studio, but we felt that Jackson was ready for his own key, being the eldest at home now. The others still have to knock; they will get their front door keys when they're his age.

Jackson is the most reserved of my children. He is very self-contained and that sometimes makes him appear cautious. He has always held back, checked everything out, deliberated. He has an analytical nature, and I wonder if he over-thinks things at times, or perhaps, being a good foster-sibling, he is just more measured and reflective.

I open the door to Lily, whose first words are, 'I hate my life.'

Standard Lily fare. I say, 'Lovely, darling. Now, come and meet Billy.'

Next in is Vincent, who is always smiling, unless he's gaming, and then he's more likely to be swearing. They sort of gather towards the kitchen. Billy is up in a shot and runs up to them. He pushes them and gives Lily a good kick.

Woah. I was not expecting that.

Jackson says, 'Hey, little fella, that's not cool.'

And just like Casper the Ghost, Billy's gone and somehow back at the table eating ice cream.

Lily is rubbing her shin and scowling. The kick clearly hurt her, and now she hates her life a little bit more. It's hard living with an emo: the dyed hair and preponderance of black are the badges of her overly sensitive and emotional character.

The evening is horrendous. I only have the chance to reply to the odd text from Lloyd, and I choose my words carefully. I don't want to paint a bad picture of Billy from the off. I know it must be hard for him to be in this new environment. It is difficult to integrate into the established routines and relationships of an existing family, whatever your background. The children mostly stay away from him, which is a shame (they normally like fussing over new arrivals) but not unsurprising given the introduction they received. Tonight they stay in their rooms and I spend the evening darting after Billy, eventually getting him to bed at 11.30pm. I close the door gently on his first night and collapse into bed.

Despite my exhaustion, I spend some time propped up against my pillows reading the messages I have received on WhatsApp. One of the foster carers has created a little group and named it 'The Blackthorns'. Message after message is filled with different foster carers describing the carnage their new wards are making inside their homes. Billy isn't the only one to eat dog food, or to snort, grunt and spit. Well, don't the Blackthorns seem like a delightful family? At least it's nice to know that we aren't being singled out for special treatment.

I reach to turn out the lamp and wonder quite what the hell I've got us into this time.

Chapter Five

I'm generally always up first in our house (apart from when Lloyd has an early morning flight), so when I wake up, I assume that to be the case. I go straight to Billy's room to see how he has spent his first night. His bed has been slept in, there is a dent in the pillow and the duvet is in a heap, but he is not in it, nor anywhere to be seen.

Great!

I know that there is no way he could open any of the doors to the outside world. They're too complicated and require a degree of local, specialised knowledge. He must be somewhere in the house.

Where can he have got to?

It's too early to go calling loudly, so I play a little game of hide and seek, trying to second guess where a little boy might like to hang out in this house. Eventually I discover him in the kitchen, hiding in the mess of chair legs beneath the table. As I approach, he begins to growl at me.

'Good morning, Billy,' I say, breezily, as though growling is a perfectly normal way to greet somebody. I then try to coax him out with the promise of breakfast. I crouch down to his level and show him the range of cereals on offer.

The temptation works. He seems most impressed by the selection and scrambles straight out. Perhaps predictably, he stabs at the chocolate cereal box with his pointy finger.

'Of course,' I say, and ask him to sit at the table, which he does.

My plan is to feed Billy and then set him up in the conservatory with some toys until the others have left for school. I do my usual calls of 'Jackson', 'Vincent' and 'Lily' to begin rousing each from their slumber. The boys come into the kitchen and ask where Billy is.

I indicate a 'shhh' by putting my index finger near my mouth, and point to the conservatory. They both look and then tiptoe back to avoid disturbing him. They choose their breakfast and chat through their gaming scenarios.

In comes Lily. 'Where's the rug rat?'

'Lily, you mustn't say that.'

'Why not? He's a freaking freak.'

I take a deep breath and decide to let it go, for now. I narrow my eyes at her, intending to communicate that we'll pick this up later. This morning I just want them to get up and away to school smoothly.

Once they have left, I go to Billy and ask him if he'd like to come shopping for some new clothes.

He's up and gets his Spiderman trainers on in a flash.

Okay, I think. *Let's do this.* I put the dogs into their cage and get out my straw shopping bag and car keys. I remember that the spare bumper seat is in the cupboard under the stairs. I say, 'Just a second, Billy,' but within a split second of me turning to get it, he's ramming the front door with his head.

Oh my God!

I lean in towards him and put my hand on his head. 'Billy, please don't hurt yourself. You scared me, there. Your precious head. You need that. It stores all your dreams and ideas.'

He turns his head towards me and gives me the wide, dribbly smile that has already established itself as a familiar feature.

'It's the most important part of you, your head. You need to take care of it.'

I reach out to hold his hand. He takes it and strokes my wrist.

A strange moment. Children don't need to stroke adults. It feels peculiar, and for some reason I can't put my finger on, a little unnerving.

We don't make it to the shops.

I manage to get Billy into the car, but he keeps on bashing his head against the window next to him. Nice words about how precious his head is don't work now. And it would be too dangerous for him – and me – to drive like this.

I abort the mission and come back inside, deliberating on how to play things. I decide to switch on the telly while I call Emma and Dara. I go through the channels and find *Bing*. Within seconds he is calm.

I'm not.

I notice loads of messages on WhatsApp. Sylvia, the policeman's wife, has resisted taking a Blackthorn child and wishes us all luck. There are various reports of the kind of behaviour that I've already witnessed with Billy. Someone has just put *WTF!!!* – which pretty much reflects how I feel, if I'm honest. But the numbers seem to have settled to 11 children in foster placements, which means the rest are in residential units. So we are 'The Eleven Amigos', as Phil, another group member, has dubbed us. Phil works nights. I remember him well from training. He sleeps during the day.

Dara answers within just a couple of rings, as ever.

I update her on the other children's reactions to Billy, his ninja-like capabilities of swift undetected movement, his very limited speech, and the disturbing headbanging. Sometimes it's helpful just to offload it all.

She is, as always, sympathetic. But I detect a faraway note in her voice. Coupled with some of the things she says, I get the impression that, having made the announcement of her departure, she's now living for the day she leaves. I'm not getting the five-star service I'm used to, but I can hardly blame her.

I call Emma next. She doesn't answer, and so I leave a brief voice message. I text, I email, and, at some stage, I might send a pigeon. Given the current workload levels that the Blackthorns must collectively be creating, I don't hold out much hope of a swift reply. Meanwhile, there is a demanding child to occupy.

I get toys out. I get some playdough out. I get lots of food out and make sure that it seems readily available, in the hope that if he's fed well and not hungry he will feel better. Hungry children can be a challenge and, with foster children, we can never be quite sure what hungry means for them. I know this only too well from bitter experience. As a fostered child myself, one of the abuses I suffered was to be 'controlled' through food withdrawal.

I'm shattered, but it's only midday and I haven't really done anything yet. Or not anything that I set out to do. I can't get ahead of the washing. It's piled up in front of the machine, and I swear the mountain has grown overnight. The dogs look annoyed because they know it's another day indoors.

Bang!

A loud noise from the hall interrupts my procrastination. I shoot out in the direction of the noise and find Master Billy Blackthorn lying on the floor, crying. I rush over and touch his arm. He has his head hidden in his other arm. I look for blood, but can't see any. His sobs come harder. I don't know him well yet, but it's a noise that suggests he's really hurt himself. I feel sick to see him lying across the hard, cold Victorian hall tiles.

'Billy, are you alright?' I sit down next to him.

He cries harder.

'Can I help you move up into a sitting position so I can try and have a look at you?' My voice is full of concern as I lean towards him. He suddenly turns around, looks me in the face, sticks his tongue out, gets up and runs up the stairs shouting, 'You can't catch me, you fat cow.'

Oh, how nice.

He properly had me there.

Deep breath, Louise. I remind myself he is five, and that I look great at the moment. A five-year-old with obvious trauma is not going to get the better of me, especially as he hasn't been here for quite 24 hours yet.

I follow him upstairs. Luckily, he's in his room and hasn't gone into the other children's. That message seems to have stuck, at least. I walk up and stand by the door. I ask if he is alright, and as he turns around to face me I can see the start of a large bruise ripening on his forehead.

'Would you like to come downstairs and play, and have some lunch?' I ask, as though the last few moments haven't happened.

I pick up yesterday's clothes off the floor and decide to wash them. They smell of an unpleasant mixture of cigarettes and toilet cleaner. I'm not sure where he's been staying since the raid, and I guess I won't get much of an answer. And actually, how would he know? He probably doesn't have a clue what's going on. I compare him to Jackson or Vincent at five years old. If they had hurt themselves that badly and cried to that degree, they would have needed a hug at the very least.

Not Billy. He clearly isn't relying on anyone else to soothe his pain. In fact, he's insulted me for trying.

I manage to get him to eat sandwiches, crisps and some of a yoghurt. I say 'some' because I'm not entirely convinced about how much goes in. He evidently has not a clue about table manners, but he also doesn't have a great deal of efficacy in his actions. He scoops most of the yoghurt up with his fingers, rejecting the spoon in spite of my efforts to persuade him. Some ends up on the table, some round his face. I'm not sure what he knows about eating. Not much, by the look of things.

I pick up my phone and see lots of WhatsApp messages in the Blackthorn group. There are smile emojis and a couple of pleas for 'help'. I see one carer, who I don't know, has written, *My Blackthorn has smashed her head against the wall.*

Mine too, I reply, in solidarity.

Emma phones back, just as I find a lump of yoghurt that has, inexplicably, found its way to the side of the microwave.

'Hi Louise, how's Billy getting on?'

I distract Billy with a pile of toys in the garden room and pull the door to so that he is in view, but can't hear what I'm saying.

I tell her straight that I'm worried, and outline some of his more concerning behaviours. 'I suspect he may be a child who has experienced sexual abuse,' I say.

She clears her throat. 'Err, let's not jump to any

conclusions. It's a bit hard for him right now, poor thing. He's just processing.'

'Processing' is a term which foster carers have to endure a lot. It's up there with the best of the Big Fat Platitudes we get at coffee mornings and training events.

I talk about my very genuine concerns for a child who is ramming their head against hard surfaces.

Emma puts on her gentle, sympathetic social-worker tone. *Are there courses for that?* I wonder. 'I tell you what, get some scatter cushions and place them in the areas he has selected.'

Oh, very helpful. Very, very helpful, thank you.

Before I have time to 'process' this conversation, I see that Billy has moved on from the toys. He is face down on the hard tiles of the garden room floor, banging his head.

'Billy,' I say firmly, swiping a cushion from a kitchen chair to implement Emma's advice, even while knowing how ineffective and inadequate it is. 'Stop that now.'

Before I can reach him and try to prevent him from doing more injury, he turns over onto his back and rolls his trousers down so that he's bare legged on the cold, flagstone floor. He pulls out his willy from his pants and makes 'naa naa' noises.

Terrific.

It seems any stage fright he might have had from arriving in a new place has evaporated. That was the warm-up act. He is just getting into his stride.

After Act One of the willy show is complete, he runs upstairs and begins swinging from his doorframe as his interval entertainment. This is perhaps even more of a feat than it might initially sound, since he is quite small and the height of our doors is larger than average. It is a high-ceilinged house, built at a time when creating a sense of space was more important than warmth. I have no idea how he has got himself up there: he must have springs in his legs.

I stand in the hall and ask him, very gently, to come down. It doesn't work. I try to distract him with other possible activities as alternatives. I try not to be cross.

I employ all the techniques from my 'conscious parenting' training. This was trendy among the professionals in care a few years ago, and is along the lines of Emma's pillow advice. Professionals, usually those who don't foster themselves, sagely offered limp advice to experienced carers who would sometimes have 'wild' children in their homes. Children who hadn't been on the courses and learnt the script. Conscious parenting is supposed to be about mindfulness driving parenting choices. In other words, parents and carers look inwardly at themselves, rather than trying to interfere with or 'fix' a child's behaviour; we strive to become more aware of what's driving our insistence on certain types of behaviour, or what makes other types of behaviour unacceptable.

I haven't got time to delve into my past and discover why I find willy-waving an undesirable activity in my house, and I'm worried about the survival of both Billy and the door frame if the current antics continue for much longer. The house and door frames may have stood for more than 200 years, but their days might be numbered if Billy has anything to do with it.

I try gently talking Billy down. I try enticing him with sweets and chocolate, but no success. He's a tough cookie. He doesn't respond to any of my coaxing and bribery. And it hasn't worked out terrifically well for me either: I seem to have comfort-eaten my way through a little pack of chocolate buttons and a KitKat while he swings and hollers.

Even seeing me eat these treats doesn't entice him down. Only the aching muscles in his arms eventually do that.

There is only a brief interval before he plunges into Act Two. This is wilder, more dramatic. He tips up everything in his room, pulling all the sheets and covers from his bed, swiping anything from the shelves. I put it all back. He does it again.

The other children are home by now, but I have barely had time to register their presence as I chase round after Billy.

Horrified by his behaviour, it seems that Vincent and Lily have taken to their rooms and barred their doors against the chaos that Billy represents. Periodically he rams their doors, and sometimes makes it through, before they learn to barricade them more effectively. The idea of barricading himself in doesn't appeal to Jackson, who patiently ushers Billy from his room more than a dozen times.

I wish I could channel more of Jackson's calm in the face of Billy's onslaught.

Billy is most definitely the star of the Allen household show tonight, and his performance, he seems to think, demands several encores. Eventually he collapses into sleep, by which point it is easy to get him into bed, because he is shattered. Too tired to get undressed and into his new pyjamas, carefully selected earlier from my emergency store since we didn't have a chance to go shopping.

I can't face texting Lloyd. He will only worry. And I don't want to think of him enjoying the bar with colleagues while I have been dealing with the firebomb that is Billy. I too collapse into bed, barely able to get myself undressed, never mind pyjamas. It is past 2am.

Chapter Six

I wake up feeling as exhausted as I did when I fell into bed.

The first thing I do is to look in Billy's room, to see if he is still asleep.

He is, thank God.

I'm not ready to face more yet.

I quietly knock on each child's bedroom door. Through the cracks I whisper to each, 'If you're quick, and very quiet, you can get out to school without disturbing Billy.'

I know my children well, and it doesn't take a psychology degree to see that Billy's presence isn't a good influence. None of them are happy.

This is probably the bit about fostering I find the hardest task of all: managing and balancing the demands of my existing family with a new foster child. Our children's lives and feelings are important, and, unfortunately, sometimes the fostering experience can ride roughshod over their lives.

But that's not a helpful line of thought: the guilt that comes with being a foster carer. It's a well-worn theme in my head. I remind myself that Lily is a foster child too, and that on the whole she is a darling, and doesn't behave like Billy.

I have no doubt that Billy is a deeply troubled child. I take a deep breath and metaphorically roll up my sleeves to get on with the day. The children successfully get through their breakfast and gather their school stuff without a sound. Who knew that was even possible? They actually seem to enjoy the challenge, and make something of a game of it, though Vincent struggles not to keep burping after rushing his cereal and juice.

As the door closes behind Lily, last to leave, I put the coffee machine on and give myself a good talking to. 'Come on, Louise. You can do this. He is only a child.'

Yeah, right. Who am I trying to kid? Anyone who has fostered a 'wild child' will tell you that size does not matter. They are like torpedoes shooting through your life. There is a possibility that Billy will do himself – or me – some serious harm if not managed well.

I can't blame the social workers for not giving me the right information. I totally understand that would have been impossible under the circumstances. We are learning as we go.

I can't find my phone.

This is a not an infrequent occurrence, but one that drives Lloyd mad because I often keep the ringtone on silent. I take the view that people who phone me have had time to make that decision and know what they want to say to me – whereas I am usually preoccupied and busy, so will never respond as well as I can. I prefer to wait for a message and then choose an appropriate time to deal with it. A ringing phone is not always convenient. I have worked with enough oppressive managers and leaders to know that it is not a good idea to respond to some calls 'in the moment'. As a result, I loathe it when people leave a message that requires me to call them back without any indication of what they want. I am also an upholder of telephone manners. I would never call anyone after 8pm or before 8am, preferably 9am, without their consent. Mobile phones have removed boundaries that previously protected our heads, hearts and time.

Nevertheless, I still need to find my phone.

Eventually I locate it beneath a pile of socks and pants that one of the children had chucked at the end of the table while they searched the laundry basket on top of the dogs' crate-bed. I didn't get a chance to sort out their clean uniforms given Billy's antics last night.

As anticipated, there are piles of notifications. Under the first Blackthorn foster carers' WhatsApp group, there are eight messages all saying the same thing, variations of: *What have we got ourselves into?* The basic theme is 'Help!'. I add a message of my own:

I don't know what's going on but my fc has been a nightmare. He turned his room upside down, he's bashed his head against various floors, swung from the rafters, and exposed himself. It didn't stop until after 2am.

I have long had the impression that the social workers, or perhaps more so their managers, dislike us using WhatsApp to communicate and share information. That way they lose control of us, and we become more powerful as a group. Knowledge is power, as they say. Foster carers' WhatsApp groups are part of the national, and probably international, revolt by foster carers who are fed up with the prehistoric system of children's social care. Of course we should be able to share dialogue with people going through the same thing. Every time I read an unleashed 'human' message such as *WTF*, I smile. Foster carers come from all backgrounds, all ages, and here we are bonded together by society's chaos.

A few fast replies ping in, responding to my message about Billy hurting himself. Three more carers talk of similar head-bashing incidents. It seems to be a behaviour exhibited by many of the Blackthorn children. That's interesting.

Perhaps the head-bashings are cries for help? Or could it be part of how the children communicated with each other? Who knows? It's horrendous, and I'm glad I'm not alone, because somehow this feels 'big'. I need to talk to Dara, more than ever. Leaving or not, she is full of wisdom and I am in need of support.

I give her a call, but it goes straight to answerphone.

If you have never heard a social worker's voicemail recording, you're lucky. They put most call centres to shame. They first have to explain why they can't answer your call, then they list all the other numbers you can call if your situation is an emergency (although in children's social care, an 'emergency' is pretty hard to define). By the time you have got through the lengthy script, you realise that leaving a message is probably futile.

I think about trying to email, too, but since the local authority launched their brand new super-expensive email system, many of us find our emails go to their junk. I haven't quite decided whether I think this is by accident or design; after all, no reporting equals no problems.

I email anyway.

I send a similar message to Emma.

I inhale as much coffee as I can and quickly make some toast before our little firecracker wakes up. I stand in front of the coffee machine and stare at the toaster as if it's going to supply me with all life's answers. Sadly, it is not forthcoming today.

Then suddenly I feel a touch on my lower back. It's not the dogs or the cat, who well know how to schmooze me when they are hungry.

I realise with a jolt that it is Billy, who is now stroking my left outer thigh.

A bit weird, I think. I turn round and see an angelic little face, smiling at me while still stroking my thigh. I reach around to his hand and remove it with a smile of my own.

'Good morning, Billy. Would you like some breakfast?'

He appears delighted by the suggestion, his face breaking into a broader smile. I place my lower palm gently on his back and guide him to the table.

'Which chair would you like to sit on?' I ask, regretting the words as soon as they are out of my mouth, realising what a stupid thing it is for me to do. He chooses Vincent's pistachio-green chair, which will probably cause conflict later.

'Mmmmh,' I say quickly, 'that one's not actually free.'

I point to two other 'spare' chairs in the hope that I can repair this and counter any possible anguish later, when Vincent gets home.

'But I want the red one,' he insists, pointing to the same green chair.

I think he's just being a bit strange, and then the penny drops: Billy could be colour-blind. I taught art to a student with colour-blindness once. It had not been recorded in his file, so I thought he was just being disruptive and argumentative for the first art lesson that I worked with him. I asked him after if there was a problem, and he explained, rather sheepishly, that he was colour-blind. I remember thinking, *Why didn't anyone tell me?!*

I offer Billy a spare red chair, which he thinks is green, selling it as the 'very special chair for special children.'

It works. He wants the green-but-red chair, and it's not Vincent's. Everyone's a winner.

I'm not sure why we bothered even to pick a chair, because he cannot sit still. He is up and down like a yoyo.

Mostly he seems to be on a mission to check every cupboard and drawer in the kitchen. I have seen this kind of behaviour before, and know that it means he is unsure of his surroundings. He has been used to surprises, and not good ones. What looks like an inability to settle is actually a systematic programme of checking on himself to make sure he is safe. What a horrendous burden for a child to have to bear. It's a survival technique that crushes any chances of experiencing 'childhood' in a carefree way. I'm a great believer that childhood should be as carefree as possible. Sadly, it often isn't. Or at least not for the children who come into care, and those children who probably need to come into care but get missed.

After several minutes of Billy getting up and down and checking things, I persuade him to have some toast with Nutella. He has not met Nutella before so is interested. In a rare moment of stillness, he sits down long enough to take a big bite of the toast. The stillness doesn't last long, though; he seems to wiggle to acknowledge that he enjoys the taste, making happy-sounding 'mmmm' noises.

'Would you like some more?'

He nods enthusiastically, head going up and down as far as it will go. How much energy must be going into even that movement response? My neck would hurt if I tried to move it that much.

I supply more generously spread Nutella toast, and sit down opposite to drink my coffee. While he is occupied with the food, I can study his face. It's a lovely little face, almost cherubic, but one that shows too early the signs of an older face. Sometimes you can look at children and see their grown self. The signs don't seem to be good for Billy; there are traces of thuggishness in those features. I know that sounds fanciful, but it's difficult to articulate. It's as if he has, by osmosis, learnt the expressions of a scary person. His forehead tells his eyes to look mean. He has a bottom lip that looks like it's out for a fight. It's the face of an adult grafted onto a child. It's hard to describe. It would be interesting to sketch.

Emma calls me, interrupting my thoughts.

'Hi Emma, how are you?'

As I hold the phone to my ear I can hear rapid fire from the WhatsApp group pinging in. I can't imagine what's going on, but something must be.

'Good. How are things with you? How's Billy?'

I hate discussing the children in front of them, so I smile at Billy, who is now singing while munching his way through his toast. We're not ready to tackle keeping mouths closed while eating yet. That can wait for another day. I head towards the conservatory for a little privacy, so that I can tell Emma about last night and how utterly exhausting it was. 'I hope he settles down soon, because I don't know how many nights like that I'll be able to survive.'

'Ah, bless him. He's processing, isn't he?'

That bloody word again. I try not to scream, settling instead for an unseen eyeroll. Emma goes on to tell me about how she has been on the case to find a school for Billy. Foster children or children who have been in care get a guaranteed place in a school, even if that school is oversubscribed. This annoys some parents, but my view is that these children have been through enough in the past to be entitled to that at the least. They are already disadvantaged, and education is their right. The trick is getting the child to recognise that school education is often their only ticket out of the lives they grew up in, but it's difficult to achieve. As foster carers we can only do so much, and we don't have long. By the age of 18, children in care are deemed adults and must fend for themselves. I can feel the fire simmering in my belly as I think about how disrespectful and careless we are with our teenagers in the care system, but it's another avenue that makes me too angry to think about.

I try very hard to listen to Emma, to appreciate all she is doing, and remind myself that she is very new to this. She reminds me of a little rabbit, trapped in the headlights. I suspect that after a year she will be thinking of another career, or will have acquired the additional armour needed to survive as a social worker. They are pulled in every direction as more and more bureaucracy is poured over them. New policy creates ever more constraint, rather than easing the workload and the worry.

As foster carers, we can be mindful of the social workers' plight, but at the same time we have to advocate and push for our foster children as if they were the *only* children in the care system. Corporate care is like an unruly dysfunctional family where the one that shouts the loudest gets the attention.

'So, the good news is that Flatfields Primary School can take Billy into reception.'

Flatfields is a very small village primary school with only about 20 children on roll, all of whom travel from different nearby villages, so it has quite a wide catchment area. It will take me 20 minutes to get there in the car, but that's not so bad, and we could work it out between Lloyd's and my working days.

I made it very clear from the beginning of our fostering journey that we could only look after school-age children. Both Lloyd and I work full time: Lloyd with his graphic design, and me as a freelance artist and illustrator. After years of fostering, we know all too well that we couldn't afford to foster if we didn't work that hard. None of the foster carers I know actually make any money from fostering – not the good ones, anyway. It's true that some people do go into fostering because they perceive it as an easy way to make extra money, but they soon learn that it is anything but that. We all help fund these children's lives above and beyond the relatively meagre payments involved.

'But it's going to take a couple of weeks to sort everything out from ours and the school's point of view,' Emma explains.

Which leaves me wondering when I will be able to catch up with my work for those two weeks, because judging by last night's performance it isn't going to be during the evenings.

Call over, I stare at the phone in my hand for a moment to 'process' all this. I turn back into the kitchen to find Billy gone. I didn't hear a sound. He really does oscillate between herd of elephants and stealth ninja as he chooses.

So, where has he got to? Though I have only known Billy for a very short time, my radar is alerting me to mischief. I walk out into the hall and call out, in my jolly, sing-song voice, 'Billeee. Oh, Bill-eee.'

He is something else. He vanishes into thin air.

Strategy: I start by looking in every room downstairs, systematically in order of the doors, calling his name as I go.

Nothing.

I go back and look behind the coats in the hall. I even look behind the collection of brollies and walking sticks, standing upright in a container in the hallway – not that they provide much cover. I look back at them, doing a double-take as I register that they could very easily become a good weapon. I make a mental note to move them when I have a minute. He isn't anywhere down here.

I walk upstairs and search every room, still calling out, but now I am beginning to worry. Where can he have got to? With rising panic, I dash back downstairs to check the front door. It remains firmly shut and, unless you know how to twist and turn the locks in exact combination, it would be quite a challenge to open, especially for a five-year-old. He must be in here somewhere.

I run back around the house calling out, 'Billy, Billy!' as cheerfully as I can muster. I don't want to sound anxious, even though I am. It's not even morning coffee time and I have already been outwitted by this strange little boy.

I check every room a second time. This time I am even more thorough, looking under the children's beds, in their wardrobes, lifting cushions and clothing piles. I look everywhere. Or everywhere I can think of.

I'm not sure what to do next. It's only the second day and I have managed to lose Billy, without even going outside. I'm supposed to be experienced as a foster carer. Losing a vulnerable child isn't exactly an ideal scenario.

I go to the guest room. I pause and look in the airing cupboard: my cupboard of sanity. The folded piles of sheets, pillowcases and duvet covers scented by bars of soap always give me a sense of hope and remind me that I organised all this, and that means I can control some things (even if it's coloured cotton bedding). The guest room contains my favourite bed, the antique Breton bed that we're not allowed to use for respite fostering because of the trauma.

I get down on all fours and look underneath.

There he is, curled up into a tiny ball. How can he make himself that small? I lie down with my head pressed to the floor so that I can make eye contact with him. Gently, I try to coax him out. He stares into my eyes, and I feel for a moment that we are making a connection, until he suddenly starts laughing. Before I know what's happened, his foot is in my face.

Jeez, that hurt! My eyes are watering, and the centre of my head stings in intense pain. For a moment I can't see anything and I put my hands to my face, which gives him the second's gap he needs to be off again, running around the house. I take my hands from my face to find that they are covered in blood.

Chapter Seven

I decide to leave him, wherever he is. I just feel defeated.

I head to the bathroom for some tissue to clean up the blood. It's nothing serious; he just caught me wrong and caused a nosebleed. I'll survive. But I look in the bathroom mirror and notice that I am looking older, more haggard. Perhaps it is just the face of a foster carer in shock.

I head back to the kitchen. *Ping ping ping*. The phone can't cope with the pace of messages as they flood in. Of course, it's the Blackthorn group. Variations of 'Help meee!'

I add my own comment to the melee of pleas and updates. *My nose is bleeding and I've lost the child in my own home.*

Within seconds two more messages ping back.

Huh, mine has been missing for about an hour, shall I call the police or the social worker first?

Good luck getting a helpful response from either in the current climate.

The other message says: *Mine won't bloody leave me alone.*

I genuinely don't know what to do.

I can't do anything until I find him. If I run around the house again he will think it's a game and that it's funny. Trust me, it's not.

If I find him, what happens then? He can't sit still for five seconds.

I don't know quite why, because I'm generally good at coping, but I feel like crying. I never usually feel like this, but I am way, way out of my comfort zone.

My phone goes: it's Emma again. I pull myself together to respond, and don't reveal that I've lost Billy.

'The school has been back in touch. The headteacher has offered us mornings for Billy for a month or so.'

A month or so. Mornings only. My heart sinks. I don't know if I have the nerve or stamina for 'a month or so'. And, with the local authority, the 'or so' might be a very moveable feast. Next they'll be asking me to do an SGO, a Special Guardianship Order. It's a legal status designed to meet the needs of children separated from their birth parents in order to provide them with a greater degree of consistency, and therefore security, than that which might be provided by long-term fostering, but without severing all legal ties with their birth parents (as would be the case with adoption).

I've encountered it before when children are as young as Billy. The authorities can ask foster carers to do an SGO or adoption. Both options are dressed up as offering the child more security, but this has always baffled me since the reality is that the parents then have little to nothing in the way of support or rights. Every time this is mentioned to a seasoned foster carer you can feel the recognition, the sigh of, 'Oh, here we go.' New carers, I'm sure, probably feel flattered to be told they are so good at their work that they are being asked to step up. It can appear to be the greatest compliment, when what it actually means is that things will be cheaper from the local authority's perspective.

I continue to talk to Emma on the phone as I walk around the house once more. I'm trying to suggest that everything is fine and dandy as I speak into the receiver, all while sneaking round my own house like an agent in a spy movie. I'm desperate to find out where Master Billy can possibly be hiding, though my movements are more cautious this time. I don't want to take another kicking.

I have no choice but to agree to just mornings at the school.

Emma witters on. 'Isn't it great that you and Billy have two weeks to bond before he begins?'

Oh, she hasn't got a clue. The only bond I need is Unibond glue to keep him in one place for more than a minute.

I am mentally redesigning my life for the next two weeks, thinking about the meetings I need to cancel, the deadlines I need to extend. It's not just wondering how the hell I'm going to do any work, it's the realisation that I'm not even going to have the energy to try.

Then Emma says one of the most patronising things a social worker can possibly say to me. 'Mornings are great. That will give you just enough time to run the hoover round and do some shopping before collecting him.'

I don't know what bloody century she thinks foster carers live in, and why she makes such gender-stereotyped assumptions. She's a woman herself. I bet she wouldn't want the domestic details of her life to be assumed in the same way.

I feel the weight of the imaginary beige cardigan coming over me.

Who does she think she is? How dare she!

I end the call, fuming. Sod 'conscious parenting'. Emma has wound me up almost as much as Billy has.

I walk up to Billy's bedroom, expecting him not to be there. But he is. He's talking to his ugly teddy, the newer-looking one, who lives on the window sill. I feel relieved that he's doing something normal. He looks the teddy straight in the face and says, 'I'm a good boy.'

I think it's a strange choice of words when he's behaving the way he is, but he is a bit unusual, so I don't really know what I'm measuring him against. I hope, at some stage, to learn at least a little about his background and what got him here. I do have one nagging question, knowing that so many of his siblings are now in care in one form or another: why the hell has it taken so long to get them there?

But, of course, I am talking about local government, and the words 'emergency' and 'bureaucracy' do not go together at all. I rein myself back in, fascinated by Billy and his fluffy little friend.

'What's Teddy's name?' I ask, trying to establish at least some sort of bond with the boy.

He turns around quickly and laughs. 'Sharon.'

Then, in a flash, he has run out of the door, disappearing down the corridor.

Oh no, here we go again.

What did he call his teddy bear? Sharon? What a bizarre name. It doesn't sound like something a child would call a toy at all. Could I have heard wrong? No, I'm sure his ugly teddy is called Sharon. This child becomes more bewildering by the minute. Perhaps there is a children's programme with a character called 'Sharon' that I'm not familiar with.

I've learned already not to chase him, but this time I decide not to look for him either. It's not quite lunchtime, but it's close enough, and I form a plan.

I walk towards the kitchen and commune with the walls, 'I wonder if Billy Blackthorn would like some Nutella.'

Sure enough, a minute later (albeit a long minute that tests my strategy to its limits) he appears in the kitchen. He stands next to me, leaning his head into my body like a tired toddler might when they've had enough of everything.

I look down to see that his thumb is stuck stubbornly in his mouth, but at the same time he is staring out ahead. It's not an ordinary gaze, though. It's disturbing: his vacant eyes don't appear to be focused on anything at all, more like the thousand-yard stare that a war-weary veteran might display, and so very far removed from the eyes of a thumb-sucking reception-age child.

'Billy, would you like this on toast, or as a sandwich?'

There is no response. I repeat my question.

A mumbled, muffled sound floats gently up to my ears. I think I make out, 'wich'.

Instinctively my hand curls softly against his hair. 'Okay, sweetheart.'

As carefully as I can, I lean towards the table to create a 'wich' without breaking this little bit of contact. Luckily the Nutella is still out from before. I have to turn myself around, but manage to do so without disturbing Billy. I don't know if I could prise him away if I tried. I suspect I must look like an orangutan carrying its young. Except that he is the one pressing into me.

Once the 'wich' is assembled, which takes some doing with restricted movements, I place my hand behind his left shoulder and ease him towards the red-green chair. It's almost as if he is on autopilot and has little awareness of where he is and what's going on.

He sinks into the seat, and I place the side plate of sliced white Nutella-heaven in front of him. I can see that he is tired. Beyond tired. The poor little boy is utterly worn out. I get a glass and fill it with water from the tap. He appears in the reflection of the kettle, yawning his head off. While he sleepily chews on his food I pretend to potter around the kitchen. When he's done, I help him down from the chair.

'Would you like to sit on the sofa for a little while, and watch some programmes on the TV?' I suggest, very softly. If he lets me choose, I know I shall go for my trusted children's friend, *Pingu*. I say 'children's friend', but I think adults who suffer from stress should watch *Pingu*, too. It's so captivating and warm, which seems an odd thing to say when Pingu the penguin lives in an igloo and is surrounded by snow.

Billy nods with a heavy head to my telly suggestion, but I suspect he would agree to anything right now, because he doesn't seem to have the energy to argue. He stays very close as we make our way to the sitting room. He is on the verge of keeling over. It's easy, sometimes, to mistake the energy of a child for the stamina of an adult. Children seem to suddenly run out of steam. When the steam runs out, so does their anger and fear. They just sleep.

I'm right. Billy is snoring within seconds of watching Pingu's mum sit down in her kitchen and eat an ice cream. I take one of the blankets from the end of the sofa and wrap it round him. It's then that I register that he's still wearing the clothes he arrived in. Just with that little realisation, all the foster carer's guilt creeps in.

This is terrible, I think. *I'm failing. I'm letting this poor child down.*

Then I tell myself to shut up and get a grip, and never to compare myself or my situation to the impossible ideal of foster caring that exists in the training manuals but goes nowhere near preparing you for the reality of dealing with a child like Billy. How could it, without making new carers want to run for the hills?

I leave him there, and Doug and Dotty swiftly take up

their positions as sleep friends, snuggling into the gaps around him. They go to sleep too, and I smile at the three of them cuddled up together. After everything that has happened in such a short space of time, it is a beautiful vision: so simple, but something quite marvellous to behold after all the chaos that has been wrought by his arrival.

It seems timely to remind myself that happiness is only ever fleeting. As, I suspect, is a quiet Billy.

I head back to the kitchen to grab a hunk of bread and smother it with butter. I don't even bother with a plate. I know I'd tell the children off for such appalling manners, but they can't see me.

I walk to my studio with my bread and phone. As I go, I see another pile of WhatsApp messages and a text from Michelle, one of the carers from the group. We've met up a few times in the past. She's one of the good ones, and something of a rarity in this area, because Michelle is a woman of colour. We're a long, long way from London, and I don't just mean in terms of physical distance. Operating within a local authority which is characterised by its lack of diversity, she is a breath of fresh air.

I text right back.

You okay?

She replies immediately. *No, I'm bloody not. This is insane.*
Typical Michelle. Tell it how it is.

Can you talk?

By the time I've entered the studio, my phone is ringing.

'Oh my good Lord God Almighty, what the hell?' (There may, or may not, be a few further profanities alongside the pleas to heaven.)

'Yes to that.'

'Louise, what have we done? Seriously, my friend. I can't do this.'

Michelle is a widow with two daughters in their late teens. Her new Blackthorn foster child is a girl, named Silver, who is seven years old.

'Louise, this is bonkers. I don't feel safe. Silver chased me around the house with a kitchen knife!'

'Blimey.' I share my story about getting kicked in the face by Billy.

'She has called me the "n" word from the moment she arrived!'

Billy's 'fuck off' and 'fat cow' don't really compare.

'And she attacked Stanley!'

Stanley is Michelle's blue Persian cat. I think Michelle finds the last of these the most unforgivable. I have met Stanley, and believe him to be almost human.

'She's like a wild animal. At dinner last night, she picked up the food and rubbed it down her front. It went everywhere. And it was just a really bizarre thing to do.'

I'm starting to feel as if I have got off lightly with Billy.

'Seriously, Louise, if it was just me, I'd probably try and get through it. But it's not fair on the big girls either.'

She means her teenage daughters.

'Silver has sabotaged their college work. She threw water all over Andrea's art project. And squeezed toothpaste over some of their clothes. The girls are livid. And I don't blame them.'

We talk about what the options are, and how she can handle this. Sympathy from me isn't enough. As a foster carer you can call 28 days' notice if you want to end the placement. It seems a long time, but is meant to give the social workers time to find a good match for a new foster placement. I've had to do this myself in the past – and who knows, I may well have to again.

If you call notice on day one, two or three, you might run the risk of looking like a complete no-hope amateur foster carer, but I know Michelle well and she is utterly brilliant. Not only is she very experienced at this, she's also wise and patient – one of the best. If Michelle is giving notice, less than 48 hours into the placement, things must be totally out of control. 'What kind of lives can these children have, Louise?'

I think she's talking about what will happen to them in the future. I don't have an answer. I don't know how they'll integrate into society and form meaningful relationships with other people. But her question makes me wonder more about the past.

How did they get into this state, all of them? What the hell happened to these Blackthorn children?

Chapter Eight

We are surviving. Days are passing. Another morning is upon us. The children are downstairs eating their snatched breakfast. Today I've left a load of cereal bars, some fruit apologies, and some love on the kitchen table. Young Billy is sitting up in his bed playing with some new Marvel figures I bought him. He seems to think they're rather marvellous. I have left him alone to play, but I can hear lots of 'voices' and swoosh-whoosh sounds, telling me that he is firmly in an imaginative world of play. I'm very encouraged by this: more swooshing and, oh! Dear me! I hear what sounds remarkably like 'cunt'.

My ears didn't deceive me.

The word is repeated.

With unmistakable conviction.

Several times.

That isn't a line from *Iron Man*, as far as I remember.

It's worth saying that our household is familiar with 'dockyard' language. I've been known to spill a few choice words here and there myself; in fact, I'd go as far as to say that I'm quite partial to a good swear, but it tends to be directed towards the lawnmower more than anything else.

Choosing to ignore Billy's language for the moment, I keep walking towards the 'nice' blue bathroom upstairs. This is a room that Lloyd and I spent ages, not to mention a small fortune, on making into 'our bathroom', away from the squirting toothpaste and dropped-towel mess the children leave behind.

This felt justified because recently we also remodelled the other bathroom, just for children. It's beautiful. There are ships, lighthouses, fishing boats, and two large lobsters and glass fishing floats from an old restaurant in Portsmouth called *Truffles*. I used to walk past it for years, looking in the window at what I thought were rich, successful people. Looking back to those days, it strikes me that they mostly looked like Arthur Daley from *Minder*. Then, when I finally reached the stage where I could afford to dine there, it closed down, and somehow I ended up with the props and decorations that hung around the bistro-style seating area. I ended up buying plastic lobsters instead of the real ones that they used to display. But the plan for the children to have their own bathroom, away from ours, failed when it became apparent that our shower was better. The little darlings just ignored our requests to clear off and go back to their allotted bathroom.

I wish I had that skill – you know, where you just ignore something, do what you want, and it becomes your norm. Children are artful at this.

I walk towards my dreamy bathroom, which always feels as though it should be special, given that I rarely secure a slot in which to use it. Alas, as anticipated, it has been 'childrened' once again. I open the window to let out that morning aroma of warm steam, spray deodorants and toothpaste. It's pouring with icy rain outside, but fresh air happens in my household whatever the weather outside. I pick up the mini-molehills of damp towels, fold them up and place them over the heated towel rail. (Now *that* is a godsend of a device in my world.) I tear off a piece of loo roll and fold it several times, then use it to carefully wipe down the mirror where greasy little fingers have been. I don't know why it's so difficult for small hands to stay away from the glass. Vincent seems to have got stuck in the stage where he keeps drawing penises and balls. It's quite artistic: his have little cartoon faces. Still, I don't especially want to look at that later when I'm cleaning my teeth. Next I spray cleaner round the taps and give the bottom of the shower a quick wipe. Living with men, and young men in particular, means that every time I want to go to the loo, I have to clean it first. This does irk me somewhat, as it means they always enter a clean bathroom, but I rarely do. I'm probably encouraging their carelessness by always being the one to do it, but I like a clean toilet and surrounding area. It makes me feel safe and momentarily happy, and you have to get your kicks where you can. It's always the small things.

I finish by gathering up the higgledy-piggledy socks and pants from the floor, then head to the laundry corner at the top of the stairs. My heart sinks when it comes into view. It's my own fault: I asked them to tidy up their rooms, which always generates more washing as they put everything that is on the floor, clean or not, into a dumping pile at the top of the stairs. I wonder how many t-shirts I have washed over the years that never needed washing. I scoop it all up into practised laundry arms and walk down the stairs. On the way I catch a glimpse of the outside world through the window, which reminds me that spring is round the corner. It's still a big fat corner, but there is warmth and sunshine and longer days ahead.

I loiter in the hallway, arms full, and clock the children stuffing their blazer pockets with cereal bars and Penguin biscuits. This is one of the payoffs for having a new foster child in the home, and I think they quite like doing it for a bit. They know that they benefit if we have a child who is highly demanding. They 'get away' with more, and they most certainly enjoy more junk food.

When they see me, the conversation turns to a well-worn permutation of the usual.

'It's about time I had a new pair of shoes.'

'And I need a new rucksack.'

'Oh yes, me too. I need a new rucksack.'

'You can't deny us a *bag* for school. How are we supposed to carry everything we need?'

The new rucksack thing is total rubbish and they know I know it. What they each have is perfectly adequate. They're only trying it on because the 'bag' is the chief signal of tribal identity in a school that requires uniforms.

I shove them out of the door, ignoring protests and demands, while calling the dogs to go out for a pee. In the few seconds that takes, the first round of washing is on. Today, instead of loads of breakfast debris, I merely have to scoop up a bunch of breakfast bar wrappers and deposit them in the bin. A quick look in the snack box confirms that yes, they've taken everything. I think there's a proverb about inches and miles, there.

Lloyd, safely back from his trip, brought more washing that has now been processed – washed, dried and returned to wardrobe and drawers. He did pick me up a rather lovely bottle of perfume. Knowing that it costs pennies to manufacture, it does hurt a little that I know he paid over £50 for it, but I'm not ungrateful. It's just that increasingly of late I have noticed the pinch on the weekly budget and, after reading about the fashion and textile abuse of landfills, I am making the most of my clothes. These days I regularly wear old numbers with renewed vigour, and a determination that this is 'my look, my style', thank you very much.

I bend down to sort the next lot of washing into a pile, attempting to fathom the day ahead at the same time.

I suddenly feel a stroke across my lower back that makes me jump a little.

It's Billy. He's ninja-d himself into position behind me and is standing there smiling and making muttering noises like an old man. He has a funny way of touching me. It never feels quite right. Not how children touch people at all.

I turn round and he's leaning across my back. He nestles his head into the back of my neck. Then he does something that takes it all a stage further and is deeply concerning: he reaches a hand round and feels my right breast. It's not just in an inquisitive way. I have to say it felt 'experienced'. Oh my, this is too horrible. I don't like this one little bit. If he was any older I would feel violated, but he's *five*. What do I do?

I ignore it, that's what I do. I dismiss thoughts about inappropriateness and stand up quickly, straightening down my front as if I'm wearing some sort of long white apron that needs the creases smoothed out.

'Good morning, Billy. And what would you like for breakfast?'

Of course, he wants Nutella and toast. I didn't need to ask by now. I set about preparing it for him, and we chat about his morning and how he's getting on with his Marvel friends. He seems happy about that. All good so far.

It's only one more day until he starts school, and I can't wait. It has been a very long fortnight. Especially since I haven't felt confident enough to really go out and about very far with Billy. We have been shopping, to the park, and for dog walks, but he is so very unpredictable that it has just been easier to be at home. I need to get back to my work. Even though we have managed to get into a rhythm and routine over the last week or so, he is not a child you can leave to play by himself for a while. He's into everything. He doesn't seem to understand the concept of something being off limits. As days and incidents have gone by, I have gradually removed all sharp and personal objects from drawers and cupboards downstairs.

Yesterday I caught him balancing on the yellow kitchen chair trying to have a look inside the medicine box. This is, of course, deliberately inaccessible, right at the top of the tall cupboard, in a basket-drawer out of sight. The whole thing did make me smile because, even though he was on the chair, he was still about four feet too short. That did little to curb his determination, though, because he quickly progressed to swinging off the drawer with one leg, reaching up to climb on the tins of beans, tomatoes and rice pudding. I asked him if he would mind coming down, telling him that 'we don't do that here.' I explained that it wasn't safe and that the medical box was really rather boring. To prove my point I got it down to show him. He was suitably unimpressed. And actually, it was a useful exercise, because I realised that we needed more bandages, sterile wound-dressings and plasters.

I need to add them to the shopping list before I forget. I rummage in the pen drawer, emerging triumphant. I'm just about to ask Billy if he'd like another piece of toast, but in his characteristic stealth-move, he is gone from the kitchen, nowhere to be seen.

I don't chase him anymore. I've learnt that it works better not to give him the audience he craves. I have been over the house with a fine health-and-safety toothcomb and ensured that it's unlikely that he will find anything dangerous. I've also taken the precaution of giving each of the other children a box to keep their precious things in and put under our bed while Billy is here.

I walk up the stairs towards his room, channelling my best 'totally unconcerned' air. As I walk past the door I notice that he's looking at what I can't get beyond calling his 'ugly teddy'. (I definitely can't bring myself to address it as 'Sharon' – it just seems so incongruous.) He's chatting away happily to it. I have no idea what he's saying, I can't make much sense of much that comes out of his mouth. But he is nodding a lot and dancing about. It's nice that he's got a friend, albeit an ugly creature in full fluff.

I leave him to it. 'Never interfere when there is peace' is a good mantra for being around Billy.

I speak to a different social worker today, because Emma is out dealing with 'an emergency'. I know that in social care, emergencies are more common than they would be if the system was better organised.

To be honest, I don't catch the new one's name.

'I'm delighted to say that Billy's school start at Flatfields is all sorted out.'

I'm delighted to hear it, although it's just as well, as he is due to start tomorrow. I don't know much about the school directly, but I do know that as well as being small, it's quite unusual, with a waft of the 1970s about it. It's in a quaint village, next to one of the stately homes often seen in television costume dramas. The estate is also famous for its historic connections with unconventional, bohemian lifestyles. Apparently there is still that vibe about it, so quietly I am looking forward to having a look and see.

'And of course, just to remind you, Billy does not need a uniform.'

'Of course,' I reply. She can't see the accompanying eyeroll. As if a detail like that would have gone unnoticed on my watch.

I put the phone down and make a beeline for the coffee machine. I'm stopped in my tracks by a *ping-ping-ping-ping* cacophony from the phone. There are three messages from the Blackthorn WhatsApp group. Part of me realises that if the social workers knew about this, they'd have kittens. No doubt we are in breach of data protection, authority protocols and the like. But in situations like this, foster carers only have each other, and this has been a bit of a lifeline for us. There's also one from the flood WhatsApp group. Its language is rather rude, but true: the messenger is talking about a couple of the councillors, and the general gist seems to be calling into question what they spend their time doing. *Not much*, is my instant thought. Our floodees' group has composed some rousing choruses reflecting this perspective: *No rivers, no lakes, no sea – just apatheee* and *Not nature, just inertia*.

You may be able to tell from our inspiring lyrics that we're a little fed up.

I flick back to the Blackthorn group and scroll back through to take in the details. One little boy has locked himself in the bathroom and will not come out. I know these carers and they live in a beautiful house, so I suspect that they'd rather not break the door down.

Oh wow, there's another bathroom incident. This time a teenage boy has pulled down the shower curtain and shower rail with it, and poured bubble bath all over the floor. The carer has slipped and banged his head, but can't go to hospital because there is no one home to look after the Blackthorn child. Luckily one of the other foster carers is a nurse and she has advised him on what to do.

Blimey, this is all a bit fraught this morning. And there was me thinking that things might calm down a bit as these children settled.

I decide to take my little curly-haired fireball up to the hills for a long walk. I have learned that wearing him out saves some of the fixtures and fittings in my home. I could probably construct a graph showing the ratio of energy levels to number of things destroyed in my home.

I pack up my special 'walking bag'. I'm well aware that it looks deceptively like something a sporty, lycra-clad person might wear. I may not have been the target audience, but I found it on the internet and it works for me. It hooks across one shoulder and under the other arm, leaving my arms and hands free. It also holds a small water bottle (I know, get me), a supply of poo bags, and a tasty selection of dog treats. I take down the dogs' leads from the hook, squeeze my phone in, and just for today, a handful of boiled sweets to help motivate Billy up the steep hill. This will be the longest walk we have done yet, and I suspect that he will need some coaxing along the way. In the shed I have some size one wellies and a warm soft-lined coat that was Jackson's. I make sure the wellies are spider and web free. I sort gloves, hats, a scarf and the kitchen sink. Today I'm optimistic that we'll get Master Billy Blackthorn tired out.

In the event, I think it's me who arrives home much more fatigued.

The walk itself isn't too bad, though I didn't anticipate having to run quite as much as I do. (Perhaps the sporty bag was the right purchase, after all.) It's a windy day, and Billy is even wilder outside. He seems to be whipped up into a frenzy by that wind. He loves to be chased, it's his favourite thing. In fact, it's about the only thing he ever wants to do:

be chased. It's exhausting and I have to be honest, the fun foster carer routine evaporated fairly rapidly after the first lengthy chase. I also have a fear of him getting too far away from me and going AWOL in the hills, so once he starts, I feel compelled to follow. I also didn't factor in the energy required to carry a small child home dripping in mud while trying to manage two dogs. I'm in need of a little lie-down, let alone Billy.

Billy is tired, very tired indeed. He has covered the same sort of distance as Douglas does off the lead. No wonder he needed to be carried home. For every mile I walk, Doug tends to run ten, zigzagging backwards and forwards on the path, or running off to chase a rabbit. I think we covered about three miles today, and Billy's zigzagging mirrored Doug's. I fix him a sandwich – no need to guess the filling – and put a packet of Skips and a chocolate Penguin next to them. I fill a big glass of water. All disappear within a couple of minutes. He drains the water and asks for more. But his eyes are glazed and his thumb pops into his mouth. He's not going to get as far as drinking the second one. I have come to know this look. I steer him out of the kitchen and towards the sofa.

But I return to thinking about Billy's chasing fixation. It is really bothering me. I think I'll let the others know that we definitely have to curb his enthusiasm for running away by not running after him.

It might feel like fun, but it's a bit twisted too. As with so much of traumatised children's behaviour, it acts as a little warning sign telling me that I might need to think about it differently. Sometimes as a carer it's important to step outside myself and my own view of the world, and imagine what it would be like to be a child with trauma, to walk those steps with them.

There is a famous maze in Greek mythology, with a man-eating minotaur living in the middle of it, half-man, half-bull. I think a good analogy for living with trauma is to picture it as being a bit like entering this maze.

According to the myth, the labyrinth was such a complicated construction that it was very difficult to find the way out alive. Perhaps others have already been in the maze; maybe they got lost, or quickly found their way out without confronting the monster. But the labyrinth doesn't only consist of the 'trauma monster'. Some of the paths in the maze that have to be negotiated are just avenues of everyday banality, but they still have to be walked down. Trauma is not necessarily experienced all the time: there's buying bread and milk too. How you navigate the maze, and what you need to take in there with you to help find your way though it, differs from person to person. Sometimes it's enjoyable, being in a maze, especially at first. Perhaps you feel a bit scared at times, or lost, or frustrated as you recognise that you are revisiting the same old paths. Sometimes you think you are on your way and close to finding your way out, but then you hit another dead end. Sometimes you can feel the monster breathing just round the corner. In the myth, Theseus takes a thread into the maze and unravels it as he penetrates deeper and deeper into the labyrinth, so that he can find the way back out when he has killed the monster. I like the idea of that ball of string, a metaphor for being able to go deep into that labyrinth, as long as you know the way back. If you know the way back then you can enjoy the adventure.

I think Billy is in that maze. I want to follow him, as far as I can, but I need to protect myself as well as him. Children like Billy are exhausting – mentally, as well as physically. I'm a professional and I know how to look after myself. But I'm not a trained therapist, although with so many cutbacks to children's mental health services, it sometimes feels as if I need to be.

He leans back on the cushions and as his eyes begin to close. He looks positively angelic.

Uh oh, this is it. It's happening: I'm falling for young Billy.

It happens with most of the children that I foster. It's an important stage, a necessary stage. This feeling of care and love will convert directly into forgiveness and understanding. I hope I've managed to show that living with a child such as Billy is like playing whack-a-mole: a game board of repetitious and sometimes futile tasks, where the successful solving of one problem just leads to another popping up elsewhere. I don't know if I could keep doing it without this feeling in place.

It's chilly in here, or perhaps I'm still wind-blown from our walk. Either way, I want to feel warmer. I go to the burner and build a fire. I place a rather oversized, over-the-top fire guard in front of the burner. Another health-and-safety rule for foster carers. It's for insurance purposes, no doubt, not us. I have noticed that if children are shown a fire and allowed to light a match and take part, they are less likely to prod and probe the fire. If they touch the log burner once and it's hot, it is very unlikely that they will do it twice. But because everything to do with children is underpinned by insurance and under the banner of health and wellbeing, we end up with a small log burner stuck behind a ridiculously large fire guard. If I want to put another log on the fire, I have to unhook the thing from the wall and drag it across the rug, just to access the wood burner.

Knowing Billy as I do, he is more likely to climb onto the fire guard and fall down the other side and hurt himself that way. I'd feel safer if it wasn't there, to be honest. But hey, what do I know? I'm only a foster carer.

After a long nap – so long that he actually sleeps through the children's return from school – Billy is not only cooperative, but actually quite sweet at dinner. He is still a little tired from his walk and it seems as if his head is, once again, slightly too big for his neck. He can hardly keep his head up. Or at least, that is, until ice cream is mentioned. That perks him up no end. While he is slurping his way through double strawberry swirl, I have the chance to observe him.

His lovely curls, that looked messy and unkempt when he first bounced through the door nearly two weeks ago, now look healthy and shiny under the spotlights in the kitchen. The children engage Billy in conversation with them, just including him in the general banter, and I can see that he loves it. Vincent has taken to talking in 'Geezer' of late (and I'm not sure he's entirely fluent), so we don't always catch what he's saying. Jackson seems quiet this evening. I study them all. Dinner is a good way to see how they are.

'Who's got homework?' I ask with a smile, as I always do at this point in the day.

They each try to wriggle out of a response, and then, when I press the issue, become defensive.

'Why do we even have to do homework, at all? It's pointless.'

'We spend over six hours a day at school already. Why should we do even more work?'

'Yeah, it ruins our social time. When do we ever get downtime?'

I refrain from pointing out that most of Lily's existence seems to be 'downtime'. I remember these same feelings, same arguments, when I was their age. And it's actually hard to respond truthfully with my responsible adult head on, because I didn't like school at all. At the same time, I know people who loved it. I suppose it depends on the school and your individual circumstances as to the kind of experience you have. A good teacher, or supportive teaching assistant, can make all the difference. But I'm also conscious that our current school model is roughly the same as the Victorian school system, and perhaps there are some things about it that could do with updating. Where else do you spend your time with people born in the same year? Nowhere, that's where. Sometimes I wonder if it wouldn't be better to finish school at 14 years of age, and then go into a different type of further education for the next four years. I have seen boys in Year 11 in full uniform with beards. I'm not sure that the system has even recognised, let alone adapted to, the fact that children are growing up faster in the twenty-first century.

I look back at Billy, on the eve of starting school, and wonder if he's experienced any kind of nursery setting or playgroup, or watched older siblings talk about their school day. How will he deal with it all? I've been concentrating on the fact that I will get some working day back, and not really focusing on the emotional impact for Billy. I wonder what he will make of it.

I have explained to him, of course, that he's going to school. He didn't look fussed or fazed. Neither did he look happy. But it should not be a surprise to him.

I plan the evening ahead inside my head, thinking that I'll get him to help me choose his outfit for the morning.

We'll lay it out ready, and that will help him to really know that it's a different kind of day tomorrow. Then I'll get him in the bath and straight to bed. I've got a lovely book I bought for the boys when we lived in Portsmouth, all about starting school. I'll get that ready.

We finish our dinner and the children ask to leave. Within seconds they're gone. I wish I had never seen films where the children stack the plates and wash up together, reciting their times tables. We, ahem, don't appear to be that sort of a household. And, to be fair, I can't really imagine living like the Waltons.

While there are chores to be done in the kitchen, Lloyd, like the children, suddenly decides that there is some 'homework' to be done. Since we work from home, who am I to question? Lily, who has a very nurturing nature, sets Billy up in front of a quick episode of *Pingu* while I clear the last of the dinner things. It has rapidly become a favourite of his. I've suggested to her that she doesn't choose the school episode. I don't want Billy getting any ideas from the playful, mischief-making, and sometimes stubborn and naughty little penguin. It's so interesting to me to see the way that Lily loves to care and nurture, and I hope she understands that she is naturally this way. I wonder if her birth mother was too, before the rot set in. I don't mean that to sound harsh. Rot is decay, the causes of which are external, a bit like the cycles of abuse and neglect. I remember my adoptive mother, Barbara, would describe people as 'rotten' when I was a child. I always thought of a brown apple core in my head when she said it, but as I've gotten older I understand more and more what she meant.

Time to see if young Billy is ready for his bath and to embark on the preparations for a very special day tomorrow.

I wait for the tell-tale burst of theme music – *Pi-pi-pi-pi-pi-pi-pi-pi-Pingu* – to end.

'Bath time, Billy!'

So far, he hasn't let me in the bathroom, and I never assume. I ask children of a certain age where they would like me to be. Sometimes I have received replies that I didn't expect, such as 'dead', and another time, 'on my face', but on the whole they say 'outside the door'. Or they can be more specific, like, 'Can you tell me a story?' Even then I will ask which side of the door they want me to stand on to tell the story.

This evening we fill the bath with bubbles and he selects the toys he loves. There is the odd flying boat across the room or out of the door but, on the whole, he plays nicely, though he splashes like crazy. I have four large old beach towels covering the floor for such purposes. I can scoop them up quickly, minimising the risk of slippage afterwards. I've learnt to look out for problems, and prevention is much better than cure, especially when you have children. And especially ones like Billy.

Today, once the bath is run, Billy invites me in rather than closing the door. He holds my hand and pulls me into the bathroom, but he does it all accompanied by strange laughter. I don't know why, quite, but something puts me on hyper-alert. Call it intuition, but I trust my old friend. I busy myself rearranging the towels on the floor by the bath. Almost before I have a chance to think, his naked bottom is in my face. I move, faster than a speeding bullet (ish), up and away from him. I didn't know my knees still had it in them.

He turns to face me, standing up on the slip mat, and holds onto his willy. That's more normal, I think. Or is it? I'm not sure. I don't remember the boys, or indeed other boys, doing this publicly at his age.

What he does next is deeply disturbing.

He turns back round and bends over, pulling his buttocks apart.

He could be trying to release a fart, or he might just be being silly, but it is neither of those things.

He puts his right hand up against the tiled wall, leans forward and says, 'Come on then, stick it in.'

I feel the air leave my lungs and my breath converts to metallic bile. This is really nasty. It is not the first time I have seen such sexualised behaviour over the years. What I have not seen before, and never want to see again, is the suggestion that he feels as though he is the one in control, asking for the sexual act.

Oh my, this poor little boy.

I realise that I'm crying. Tears are spilling down my face. I try to wipe them away before he sees.

I want to ignore what I saw, to push the image from my mind, but I can't, quite.

While he was striking that horrible pose, I noticed dark red bits poking out of his anus. I'm not a doctor, but I think he has a prolapsed rectum. Oh my.

'Would you sit down, please, Billy?'

I don't really know how to carry on, but I want Billy to just enjoy a lovely warm bath with his new bath toys.

He sinks down into the bubbles.

'Sit down by the bath?' he asks in return.

I grab the Lloyd Loom basket, move it to the tap end of the bath, where his feet are, and sit on that.

His behaviour reverts back to a five-year-old's, as though nothing has happened. He starts making engine noises with one of the plastic boats, splashing most of the water out as he makes it travel the distance of the bath, but right now I could forgive him for anything. I begin to imagine the detail of the kind of abuse he might have suffered, even though I don't want to. It's one of those moments where I'm grateful that I'm in this position, grateful to be able to offer a home to a child, grateful that he has been removed from whatever toxic environment he was existing in before he and his siblings were put into care. I wonder how many abused children grow up without any help or support and end up being demonised by society.

He stays in the bath for what feels like days. I stay with him, but keep the bathroom door wide open. I feel as much in need of making sound effects and silly noises as Billy seems to be. He plays innocently and unselfconsciously with a toy shark, a souvenir from a day out at the Sealife Centre with the boys a while ago. I bet Billy would love a day like that. I hope we can get to a stage where I can do that sort of thing with him, though we're a long way off that yet. He would be too overwhelmed by the whole thing at the moment, and I couldn't cope with him through a train journey, crowds, and hours away from the house. I get the impression that young Billy didn't really go anywhere very much or do anything beyond being at home.

I breathe out a deep sigh, imagining that all his cares and woes and everything that has happened to this poor boy can just sail away on it.

Eventually Billy stands up to get out of the bath. I help him out, but when he puts his hand on his willy I quickly wrap the towel round him to prevent either of us having to go through another uncomfortable scenario.

I will write all this up later in my log, to be shared with the social workers so that they know exactly what has happened.

When we're in his room, he seems happy and light. He skips around the room and today he actually introduces me to his two rather raggedy old teddies that were slung on the bed the first day. Suddenly they are called Ant and Dec. I wonder if he has seen Ant and Dec on TV.

'How long have you had Ant and Dec?' I ask.

He shrugs his shoulders.

Conceptions of time are difficult for younger children, I know that, so I approach it differently. 'Did you get them when you were little?'

Again he shrugs his shoulders.

I point to the ugly teddy on the windowsill. I wonder why he keeps them separately.

'What about Sharon? How long have you had Sharon?'

Once more he shrugs, but this time I notice a little delay, like he had to think hard about it. I don't want to bombard him with questions. Child brain, timelines, so much happening recently, there's bound to be confusion.

I return to Ant and Dec.

'Do you like Ant and Dec on the telly?' I ask. 'I think they're funny. When my stepdaughter was young she used to watch them on Saturday mornings. Oh, what was the name of the programme? "Gimme 5" or something like that.'

As I ramble on, I realise that must have been back in the 1990s. I don't know where he would have encountered Ant and Dec, or how much meaning they might have to a five-year-old. He does seem to have odd choices of names for his toys.

I open the top drawer and take out his clean pyjamas. Turquoise with a beige dinosaur pattern. He looks very cute in them, younger and sweeter. Sometimes when he's in his jeans he looks a little thuggish, but that's not a great way to describe a youngster, and perhaps I'm just remembering the kick in the face.

For school in the morning, he chooses a pair of dark blue jeans with an elastic waist and a red t-shirt with a dinosaur. I choose a dark red hoodie to go with the t-shirt, which won't be enough on its own in this weather. I lay it out on the chair, along with socks and pants. I get him into bed. This has become much easier. In the first few days he was like a rocket taking off: as soon as I said good night he was up and following me out of the door. I couldn't get him to stay there. The first four or five nights, while Lloyd was away, I sometimes ended up sleeping in my clothes, just in case something happened. I didn't trust him to be safe, and I was worried about all of us. He's much better now, and I have to say the old winning formula of fresh air, exercise and good meals, plus lots of positive healthy attention, has helped him settle. And actually, given how difficult those first days were, he's responding much faster than some of the other children we've looked after.

He lies in bed, holding the duvet with both hands, and kicks his feet up, laughing as the end of the duvet goes up in the air.

'Right, Billy, that'll do,' I say in a firm voice that he now recognises and complies with straight away, flattening down the duvet and looking meek.

'Would you like a story?'

At this suggestion he gets excited again and throws up the duvet with his feet once more. I let him be, and notice that he checks himself and calms down as I reach for the book.

I placed *Topsy and Tim* in position there on his bookshelf earlier, all ready.

I shift his fresh clothes for the morning over to one side of the chair, sit down and turn to the first page. Even on page one I already have to do what foster carers always do with children's books: rewrite it as I go along. The first page talks about starting school after a lovely summer holiday. I don't think Billy, or any of the Blackthorn children, have had lovely summer holidays. And it's the middle of February. The world misses out looked-after children, the books certainly do, but this is to the detriment of all. Sometimes when they're mentioned and given a voice, their stories can strike a chord with all children.

Billy is very tired tonight. The thumb is firmly in, the eyes are heavy. I finish the story.

'Nestle down now,' I say. 'Big day tomorrow.'

He smiles while sucking his thumb.

Yes, I am beginning to adore this little fella.

As I walk down the hallway to the top of the stairs I hear something. I quietly walk back along the landing and move my head round his semi-open bedroom door. He's up and standing in front of ugly Sharon teddy, moving from foot to foot saying, 'Yes.'

I leave him to it. He seems to have created a real bond with toy-Sharon. I really must stop calling the thing 'ugly'.

I do a quick round of the other children, knocking on each bedroom door to check they're okay. They are all fine, though they barely register my presence. The boys are in front of a screen, headphones on, plugged in, playing something together. Their reactions are so visceral to whatever has happened in the game, and I've noticed that

Vincent's language has become a lot more colourful lately. A big transition occurs when they move up to secondary school and the floodgates open. He has become fluent in Dockyard himself.

I head downstairs and along the hallway to my studio, my sanctuary. I haven't spent much time in here of late. I tune in to Radio 4, hoping that it will calm me. Instead I catch part of an episode of the *Moral Maze,* a conversation between Michael Buerk and some well-known (but unheard of to me) clever-clogs and members of think-tanks. What a way to earn a living, eh? In the context of everything else that is going on, I find the talk deeply annoying and turn it off. Sometimes the arrogance of the middle classes drives me up the pole.

I answer my emails. It is a bulging inbox because I just haven't been able to get on top of it lately.

Yikes. Jane, my writing agent, is chasing me for a synopsis I need to send her, and James, my art agent, has reminded me about an interview I have been offered on Soho Radio to talk about my illustrations for the seahorse book. Neither are anywhere near completion. I spend every spare minute I have in the day battling Billy's erratic behaviour, or thinking about what has gone before for the Blackthorn children.

Something terrible has been going on for them. There is no doubt about it. I think about Billy showing me his bottom and what he said, and I feel sick all over again. It seems that there's no limit to the exploitation of children. I write emails to whichever social worker I've seen the name of, to update them on this latest episode. I include Emma and hope she's okay. I also include Dara. Even though I know she must already be in de-mob mode, and who could blame her, I still want to keep her in the loop.

More than ever, I understand that they are overwhelmed. More and more children are coming into care than ever before. Our local authority has been inundated because of the Blackthorns, but the picture is bad all over the country. I am convinced that if money went into prevention, helping those who struggle to have support and confidence, a fraction of children would need to be in care. But the money isn't channelled that way, and so we have to pick up the pieces. Money, money, money. It always comes down to money. I hate it.

I can't settle down to any work tonight. My mind is all over the place. I leave the computer and pop upstairs to have a peep at Billy. Perhaps he's having trouble sleeping with the knowledge of what lies ahead in the morning.

I'm wrong. From the crack in his part-open bedroom door I can hear that he's snoring away, and his curls against the pillow make him look positively angelic.

Chapter Nine

I wake up early. Lloyd is already up. One of his clients wants all-new branding: a huge job, but good money, which is just as well right now. We are feeling the pinch. Fuel prices have gone up, everything seems to have gone up. Everything apart from the fostering allowances, that is.

I feel fresher than I have done for weeks. Well, since Billy arrived, anyway. First port of call is Billy. I head along the corridor to check on him, but he's still snoozing away. Good. I have half an hour until the others need to be up. Coffee is calling. There's a chill in the air, and I put on my big woolly outsize cardigan-coat. It's quite a natty piece of knitwear, a charity shop find from years ago, and I like to use it as a dressing gown. It's warmer than any *actual* dressing gown I've known, and I love the comfort of being wrapped up snugly inside it. In the summer I prefer a cooler, kimono-type garment, but in the winter this little knitted number does the job perfectly.

I unplug my phone from the charger and see bundles of WhatsApp notifications. Once again, it is two groups generating all the activity. No surprises which: the flood group and the Blackthorns. I take my steaming coffee to the kitchen table and sit down to catch up. I find WhatsApp chats can be difficult to follow when you're not 'in the moment' with what's happening, so I track back carefully.

The flood group members are getting lively, and

comments are taking an increasingly political turn. Corruption is mentioned several times, but I suppose it isn't surprising under the current regime. I think we'd all be shocked if there was a party in existence that was wholly lovely, kind and honest.

Oh blimey, it's all kicking off in the Blackthorn group again. These children are wild. The older ones are off the wall. I'm lucky to have one of the younger ones, it seems. One foster carer, Trudy, reports that her 'young lady' (and she seems to be using that term with heavy irony), has:

Only gone and dragged her used tampons across the hallway walls.

I've seen those hallway walls. They're pristine. Pale apple green, if I remember.

It looks like the cats have dragged dead birds along the walls.

Trudy will not have coped well with this. She is lovely and always wears well-ironed outfits. It's a detail I notice because I don't.

There's a third message from Trudy, explaining how the tampons then ended up in the biscuit tin.

Delightful.

There are more, loads more, but I decide that I will have to come back to them later. I must get all the children sorted and want to leave myself plenty of time for Billy and his first day: I need a good half an hour for the drive to the primary school, and ensure that everything is ready for a smooth departure.

Lloyd takes over the morning shift so that I can concentrate on Billy. This is a novelty for all, as Lloyd's normally on international calls at this time of day. His clients are mainly in Switzerland and Germany, which means that when I'm flying about looking for pants and PE shorts, lunch boxes and breakfasts, Lloyd is usually in a Zoom meeting. I wonder what would happen if I got a publisher in Italy. Perhaps the children would have to fend for themselves.

No prizes for guessing what Billy chooses for breakfast. But I'm not the worst person in the world for giving this little fella Nutella. Although it will sound as if this is all I feed him, he's already looking a lot healthier. He's no longer ravenously hungry the whole time, as he seemed to be when he first arrived. And he's definitely filling out, looking less bony. At one stage I thought he might have knock knees, but I think it was just the impression created by his skinny legs. They seem fine now.

He's soon fed and dressed, looking good, ready for his big day. I carry my green furry coat out to the car. I don't think I'll need it because it's a crisp sunny day, perfect for the first day of school. Because he's only in for the morning, there is not really enough time to go home and come back, regardless of what Emma thinks about giving me time for 'running the hoover round'. Thinking about her comment makes me cross all over again. I know it's a throwaway remark, but what kind of a sister is she to feminism and anti-misogyny? I don't believe that social workers should still be using the same old narrative that it is women who are responsible for the domestic chores. Nor that foster carers are mostly women, looking after children for a bit of 'pin money'. It's just a totally inappropriate perception of what we do.

'Goodbye,' I call out to anyone who's listening. Only Dotty and Doug give me any kind of response.

Billy jumps enthusiastically into his car seat. He seems to like being on his throne. I have created quite the little kingdom in the back there, surrounding it with toys and books and games: things to occupy him. Sometimes none of it is necessary. From time to time when we've been driving, I've caught him staring out of the window in absolute wonder. Children like looking out of moving vehicle windows. It must be quite mesmerising. I remember doing it myself.

The drive does me good as well as Billy. My head clears of all its day-to-day nonsense as we approach the school. The only signage is a little brown street sign with a graphic illustration of children. The area is beautiful. Winter trees are illuminated by the bright white sky, creating majestic silhouettes. It's a lovely day. We head down a little country lane. Now there is a wooded sign which looks rustic and homemade, but by a skilled person. So very different from typical primary school signage in corporate colours. There is a childlike painting of three flat fields in different tones, with dark green at the back to suggest perspective. A smiling yellow sun floats above with orange and yellow rays. I have always loved looking at people's depictions of the sun; they never fail to make me feel happy. We continue past the sign, passing through an orchard on both sides of the drive, albeit an orchard that is resting through winter, grey gnarled branches catching the light.

What a location. I'm thoroughly enjoying this experience.

Ahead I can see what looks like a gorgeous little car park surrounded by bushes and last year's planting weighted down by old seed heads, but before that I spot a pen of sheep. There are four piebald Jacob sheep munching on hay. I love it all, this beautiful, tranquil setting.

Beyond the bushes nestles the little school building, made from wood. As I lock the car and try to hold on to Billy's hand, I suggest that we say hello to the sheep first.

He immediately jumps up on the pen. I know that we will be being watched, not out of malice, but because we have arrived and there are big windows all round the building. Leaping up onto the side of the pen is probably not creating the best impression. Distraction is the answer.

'Right, Billy. Where's the blue car?' I say, quickly inventing a look-see game to persuade him to walk with me.

'Where's the red car?'

He doesn't respond. Ah yes, colours. Not his strong point.

I change tack. 'Which is the biggest car?'

Nothing. But he does at least leap down from the pen and run beside me up the ramp to the main door.

I assume that the ramp means there must be a child in a wheelchair. Even if there isn't, this is the sort of place that would have factored that potential into its design.

The door itself is dark glass, like a mirror reflecting the surrounding trees. A man immediately appears and opens the door to let us in.

'Good morning, I'm Max, the headteacher,' he says by way of introduction. His voice is deep and warm and welcoming. Max has a balding head of red hair and a beard, neatly trimmed. Nearly all men seem to have beards these days. I remember that I was scared of them as a child: I wouldn't go into my new classroom because Mr Churchill, the teacher, had a bushy beard. I wouldn't go anywhere near Father Christmas in Debenhams for the same reason.

Holding Billy's hand, I can't tell anything about his feelings. He appears neither nervous nor excited, just quiet.

'I'm Louise, and this is Billy.'

Max is wearing a lovely mustard-coloured jumper, good-quality cashmere, with a thick red tartan flannel shirt peeping out from beneath the V-neck. Beneath faded black jeans I notice his shoes: handmade, welted brogues. They are clearly old, but like the rest of him, exude quality. I don't know about Billy, but I'm in awe of this man and this place. I want to come to school here. I would have loved for all my children to have come to a school like this. What a great opportunity he has ahead of him.

We walk through the large hallway, where there are framed paintings on every wall, mostly abstract. Some is the work of pupils, children who are evidently talented, and I love that their work has been framed.

All Max's attention is focused on Billy; he's chatting away and pointing out things to Flatfields' newest pupil.

It gives me a moment to notice one particular painting and the signature. It's by a well-known artist from the fifties, not Tate-Gallery-famous, but I definitely remember being shown his paintings at art school.

I am fascinated by everything here.

The walls are painted a peach colour. I know that some Steiner schools use colour to help children feel recognised at different stages in their development. Years ago, one of my friends was an artist in residence at a Steiner school; she got the gig via the old Arts Council based in Winchester. I was a bit envious, I have to say, because I never had any success myself with funding bids. Later I learnt that her mum's best friend was a teacher at the school. As ever, it's not what you know, etcetera. But I learnt from her how important colour was to their curriculum. She had painted the classrooms various colours for the different ages. The little children were in a room painted various shades of pink, to represent newborn (at least to a white demographic, I suppose). I remember her talking about how they painted the colour peach so that it faded out at the edges, just as it does here.

'Now, would you like to come into my office so that I can introduce myself properly?' Max asks, interrupting my colour reverie.

We follow. I think Billy is checking everything out, and I keep a firm hold of his hand. I think I notice Max looking at my hand with a slight glimpse of disapproval. I don't know what the social workers have told him in advance, but my instinct is 'probably not everything.'

'Please, take a seat,' Max gestures.

His eyes linger on my continued hold of Billy's hand. Maybe he's right. I shouldn't hold his hand firmly. But I'm pretty sure that he will run wild and pull this room apart if I don't.

We wait as Max invites Billy to sit on a beanbag. Thankfully, I'm offered a chair. I don't think I'd ever get up from a beanbag after the last few weeks with Billy. My body feels stiff and painful. Billy throws himself down on the indicated yellow beanbag, with the force and energy that I recognise and can feel mounting further. I want to talk to Max without Billy in the room. I want to tell him about Billy's behaviour. I don't suppose that I'm going to get that opportunity.

Max begins to talk about all the exciting things they do here. I did notice the most beautiful nature table in the hall, which looks like something from *Country Living* magazine, but he talks about the animals here, the agriculture and planting, as well as the art. I can see that Billy is not interested in the slightest. But I think I can also detect the beginnings of his unease with the situation.

Max is also watching Billy, and wisely stands up to move things on. 'Well, Billy, since this is your first little getting-to-know session, I think it's time you met your new friends.'

That is that, then: me done, and no opportunity to speak to Max in private. If nothing else, I just wanted to have the chance to warn him to be careful. Billy exits the office first, with Max walking behind. I can see that Billy is fast approaching the nature table.

'We're a trauma-aware school. Billy will be fine.'

Just at that moment, a loud bang and crash resonates through the hall.

'Oh dear,' says Max gently. 'That's fine, it can be replaced,' as he gestures to the main door, my signal to depart.

Back outside, I look at my watch and realise that there won't be time enough for me to do anything much more than drift round the local estate and the village shops.

I have been tipped off by a friend who sells vintage fashions online that there's a fantastic charity shop in the village. She is very much in the know, sniffing out where the well-heeled live in order to target their local charity shops. I decide to save that treat for another day, and have a look around the estate this time, the gardens being my real interest ahead of the house. And these gardens are stunning. Topiary trees and well-trimmed hedges give it all a feel of *Alice in Wonderland*. I bet the Flatfields children come here. How wonderful for them.

I find the coffee shop and treat myself to a piece of walnut cake and a cappuccino. I sit down and imagine the mornings ahead. I can sit in this wonderful wood-panelled room, enjoy a coffee and do some work on my laptop, if I get myself organised. I look for a sign to indicate the possibility of wi-fi access, and there it is, in a gorgeous Farrow and Ball green-painted frame. Green Smoke, if I'm not mistaken. Good, a plan for tomorrow. Meanwhile, I catch up on my phone messages while enjoying my cake.

The flood WhatsApp is as busy as ever, but so is the carers' group.

Shane is a fellow carer, and an ex-soldier and ardent biker. He has one of the Blackthorn boys. I always find him hilariously funny. But I'm surprised he has a Blackthorn. I thought his household was full. He and his wife Bev only look after boys. They do a really good job, and despite his 'hard man' image, Shane is a gentle pussycat. His first message says:

Our Blackthorn is at the police station after hitting his teacher, a woman, at school today.

Oh my, that's terrible, the poor woman.

His next message sounds more frantic.

I've got to go and get him from the station, where's the bloody social worker?

I scroll back and realise that it's Shane's Blackthorn child who pulled the shower curtain and rail down and wrecked the bathroom.

One way or another, even without my laptop, I keep myself happily amused until collection time for young Billy. One part of me wants Max to have waved some sort of magic wand and completely sorted Billy out so that I will arrive to collect a transformed child. The other part knows damn well that it is never going to be easy, and definitely not in one morning. In real terms, I just want Billy to have made a good start, to have enjoyed his day, to have something to build on.

I look at my watch and head slowly back to the car. I savour seeing my breath vapour in the air as I walk. I'm reluctant to be leaving this wonderful place today but charmed in the knowledge that I will soon be back. I anticipate the delight of seeing the season change as we head towards spring. I have no doubt that I shall find it inspirational for my art and my writing.

I take the short but picturesque drive back to the school grounds, calculating how long it would take to walk rather than drive between the two. I park my car and head towards the entrance. Max is standing framed by the glass doors, wringing his hands, not looking that great.

Oh no, something must have happened.

'It hasn't gone quite as well as we hoped.'

He escorts me in quickly, circling one arm a distance from my back but very keen to usher me through the door. He takes me directly to his office. I sit down without waiting to be asked this time. Max seems genuinely fraught. I sit and wait for him to speak.

'I don't think this is the right school for Billy.'

My little fantasies of eventually getting a gardening job at the big house while Billy thrives at Flatfields School are shattered in a second.

'What's happened?'

Max looks defeated. 'He's hurt several of the children, kicked a teacher in the shin, punched me in the stomach, and pulled two classrooms apart.'

He clears his throat, which alerts me to the fact that there is more to come.

'He then stood in front of all of us when we tried to calm him down and pulled down his trousers. He urinated in the classroom bin, then started playing with his penis and said, 'Suck this c-u-n-t.'

He spells out the letters rather than repeating the word himself.

'So, as I say, I think perhaps this is not the place for Billy. He needs somewhere that can cater more effectively for his particular needs.'

Doesn't he just. *That was supposed to be you, with your 'trauma-awareness'*, I think, but I don't trust myself to speak and be polite, so I just nod.

'So, we won't be expecting him back tomorrow,' he says, gently, just to make sure I have fully understood. Next, I'm escorted to Billy, who is fast asleep under the teacher's desk, his exploits evidently having worn him out. The classroom is otherwise empty, all the other children having been placed in another room away from Billy for their own safety.

I wake him, then pick him up to carry him straight out to the car.

There are no words of goodbye.

I have so many mixed emotions. Part of me feels furious at having been taken in by Max's cashmere sweater and nice shoes. The arrogance that the school prides itself on being 'trauma-aware'. Really? What nothingness did they have to do to get that stamp? How dare they just wash their hands of their new pupil? I know I'm not going to let this go quietly with Emma or whatever social worker is on duty today. It's not fair. I see a boy who is suffering in ways he cannot describe, and reacting violently to that suffering. And of course I get both sides of it. I really do. How could Max allow staff and the other children and their families to be put in danger? At the same time, something has to happen for Billy. He has to be educated, and I'm definitely not offering free home-schooling. I know private children's homes that charge in the region of a £100,000 a year to offer 43 weeks' part-time teaching to children like Billy, but where's the money for that going to come from? The whole thing is mad. I don't know what to do.

I call Emma and Dara as soon as I'm home. Both of them are busy. I miss Dara. Really miss her. I've tried to be professional about it, but, if I'm honest, I'm heartbroken that she's leaving, and to all intents and purposes has already gone. The best ones always seem to leave. The system must have some fractures in it if that's the case.

I try to imagine what Dara would say if she did pick up. Something funny no doubt, something bordering on unprofessional, something that would make me feel a whole lot better than I do right now.

I'm full of different emotions. I'm more than deflated by how things have gone at Flatfields. I'm cross with Billy for behaving like that, but cross with myself for feeling cross because I know that this behaviour is a form of communication in itself and we, by which I mean society at large, need to be able to do more to help him. The other emotion that I have is worry. I'm concerned that my work, my living, will suffer again. And then, of course, I feel guilty for thinking that way. But it's *always* my work that gets the squeeze. I sometimes wonder if that's because I'm a creative. Most people's perception of 'creating' is that the work is just magicked up from the air. If people knew how much time, energy and skill goes into art, they might feel differently. I suppose I'm feeling bitter after hearing a bunch of writers talking on Radio 4 recently about how hard their lives were. It seemed as if they belly-ached their way through the whole programme. One woman described having to work in a purpose-built writing room with a view over an estuary. It had been a gift from her architect husband. Poor love, sitting there wrapped in a cashmere blanket from Liberty, sipping herbal tea, waiting for the muse to strike. Oh, stop it, Louise, I tell myself. It's the pompous privileged creatives who give us normal hard-working ones a bad name. Imagine having the time to gaze into an estuary for hours before writing. Actually, that sounds amazing. And it was a version of the little life I was carving out for myself just a few hours ago when I envisaged writing in that oak-panelled loveliness.

My phone is pinging. The Blackthorn group again. I'm not entirely sure who everyone is. I think I know, or have met, about half. It's interesting to me that the local authority hasn't placed any as sibling groups; each child is on their own. That's unusual. Without wanting to sound like a duchess from *Downton Abbey*, I wonder who the father is, or perhaps fathers. I would love to see the others, to see if they look like Billy with his winsome curly hair. Of course, no one on WhatsApp would post a photo of any of these children. Seasoned foster carers well know the drill. We know not to do that. We're all professionals.

However professional we are, though, I have to say that we do have names for some of the staff, like 'the fat controller' for one of the area managers, who is known to have his fingers in lots of pies. There are sometimes comments that are a little near the mark in relation to certain figureheads in the authority, but, above all, we endeavour to protect these children. We keep them safe.

I flick through the new messages. None of them are good. Like Billy, several of the children have been sent home from school or refused to go in the first place.

There's also a flood group message that worries me: *Stand by. Looks like heavy rain later.* Great. Just what you need when you've got a wild child, with no immediate prospect of school, confined to the house. I look at Billy, the main source of all my woes at the moment. He's busy arranging the batteries in the recycling box. I guess they are a nice weight and make that wonderful sound when rolled together. Quite mesmerising. I can see the attraction of that game.

My more general observation of Billy is that he is okay when he's with me, Lloyd and the children here, but can't easily cope with being in a new environment, or with new people. That makes me think that he must have not felt safe in the past, and also that he hasn't experienced many environments or people. Perhaps he has been hurt. He certainly seems to have been sexually abused. His reactions are more extreme than other children that I have looked after, though there are some similar behaviours. But Billy's behaviour makes me feel more uneasy than that of any other child I have worked with. And weirdly unsafe. There's always an undercurrent of threat in his behaviour. If I'm honest, I'm scared of him. Frightened of a five-year-old. He worries me in all sorts of ways – not just getting through the here and now, but in terms of what lies out there for him later in his life.

I try the social workers on the phone again, but I'm not getting much response from Emma, or indeed the other social worker, who, it turns out, is an assistant. They are so short-staffed anyway, and with the Blackthorns coming into care I doubt if they have anywhere near enough people to handle everything. Michelle reported on WhatsApp that she had a visit from an unaccompanied student social worker. I know that this would never normally happen with the local authority, and it doesn't help me feel confident about looking after Billy. Does *anyone* know what's been going on for these children?

I send Billy and the dogs out to the garden to play. I hope I've done the right thing, because it's starting to get wetter and wilder, but Billy is all wrapped up and warm. I remember when Jackson was at nursery school, the headteacher there would tell the parents to bring waterproofs. She was a firm believer in the old adage that there is no such thing as bad weather, just unsuitable clothing, and that all children should be outside for some time in the day. I used to totally agree with her, but since the flooding has got so much worse as a result of the heavier and more unpredictable rainfall caused by climate change, I'm not so sure. I call the rain the 'rain from hell' and I know that it only takes four inches of rapid-moving rain to knock a big, grown man off his feet. I wouldn't hold out much hope for a child. I move myself into a better position to view him. While two and four legs run around the garden, I stand at the kitchen sink with my laptop and email the social workers. My phone pings again. Not the Blackthorn carers but the flood group. George, who is a retired fireman, is advising us not to bother with gel bags.

Complete waste of time and bad for the environment.

Instead, he suggests buying builders' sand and filling the bags up ourselves. Something else to do before it gets dark. Lloyd's out today and, by the time I've explained what to do to the children and waited for them to stop arguing or being silly, I really could have done it myself.

So I take my eyes off Billy for a moment. That is a mistake.

Our two giant terracotta pots look empty from the window, because they are packed with layered bulbs. I saw Monty Don do it on *Gardeners' World*. My friend calls it a bulb lasagne. I put daffodils at the bottom, then a layer of soil; tulips, then soil; anemones, soil; then crocuses on top, before the final layer of soil. It makes it look lovely for months. I have placed the pots there so I can see them from the window when I'm washing up.

But not this coming spring.

Billy has pulled them over and pushed them down the steps, where they've shattered: a million pieces everywhere. I'll have to write them off, and I'm looking at a couple of hundred pounds. If I tried to claim for them, the social worker (if not her, then her manager), would say, 'You shouldn't have them, it's your risk.' Or something equally unhelpful that will make me want to spit.

I sigh and close the laptop, putting it against the kitchen window, well out of reach of the hands of a certain small person. I go out into the garden following the dogs, who are happy to greet and lead me, because they love mischief. Though Doug always looks guilty if he's taken part in a crime. I look at my garden, gazing in disbelief at the total devastation of the broken pots.

That's not all. I look again and see worse. Two of my statues, works of art that Lloyd bought me for birthdays long past, have been pushed over and smashed on the patio. It's a lovely space for eating in the summer, formerly a pond. Now it's home to a pile of rubble. I feel wretched. They're one-offs. Objects that can never be replaced. Like the terracotta pots, they were in a sensible place and Billy must have really wanted to damage them. I realise that I'm looking at about £500 of damage in the last few minutes alone, and I know I will have to suck this up. Not only that, but I shall effectively have to home-school Billy for free for two and half weeks, and sacrifice my own work schedule. It feels like an impossible position. I've known carers who recently had to pay for two new front doors for their Aga after an 11-year-old foster child kicked them off their hinges. With the labour factored in, it cost them £800. That was the same as working for free for a month as far as they were concerned.

It's hard to take, and there are no easy answers, but it's just another reason why so many foster carers are leaving the service. Sometimes it doesn't add up to seem worth it. I'm extra sad because the two figures he pushed over were given to me by Lloyd when the boys were little. The figures look like devils. I used to think of them as my 'little devils' and think of the boys, but their devilishness is nothing compared to young Billy's. And yet at the same time I know that he's no devil. I am watching a deeply traumatised child, feeling out of control. I catch a glimpse of him before he disappears at the other end of the garden. Yes, he's smiling, as though he enjoys my sadness, but I don't believe that. I somehow think that's his default position, as if he's been told to smile. It's a bit like a child I looked after years ago who used to kick me because his mum's boyfriend had kicked him and more. The boy's mum would then explain that in spite of the kicking, 'he loves you'. So this little fella kicked me because he liked me. While it makes no sense if you haven't been abused, from another perspective it seems perfectly logical behaviour.

Asking a child 'why' is one of the world's greatest wastes of time. They don't know why, especially not a traumatised five-year-old. I guess, at the most basic level, it must have felt quite satisfying, pushing the pots and statues over. How do you know how to behave if you haven't been shown? He may well have lived in chaos and not been allowed out of his area. There is something deeply wild about Billy but, ironically, I sense that it's wildness born out of limitations.

I look around the garden for him, since he seems to have evaporated. After a moment he runs up to me and throws himself against me, smiling and laughing.

I sit on the stone steps so I'm at his level. 'What happened here, Billy?'

He wriggles about and starts laughing, and in typical Billy style, shoots off back to the other end of the garden.

I wonder if his movement, which looks like taunting in the wake of his vandalism, might actually be fear. Is he scared that I might do something to him, hurt him in some way? He seems to love playing cat and mouse, but I don't like it at all. In fact, it makes me feel uncomfortable and unsafe. I also dread to think why adults might have wanted to play this game with a little boy. I shudder.

I decide to leave him to it, and return to a tried-and-tested foster carer classic. One that isn't in the books about trauma. As I walk back towards the house, I call out, loudly, 'Nutella'.

It works. In he comes. Coat off, boots off. I hold his hands, cold from the rain and wind, and rub them. 'Let's warm you up,' I say.

He starts shifting about, laughing still, and asks, 'Am I touching willies, then?'

Oh my God.

I feel sick. Sick to the core. I don't know who he's talking about, but I want to poke their eyes out. This boy has been used. I have such a bad feeling here. I will never be okay knowing that adults exploit innocence at this level. People always have. I know that. But surely not now, not these days. And yet I know it still happens. Bad people will find a way to be near children, and this is what must have happened to Billy. I'm pretty damn sure that's the case. I find it one of the hardest things to know about. It is truly evil. Yes, I've read and heard all the accounts of child sexual abuse. Some say 'it's an illness'. But I think that it's much more than that. It's a culture that we've sadly hidden for years. Worse, it's an economy, with pornography at the heart. Consider the ease of accessing porn. Why *do* people watch it? It's always exploitative, and it seriously messes with people's heads. For years people's bodies have been described as objects. 'Look at the tits on that,' was one gem I had to endure as a younger woman. Even men in my own social group would say things like that when we were out. Who the hell do these people think they are?

The day I've had: Billy's effective expulsion from school after just one morning, the horror of this confirmation in words of something I'd already suspected, the unfairness of everything. It all makes me bolder. I'm definitely in the mood for some reckoning. I take the plunge and pursue the conversation.

'Did you touch men's willies?'

He laughs and performs a fake gag. Mine is a real one.

'I play with the snakes, sssssss.'

'Oh, Billy.' I realise that I'm still holding his hands to try to keep him still, because he wants to be jumping up and down. I let go, understanding that it may feel restrictive.

He reaches for my hands back immediately.

I oblige, and we stay rooted to that spot for a moment. We haven't even moved past the tumble dryer, now living in the conservatory by the back door. I crouch back down so that I'm right at his level, and can see straight into those large eyes that have seen, well, God knows what.

'What would master Billy like?'

'Nutella,' he replies.

Thank the Lord for that. I thought for a moment he was going to say something sexual.

It feels awkward holding hands, but Billy clearly doesn't want to let go, so I show him how to do the fingers game.

'Here's the church and there's the steeple, open the door and see all the people.'

I hate it when I know a child has been sexually abused. I've heard it said that men think about sex every seven seconds. I don't know quite how true that is, but imagine how much brainpower that must consume. Then factor in men who watch porn regularly. I feel, bizarrely, that Billy's disclosure leaves me with a trace of their toxicity. I look at Billy wiggling his fingers to make the people. All I see is men's penises, legs and arms, and exploitation. I hate feeling like this. It isn't Billy's fault. He's innocent. But I can't unthink things. I wonder for a brief moment if the world would be a better place without men. Then I remember that Lloyd is a good man. They're not all bad. My thoughts are all over the place.

When Billy is finished playing 'here's the steeple', he reaches for my hand once more. More than that, he is hanging from my wrist. I look at him and suggest that the hand will do nicely, thank you. He seems happy with that.

In the kitchen I make some toast.

'Would you like a hot chocolate?' I ask, while I'm waiting for the toaster to pop.

Of course he does. I make two pieces of white toast. I've learnt my lesson: he was a bit fazed by the seeded loaf I used the other day. I cut the toast up into little triangles and place it on the table. I make his hot chocolate in a revolting mug he chose when we were in Primani. That's a whole other story: I'm surprised we weren't arrested, frankly, when he pulled everything off the rails. When I quickly grabbed a new hair band for Lily, he pushed the nail polish display over. It was awful. One of those days when you wish you had a digital sign above your head. 'Forgive us, I'm his foster carer.' But it seems that there is no harsher judge than 'other people' in the context of a woman with a child behaving badly.

I make myself a coffee. I have earned another one today, I think. I sit down at the kitchen table next to Billy and play a podcast through the speaker: *Woman's Hour*. I haven't quite adjusted to the new presenters. I had only ever known Jenni Murray, who I always imagined to be quite a force. I will give them time, I need to get used to them. I always used to enjoy Radio 4, because it felt like mature sages were informing and amusing me. Now I feel like the presenters are students. But I know that this is an impression I need to be realistic about. A result of me creeping along the conveyor belt of time. They are just younger, that's all. I need to get a grip. But I am struggling to hear the 'voices' – I mean the actual voices. Coffee and life. Today this lot feel too much like crushed avocado and almond milk, and bed by 10pm. Too clean, too sensible, too divorced from my own perception of the world that has tilted horribly in the light of Billy's revelations.

I turn it back off.

'Would you like to do some drawing?'

He nods and presses his face on one side against the kitchen table, dribbling onto the wood.

I ask him not to do that, and feel some comfort in knowing that I still have anti-bac spray in every cupboard in the house. He pushes the dribble round on the table with his fingers. Blimey, if that's entertainment, he must have had some bored days.

I get a supply of materials from the grey cupboard in the conservatory. I suggest we draw some animals.

'Which animals are your favourite?' I ask.

He looks puzzled.

Okay, I will try a different approach. I look at Dotty as she heads away from the table on her way to her bed in the corner, reluctantly accepting that she's not getting any of Billy's Nutella toast.

'Do you like dogs?'

He scrunches his nose. 'I like Dotty and Douglas.'

That's good news, I think to myself, and a good place to start. I go to my laptop and look up 'pictures of dogs' on Google.

Puppies everywhere. Lots of fluffy, adorable puppies. Plenty of inspiring material here. Billy and I sit there and 'aww' and 'ooh' at one after another. Suddenly he sees a picture of a black Staffordshire Bull Terrier, from an insurance company advert or something similar.

He points at the Staffy excitedly. 'Dec!'

A little further probing reveals that Ant and Dec are the names of two Staffies belonging to the Blackthorns. He seems happy to talk, and it strikes me as a good way to ask a few more questions and to understand what might have been going on for Billy, what his home life was like.

'What were Ant and Dec like?'

He shrugs.

'Did you take them for walks, like we do with Dotty and Doug?'

'No.'

'Did you help to feed them?'

'No, no.'

'Did you like to stroke them?'

'No.'

I'm getting nowhere, fast, but have a flash of inspiration. 'Were they guard dogs?'

He nods as he stabs at a piece of paper with a pale blue felt tip.

Now, why would a family need guard dogs?

I show Billy how to draw a cartoon dog face first, and then a real dog. Not bad efforts, even if I say so myself. Now, normally if an adult draws something reasonably okay, children seem to think we're amazing. But not Billy. He just watches, sitting up with his arms folded. After a while he leans on the table and dribbles over my drawing of a dog. One of my best performances, and it evokes no response. I resort to cheaper tricks as the afternoon goes on, sticking a film on and making a lovely comfy zone from the larger cushions. This will enable him to be all set up for a snooze if he wants one. I have noticed that he fades in the afternoons, almost always needing a nap. If I think about it, that behaviour suggests that he may not have been quite ready for school after all. It seems to add weight to my hunch that Billy has just been left for long periods, perhaps ignored and left to get on with things for himself. There's other evidence of neglect. His hair badly needs cutting. It was unkempt when he arrived, and is now hanging in his eyes. The rules are different all over the country, but under our local authority guidelines I need to have permission from the birth parents to get a haircut. Who knows when I'll get that when I can't even seem to get hold of a social worker to discuss what's going to happen next with regards to school.

I was planning to do it anyway, but after what Billy has said, I make a quick phone call while he's in front of the TV to organise an appointment with the doctor. Recent experience tells me that I'm unlikely to get to see our family doctor in person at the moment. The last few times we've had to see a locum. But I need to see someone, or rather Billy does. I'm concerned about the state of Billy's bottom. I was very unhappy at what I saw when Billy was in the bath last night, and from everything else he has revealed I am pretty certain that something very bad has happened to him. When I lived in Portsmouth, I knew a beautician. This was in the days before children, so I had some extra time and cash to spend on luxuries. It seems laughable now, but my weekends back then usually included a beauty treatment. I had been seeing the beautician for about a year or so, and we had got to know each other quite well, perhaps as a result of the forced intimacy of the treatment room. She told me that her mum's brother had sexually abused her for years. He forced anal sex onto her. When she was in her mid-twenties she had to have surgery to repair the damage to her rectum. I have been thinking about her since last night after seeing what I saw during Billy's bath.

Appointment successfully made for tomorrow morning (now that there's no school to worry about), I catch up with my paperwork while Billy lies down in his nest of cushions. I make sure to sit in the same room with my laptop. I daren't let him out of my sight after today's shenanigans.

I'm suddenly overwhelmed by a series of big yawns. I know that I yawn when I'm stressed, or when I have stopped feeling stressed, as well as when I'm tired. It could be a combination of all three. I have definitely felt stressed, and this wee fella is certainly tiring. But there is the after-school decompression zone and an evening to negotiate before I can think about being reunited with my bed.

When the children troop in from their school day, they perform their usual locusts' manoeuvre, roving through the kitchen croplands and flattening everything in their wake in a devastating blitz (by which I mean opening and closing the fridge, bread bin, then the cupboard of doom). Even though they know what's likely to be in each location, I think they think that there is a secret shelf that will suddenly appear full of cakes, chocolate and sweets with a sign saying *Help yourself: fill yourself up before dinner! Why not?*

It's quite a ritual and a sight to behold, something weirdly primitive about the young teenager's sense of survival. Vincent always stuffs something else in his blazer pocket, thinking I haven't seen. I keep vases on the top shelf and every morning I put back what they pull out. Once they've acquired their stash they head upstairs, stepping over their own bags, coats and shoes on the way. No matter how many times I ask them to pick up their stuff, they ignore me. I suspect their bags are not as interesting as gaming. In benevolent moments I tell myself that it happens because they're actually quite relaxed and happy. When I lived with my adopted mother, she was so scary that I could never imagine myself being brave, brave enough to just be a child. Instead I was always on tenterhooks, awaiting the next violent explosion. That's one of the reasons I know that I can tune in to foster children and their needs: it's rare that they haven't experienced heightened fear and manipulation from adults. I knew it well, once.

It's not a secret that the other children still find Billy challenging. So, going off to their rooms is also their way of avoiding his sometimes very strange behaviour. But I know in my boots that this is not sustainable, and that the other children should not feel the need to shoot up to their rooms to avoid conflict with a five-year-old. After all, we are only a regular household who foster, without much scope, particularly in terms of resources, for us to do the intense work that some of these children, like Billy, need. I know myself well enough to know that I will always put the whole household's needs before the latest arrival. But I also know that my children – and Lily, who is part of this family – learn a great deal from each child, even if that's finding ways in life to be distracted from negative behaviour. Fostering is all about balance, and any household requires a healthy balance to thrive.

To begin to redress some of the balance, I decide that I will put their needs first this evening. I will see each one on their own in their rooms and gauge how they are while tidying up their clothes and chatting. They know me well enough to know that when I do this it's their opportunity to truthfully tell me how they feel. In these moments I listen. I really listen.

First, I return to the sitting room to wake Billy, who has somehow continued to sleep through all the kerfuffle. He looks cherubic once more.

But I know that Billy will not be transferring into permanency here.

I know that Billy will need more, much more, in the long term.

Chapter Ten

We sit in the waiting room, ready for Billy's appointment with the doctor. The large, brightly coloured mural of a toucan is a familiar sight to me, but it is always a joy to see new children notice it.

We don't have to wait long before Billy's date of birth flashes up on the screen. The world of GDPR has made it so that at this practice at least we are now summoned by our birth dates, not our names. Standing outside the doctor's door, I give Billy's hand a little squeeze for reassurance. I never know how he will behave, what will freak him out, and what I'm then going to say to the person whose room he has just wrecked. So perhaps it's a squeeze of reassurance for me, too.

I go in and wait to be asked to sit down. I move the chair that the doctor points at so that it is positioned next to Billy's. The doctor looks at her screen and I see the look on her face when she notices the 'child in care' label. This is a look I have seen many times. It's not a good or bad look, necessarily, just a shift in their approach, and it generally comes with extra kindness.

Dr Jones is a middle-aged woman, warm and friendly.

'Hello Billy, good to meet you.'

Billy is wriggling in his seat. I suspect that he won't last long in it, so I get going straight away. I have learnt to write all of my concerns down in bullet points on a piece of A4 and hand them over to the doctor, which I do. I hate discussing their intimate details in front of them. This way I have found to be more efficient and to offer the child a little more dignity.

Dr Jones does all the usual checks. Throughout the examination I continue to hold Billy's hand, mainly because he wants me to, but also because it means he can't so easily destroy something nearby. It does mean that we do a funny arm dance around Dr Jones as she moves to look in his eyes and ears.

By the time she sits back down Billy is laughing, and a bit of dribble in one corner of his mouth drops onto his lap. She doesn't seem to mind. Instead, she sits forward with both arms on her lap.

'Billy, does it hurt when you do a poo?'

He nods, and my heart sinks. I didn't know he had trouble going, and that makes me feel a little bit of a failure for not asking.

'Can you tell me what your poos are like?'

To help answer this question, she has a card with pictures on.

I'm less worried about this question. I have seen what he has produced in the bottom of the toilet pan. They look alright to me, and smell alright too. It's an instinct with people who look after others to sniff the air after a child has done a poo, and his are fine, I'm sure. Perhaps that's why I didn't think that he had any trouble going. Until that bath I wouldn't have known that anything was wrong there.

'Is there any residual in Billy's pants?'

This question is directed at me. We're at the stage with Billy where we're working hard to broaden his diet, but Nutella is still pretty ubiquitous.

'Yes, a little. But I thought it was from eating way too much Nutella.'

She smiles. It is a smile that tells me she has enough experience to know that food issues and children in the care system is a whole other subject. But there is genuine sadness in her eyes. I brace myself for more.

'Is it related to ... ?' I trail off and wave my hand in a circle.

She understands my body language. 'Perhaps. There is certainly a rectum injury. I think I may refer Billy to a colleague at the hospital.'

Then she turns to Billy. 'To see if we can't get those poos sorted out for you.'

Even though I had anticipated this outcome, it still hits hard. This is a vile world sometimes. How am I supposed to feel? How am I supposed to deal with this? Therapists I've met who work with sexually abused children are offered counselling themselves. My family and I cannot opt for support or a reduced workload to compensate for the emotional drain. Foster carers have to keep plodding on without help, and little recognition that they are human at all. Billy, though, is none the wiser, and as a treat I take him to the nearby newsagents, a familiar stop to all the children after a doctor's appointment. Though he must have undoubtedly felt nervous, Billy was exceptionally good today. I didn't think for a minute that he would sit still, let alone let the doctor touch him. That was a good hour he sat through, in the end.

Later at home I pull out the pots and pans to begin preparing for dinner.

'Make sure you keep away from this corner of the kitchen,' I warn. I explain that I'm busy moving about with the kettle, toaster and cooker. I'm toasting a load of paninis to fill them with turkey, ham, cheese and salad. I say 'salad', but Lily always has double cheese, and it's only if she's in a very good mood that I might be able to entice her into having some sliced tomato and lettuce to keep the cheese company.

Billy rushes into the back of my legs.

I send him back to the other side of the kitchen with a stern word.

He keeps doing it. I explain that I'm boiling water in a pan, 'because Vincent likes a side order of pasta twirls with a flick of parmesan. I can do some for you, too, if you like?'

Billy quite likes plain pasta too. I show him the pasta bag. Lidl had a good selection of Christmas food back in December. I bought the children something foody each for their stocking. Vincent's was a large bag of coloured pasta Christmas trees. He loves them. I also think he needs the extra carbs. He's having another growth spurt. After eating a huge meal, I know he'll be back down in fifteen minutes to start again.

But Billy isn't interested in the pasta. I can sense that he's becoming increasingly restless. There's a strange energy about him. I don't want him to become unruly while I've got so many different appliances on the go. I decide that, for a few minutes whilst I sort the food out, he can go into the sitting room. It's much warmer in there than it is in the conservatory.

I entice him into the sitting room with the promise of children's TV. They are only short programmes, so it will not be too hard to pull him away for his dinner when the time comes.

Just as I am close to finishing the food preparation, Jackson walks into the kitchen with Lloyd. I look up to see that Lloyd is smiling.

'Billy is humping the cushion.'

I am not smiling, and neither is Jackson, who has obviously just seen this and appears shocked. I realise that Lloyd's smiles are about trying to make light of whatever is going on in there.

I down tools and head to the sitting room. Lloyd and Jackson follow behind me.

Bloody hell!

To my horror, he isn't lying comfortably on the cushion where I left him.

No. Instead, he is semi-naked on the sofa, top on, but pants and trousers off, one hand on his 'area'. The other hand is in his mouth. He is sucking his fingers in an overtly sexualised way that makes me feel ill.

I shoo Lloyd and Jackson out of the room. Thinking quickly, Lloyd mutters something about showing Jackson a picture of his cousin in France who has helped to clear some woodland with his dad.

Now what do I do?

I sit down on the armchair next to the sofa. I look at the log burner rather than at Billy's performance.

'It's dinner time.'

He stops what he is doing, sits up and laughs, dribble all around his face. He wipes it and licks his fingers. I'm certain that he's about to make a sexualised sound.

Before he has a chance to do that, I jump up and clap my hands in my best, upbeat Mary Poppins way.

'Off we go then. You wash your hands while I call in the others.'

Chapter Eleven

Another week passes. Billy has been with us for over a month.

The children are having their dinner. This evening I have cooked them an earlier dinner than usual to keep up with the combined demands of Vincent's growth spurt, Billy's increasing appetite and Jackson's volleyball club. I plan to make a paella later for myself and Lloyd. I have some lovely bread that I can heat up, slather with butter and dip into the steaming paella rice. Just lovely.

I am in the conservatory packing away Billy's toys when chaos breaks out. Suddenly, Billy decides to be a dog. He leaps down from the table and, on all fours, scrambles around the floor under the table, attacking the children's legs. I fly back into the kitchen to see all the children looking horrified, surrounding Lily, who is crying.

'He's bitten my ankle and made it bleed!'

'Billy!' I shout before I can help myself. I am so shocked.

By now, Billy is shunting himself along the floor, barking and growling. At my word, he stops, changes direction, and comes straight at me. The children now take up a chorus of screaming which brings Lloyd running.

He hurtles through the kitchen door. 'What the hell ...?'

I take my ankle back from Billy's mouth, but not without some effort. He lets go, then goes straight for Lloyd, sinking his teeth into the back of Lloyd's calf.

'Jesus,' cries Lloyd, Billy still hanging onto his leg with his teeth as Lloyd tries to walk away.

The situation has gone from dramatic to insane in the space of a few seconds.

Jackson moves towards Billy. 'Billy, let go! Let go of my Dad!'

Lloyd is doing all he can to drag his leg away, but Billy's teeth remain firmly clamped to his leg.

'Lloyd, stand still!' I call.

I approach Billy slowly and manage to coax him away from Lloyd's leg.

'It's alright, Billy. It's alright.'

Then I pick him up and hold him as tight as I can, using my right hand behind his head to steady him. I leave the room and walk him into the sitting room. I sit down with him on my lap and hold him close, doing my best to rock and soothe him. Before long he turns into a baby, snuffling and staring into the space behind me.

I can hear the kitchen gradually settling down. Vincent is saying, in rapid 'Geezer', something which sounds remarkably like, 'Bejesus cohesive.' I don't think that's exactly what he means to say, but we all get the gist. The experience is rapidly turning into the post-event reportage of exciting conversation. A minute or two more and I hear laughter. This one's going to go down in Allen family folklore.

When Lloyd comes in to check on us, I'm just swaying on the sofa with a very confused, hurt little boy. Lloyd disappears and returns with a cup of tea, which he gently places on the side table. I can hear the sound of the freezer and associated excitement as they take full advantage of my compromised situation to tuck into the new raspberry ripple ice cream that I was saving for the weekend.

Ah well. Under the circumstances.

Next I hear the sizzle of onions and garlic.

Oh good! That means Lloyd is cooking the paella, and his is far better than mine.

Chapter Twelve

I am exhausted.

Today, the flood water has been as bad as it has been in the ten years we've lived here. I become tense as soon as I see the telltale brown water merging with the surface water on the road. It only takes one inch of filthy disgusting water to wreck homes and cause damage for months. Not to mention the expense of it all, especially as we can't claim anything on the insurance. Since the dog incident a few days ago, the house has been relatively calm on the Billy front. But today there was flood drama. The rain began pelting down non-stop this morning. The ditches and the gullies became blocked, meaning that the run-off from the fields was at tipping point. By lunchtime we knew that any more and the water would be rushing into our home. It's become much worse since the new development. More cookie-cutter houses in the fields. They're meant to be affordable starter homes, but I don't know many young people from around here who could afford the mortgage.

It's been a tough day of battle while Lloyd and I have been doing whatever we can to defend our home against the flood. It feels as though we are living in a dystopia. Everyone has a job to do when the flood-threat is imminent. The main work is the preparation. Lloyd fixes the flood gates. I generally run around with old beach towels to mop up any residual water seeping through the enormous sandbag and plastic sheet construction I made the other day when we looked at the Met Office forecast. For most of the afternoon, Lloyd and I play tag outside. At some moments we are both out there along with our neighbours, trying to slow down cars who just don't seem to realise that they make the water worse, or chasing more debris from collecting in the grid of the already-blocked drains.

Through it all, Billy has been an excellent helper. Bizarrely, he seems to have enjoyed the mopping up job. I think he rather likes being part of the team effort to fend off the rain. But there is nothing more to do now other than wait and see. We have done all the preparation we can.

The children like to watch the progress of the flood water from our bedroom window, where they sit atop the old Swedish wedding chest. Jackson, Vincent and Lily discuss every little detail, including the excitement of an orange Sainsbury's carrier bag floating along outside.

Billy, trying more and more to belong, pops in to join them.

And then he does something gorgeous. A little thing, but one that gives me hope. He goes into his room and takes ugly teddy Sharon off the windowsill. He brings her to the window and sets her down on the chest.

'Sharon make it better,' he tells them, firmly.

Bless him.

They stay there as the light gradually darkens. This adds to their excitement, but for me sunset is when flooding becomes even worse. The darkness and the water merge together in dark threat.

'Great job, today,' I say. 'Now time to think about bed.'

I think it's going to stay calm now. The rain looks to have moved off in an easterly direction. There will be at least a few hours of respite. Even so, I can't stop thinking about it. The rain, the rain.

Heavy and consistent, it just pours off the fields and into our lives. Yet we have no sea, no river, no lake nearby. I feel sad and defeated. I try to pull myself back from the brink, reminding myself that feeling sorry for myself will achieve nothing at all.

Lloyd is lying by the fire, his head on a cushion, sound asleep. I take one of the scatter rugs and lay it across him. His lower back is exposed, and it makes me feel cold. The TV is on, the animals are all relaxed. The bedtime bathroom scramble is over. Peace has descended.

I leave Lloyd sleeping to run a bath. While I wait for it to fill, I head downstairs and pour myself a glass of red wine. The bottle's been sitting on the side since Christmas, but today's flooding activities require a glass in the aftermath.

I take a sip and wander back towards the bathroom.

What a day, but all the tension is slowly releasing. We could all really do without the drama, especially when our flooding is caused not so much by a so-called act of God, but the inertia and greed of man.

The bath is almost ready. Before I go off duty for half an hour, I do a final check on all the children. They are all fine. Lily is painting a picture in her room even though it's way past her bedtime. I smile and pull the door to. She likes to do something creative, and she seems to like it particularly after any sort of drama or event. I can understand that. Jackson and Vincent are gaming with each other from their individual rooms, a setup I will never entirely understand. Billy is fast asleep. He must be exhausted from all the exertion. He is lying flat on his back, head back, snoring. I gently touch his arm and he turns over. I pull up his duvet and tuck his extra blanket in at the sides to keep all the heat in. It's cold outside and the air is damp from the rain.

I take a final check on our flood defences before locking up the house. Lloyd's still asleep. I call him to wake up. He can take another hour to move when he's this warm and tired. I put the dogs in their cage, close the log burner door and turn most of the lights out. I shall have my bath and leave him to it. I've known Lloyd for over 35 years and I don't need to fuss around a fully formed adult.

The bath is a thing of gorgeousness. That's another good thing about the months after Christmas: lots of luxurious smellies. What can't be worn or poured in the bath goes into the airing cupboard and drawers to make everything smell lovely.

I hear my phone ping and ping and ping. It will be the flooding, and I don't want to know anything more about it. Whatever it is can wait.

I sink beneath the bubbles and try to release all the cares of the day. I'm so tired anyway, even without the flood. I've been preoccupied with Billy, and with managing the guilt of wondering how much Billy's behaviour is harming the other children. But today he did us proud. Instead of his old behaviour, Billy was fine. I'd go as far as to say he was sweet and caring. So cute with the ugly teddy. So quick to do whatever he was told with towels and sandbags. Another moment from the day pops into my head. I was talking to an elderly neighbour whose front door was leaking. She was obviously very scared. He sat on my lap while I was trying to reassure her, popped his thumb in his mouth, and with the other hand stroked her hand.

'What kindness!' she said, with a little tear in her eye.

I realise that today at least, I'm proud of him. He was a good boy, and the flood has brought out a completely different side to him. Now that I've seen him do that, behave like that, I want to understand why. Why today? What was it about the flooding that channelled such different behaviour? It cannot be the flood that made him feel safe, but maybe being part of something bigger, working hard to keep everyone else safe, has helped. I don't know. Perhaps the wine is making me fanciful. It was such a physical enterprise today, to fend off the bogeyman of the flood. Perhaps witnessing that communal effort has restored some faith in adults.

Who knows? Let's hope so.

Chapter Thirteen

Refreshingly, my first thought as I wake up isn't 'Billy'.

Instead, it is 'flood'.

I test the atmosphere by listening. If it's been bad, you can hear people outside sweeping and talking. But all seems quiet on the western front.

Lloyd is still asleep, which doesn't surprise me. He slept through all the boys' night-crying when they were babies.

I head downstairs tentatively, not knowing quite what I will find. This is flood number 16 since we have lived here. The government used to measure one flood in 100 years as an act of God. 16 floods in 10 years is not, then, an act of God. But the powers that be can't just pin it all on climate change and absolve themselves of all responsibility.

I reach the bottom stair and I am relieved. It's not as bad as I thought. The old towels and dust sheets have soaked up any leakage from our *Dad's Army* style flood-defence.

I'd forgotten about the pings last night, but they are still there waiting for me when I pick up my phone. And it isn't the flood group, as I'd thought.

There are more than 100 messages in the Blackthorn group. A hundred! This is going to take some catching up with. Martin is another foster carer. I don't know him particularly well because he lives right on the other side of the county, but we met at a training event a good while ago, so I've known of him and his wife, Julie, for some time. They are retired and still foster, which I admire greatly. I think they're amazing but perhaps also a bit mad, when they could be having a much easier life without the fostering. Martin was very supportive after the Billy-dog-biting incident. Like most of us who hang on through gritted teeth, though, we do it for the children. He's left several messages in the WhatsApp group.

I'm now stuck in a Travelodge.

Eh? I scroll back to find out what's gone on to lead to that little scenario. He reports that he is staying away from his own home, after being told by the child's social worker that an allegation has been made against him that he French-kissed his Blackthorn foster child.

What?

His two long-term foster children are now considered to be at risk, and his wife is on prescription antidepressants. I scroll upwards further to get the whole story. It's a nightmare.

It was the girl who tried to kiss him. He was alone in the kitchen with her for a matter of minutes, chatting about the rugby. I remember now that Martin is a big sports fan. As he turned around to get past her she reached up, stuck her tongue in his mouth and put her hand on his testicles.

Jesus. Their Blackthorn is 14 years old. Apparently, she is at a holding centre. Not the language the authority would use, but that's what we call this particular 'children's home' colloquially. The allegation the girl has made against him is horrendous and, as far as I can see, incredibly believable from the point of view of the authorities. But I don't believe it. And not just because of my admiration for Martin and Julie. I have seen enough of Billy's behaviour to know that these children have been sexually exploited. Not just once or twice, but systematically.

Poor Martin. Allegations like this can destroy your life. It's only recently that foster carers were finally permitted to join a union. We all belong to the NUPFC (National Union of Professional Foster Carers). Somebody else has already asked the question in the group. Fortunately, Martin and Julie joined a year ago, so will be fully supported. Their union rep has already negotiated that children's social care foot the bill for Martin's hotel. I'm struggling slightly to understand why a social work manager is digging her heels in so much. From the comments, she sounds horrid and vindictive.

The pressure each of us has been put under is crazy, and doing something like this is only going to bring our fragile morale down even further. Bloody idiots. They must know this is likely to be a mischievous allegation. There is no workforce that has as few rights as foster carers. Sometimes it feels as if we're lambs to the slaughter. I'd love to meet this stupid manager and give her a piece of my mind. I put words to that effect in the chat.

Sometimes I think they are sociopaths who end up in this sector because they want to hurt people.

In spite of my elation at the flood defences holding up, I now feel deflated. I know what Martin will be feeling. We've been through allegations in the past, and there is nothing good about them. One was a bitchy fabrication from a social worker who was terrified of her locum manager. After nearly destroying ours and a few other foster families' lives, she left our authority and got herself a top job somewhere in Wales, earning over £150,000. I will never understand how things got so bad in children's social care. It's a cesspit of sick opportunity.

I send Martin a private message of hope, and switch to reading the rest of the flood messages. One of the local residents has a drone. He flew it up the hill as the flood started and is convinced that he's pinned the source down to four fields at the top of the hill. Wouldn't it be maddening if all the farmer had to do was plough the soil the other way, so the run off didn't face us? I feel like I've already had enough for one day and I haven't even got through breakfast.

I turn around and I see Billy. He's looking up at me with his little dribble and laughing. He tugs my arm and drags me along the hall and into the kitchen. He opens the tall cupboard and reaches up to pull down the Nutella. Oh, my what have I done? I have created an addiction. But how can I refuse this gorgeous sweet little boy? They aren't adjectives I could have used to describe him before, but after yesterday I feel that he absolutely is those things. When children as young as Billy have suffered abuse and neglect, the way out of that maze is arduous and the trauma may take years to release its grip. We also don't quite know exactly what has gone on with Billy. I feel that perhaps we are only scratching the surface. I know he can dart from one emotion to another in an instant, like a little bird pecking at the ground, its attention suddenly taken in a different direction. The maze of trauma goes here and it goes there, but at the moment we are not stuck at a dead end. I feel as if we have made some real headway.

And sexual abuse is different from other kinds. I know that. It's not just the effects on the child, but on the teen and then on the adult, and on everyone that child, then teen, then adult comes into contact with. It goes deep. Because how the hell do we talk about it? I'm quite comfortable talking about my abuse these days, but I struggle with the faces and body language of those listening, and sometimes I'm conscious of their self-referencing. The 'how will this impact on me?' attitude can sometimes feel more degrading than anything that has ever happened to me.

But I'm sure now that this little boy has a good heart and a good soul. I also know that if we had no other children, we might really be in a position to help this young man. But we *do* have three other children, and their needs matter too. I am not a 'rescuer'. I think I was, once. I remember when I was a teenager, my friends would phone me to help them when they were in a pickle. I told myself at the time that it was because they recognised how mature and capable I was. I soon realised that their scrapes weren't worth the 'p' in pickle, and they didn't actually need my help. In fact, they were drama queens, making a meal of everything. It wasn't an honest exchange. So I curbed my need to rescue them. I like the idea that if you want help, you also have to be able to receive that help with honesty, not because some of your basic emotional needs haven't been met. Honesty means the person in the parent role saying 'no' occasionally. But Billy needs far, far more than that. I suspect that he and the other Blackthorn children (given the collective reports of their behaviour) are going to need good therapy for years. And that costs money. Lots of money.

I let Billy carry the glass jar of Nutella over to the other side of the kitchen, near the toaster.

'Which bread would you like to go with it?'

I have two sorts on display: rubbery white sliced, and gorgeous crafted bread from Tesco's topped with crisp sunflower seeds. I salivate just thinking about the latter, but of course it's not so tempting to a five-year-old. Billy bends his knee, then springs back up, pointing his finger at the white sliced.

I put two slices in the toaster, pulling it a bit closer so Billy can see his distorted face in the reflection of the stainless-steel sides. I crouch down beside him and try to make the same silly faces as he does. He puts his hand onto the top of my head and plays with my hair.

I stay down there awhile so he can enjoy making faces, but I have to slowly stand up after a minute or two because my knees are hurting. I make a mental note to fit in some Louise-Allen-style yoga to get me back on track as soon as possible. It's a bit of bending and stretching, then a dance to a blast of Tori Amos' *Professional Widow*. That'll do for me.

The toast pops up and Billy claps with joy. How utterly delightful to see. He keeps checking my face. He still needs to know that I can indeed be trusted, that I am safe to be around.

While Billy munches into his toast, he communicates such enjoyment of the experience that I fancy a piece myself. I cut a slice of the sunflower seeded bread and toast it until it's crispy on the outside. I sit down opposite Billy and enjoy smoothing the salted butter onto it. Then I reach for a jar of peanut butter. It's no ordinary jar of peanut butter, either. It's only just still in date, but brings back a memory. I actually got it last year from a lunch out with Lloyd. He took me to a lovely little country restaurant. I say 'restaurant', but it was made up of a bus and an old cattle shed next door. These eclectic spaces also housed an organic ice cream parlour and food store. I was so shocked at the price of a carrot I sent myself into a spin. There was a Canadian woman there promoting her homemade peanut butter. She told me her entire life story and how, trying to feed her 24 children (I know, I raised my eyebrows there, too) on a budget, she had begun to make peanut butter in her kitchen. Before she moved to England

212

she had worked in marketing, hence her enthusiasm. I was given a piece of cracker smeared with a disgusting brown and pink goop. Somehow I walked out without the carrot or any vegetables, and came home with the most expensive and disgusting peanut butter I had ever experienced. I decide that today I should actually open it and try it.

I manage to get the lid off and sniff inside. I spread the toast with the goop. After reading the label I realise that the pinkish bits are strawberry jam, also made in the Canadian woman's kitchen. I have to say that it isn't as bad as I remembered. Perhaps my taste buds had been affected that day by the high prices in the farm shop.

I look up to catch Billy's little face smiling.

'Right then, Billy. What do you think you might like to do today?' I ask him.

I look out of the window at the weather. It's only misty rain, nothing like yesterday's deluge. It'll ruin my hair but not much else.

'Sheep!' he says, screwing up his eyes.

He must have been listening when we were out driving the other day. I find myself continually pointing things out. 'Look at the DAF lorry,' or 'Can you see the tractor?' The other day before the storms, I spotted 'sheep'. Or maybe he even remembers our visit to Flatfields Primary School. I still can't think of that place without sniggering at the idea that they considered themselves to be 'trauma aware'.

Well, I can't really deny a five-year-old 'sheep'. Especially not given where we live. I have a quick think. Not far from here is another large country estate. Like the one by Flatfields, it features in costume dramas and has been on the *Antiques Roadshow*. I know that it has a petting farm. I will take Billy. The more I think about it, the more it seems like a good idea, until I'm more excited than he is. I feel a Tupperware lunch coming on.

I stick two eggs on to boil. Because it's the weekend and the others are home, I go upstairs to see if any of them want to come. I receive a definitive 'no' from my peri-teenagers. Oh, I love my children. Lloyd is sitting up in bed looking like he is ready for a first cup of coffee of the day. I head back downstairs and rummage in the coat stand for a scarf for Billy. I bought him his own but, as is the way, he prefers the old one that Vincent used to wear. It's a fox head with scarf bits attached. He looks adorable in it, with curls poking out all over it. I quickly put together the lunch (which I know will actually be eaten at coffee time).

I load up the car and strap Billy into his seat. We head off to the next town, where we stop at traffic lights for a moment, giving me an opportunity to gaze wistfully into the gift shop window. It's a gorgeous shop, run by two women who were openly gay back in the early '90s, marrying as soon as same-sex civil partnerships became legal. Apparently, this caused a bit of a ruckus around these parts back then. They have great taste, and so many beautiful cards. I used to make all my cards by hand, but those days have long gone. They coincided with the arrival of children, as I recall. The shop always smells lovely, with the waft of scented candles and room scent. The atmosphere is enhanced by the rustle of tissue paper and crackle of paper bags. They always have nice music playing too: k.d. lang or Bob Dylan, or something along those lines. It's lovely: a small bit of frivolous nonsense in a world that feels increasingly drab and challenging. But while I'd love to stop and look around, even with Billy being 'good' I don't fancy my chances of escaping without a breakage, so I put the car into gear when the lights change and drive on.

We drive out of the town and along a winding B-road. For a moment the road passes alongside a river, where I slow down.

'Look, Billy, can you see the ducks and geese?'

He loves it!

We continue along, chatting away, and after the ducks I make the Daffy Duck sound that I used to make as a child. He seems to find it hilarious, and we have a lovely old time. Even though I delight in his laughter, a shadow lurks behind. I struggle to see the child, knowing that he has experienced exploitation from adults for sex.

I once worked as an artist in residence in a men's lifer prison. I got to know some of the inmates quite well. I had recently had Jackson; he was perhaps about six months old. At the time there was a news story about a man arrested for raping a two-month-old baby. It stuck with me because I thought of my own child. I remember a prisoner, Mark, a fearsome-looking Hell's Angel, complete with full beard and tattoos. We got on well together because I smuggled in a tape of the folk and blues singer Lead Belly for him. At one session I noticed that he was quiet, so I asked him what was wrong. It was the story of the rape of the baby that was eating him up.

'I just don't know what's wrong with people,' he said.

Mark was himself serving a life sentence for murder, so perhaps his judgment of someone else seems weird. But one thing I learnt there was that not all crimes are equal, no matter the sentence that is handed down. Paedophiles are not liked within the prison walls. I chatted at length to Mark, the murderer, understanding that his moral compass and personal morality would never have allowed him to abuse a child. I remember that conversation well, and it is one of the reasons why I live by the adage that people are not always as they seem or who we think they are.

I drive past the tall walls that mark the boundary of the country estate and along the recently tarmacked road, though I notice that the surface is permeable; they must be worried about the flooding here too. We park the car and my little friend looks out of the window.

'We're here!'

He is kicking his feet with excitement. There is only one other car in the car park. Not so surprising at this time of the year. In the spring and summer it's packed: cars end up in the fields as overflow from the main car park, but not today. We get out and Billy dashes straight towards me to hold my hand. It's another very little thing, but it makes me happy. So happy that I find myself wiping away a little tear.

He doesn't notice, since he's too busy skipping and jumping. This child loves going out. I keep hold of his hand. I definitely think it's the hand-holding that keeps him feeling safe, emotionally as well as physically. We head towards the gift shop, where visitors pay to get in. Not us, though: we are members of the National Trust, and when you have children that is a great investment. We show my card, and I am pulled by the hand to look at the beautiful jars of chutney and jams. It's a bit more expensive in here than it would be in a supermarket, but I know that Lloyd and Jackson can't resist the garlic pickle.

'Maybe on the way out,' I say. I realise that Billy is showing me things because he has worked out that I might like them. He can have no interest in the chutneys for himself, but he knows that I might and he's trying to please me, to do something lovely for me.

What a kind-hearted little fella he is.

We head towards the first garden, and eventually to the sheep. After watching *Countryfile* one Sunday, I learnt the breed names of the sheep here. North Ronaldsay are from the Orkney Isles and are fed seaweed because that's their natural food from living near the sea. My favourites are the Hebridean – small black sheep with pointed horns and impenetrable expressions. I love them. The ones I think Billy will enjoy meeting are the Castlemilk Moorit, dainty little sheep with enormous curly horns and soft fleeces. I can't wait to show him, but right now he is running round and round the paths of the Victorian kitchen garden.

My phone rings. It's Dara, at last!

'Hello Mrs, how are you?'

'I am okay,' she says, with her gorgeous inflection, 'but I wanted to catch up soon because I'm leaving next Friday. On Thursday my colleagues are taking me out to dinner, which is making me understand that it is all really happening. I feel very conflicted about it all. This system is broken, you know as well as I do, but I love the children and I love most of my foster carers.'

I know I'm one of the loved ones. I smile like a child who knows they're the teacher's pet.

'But enough about that, Louise. How are you? How is Lloyd? What about Jackson, Vincent and Lily?'

I tell her we're all fine.

'And Billy? How is Billy?'

I walk round in circles, loosely following Billy, who is zooming round all the paths, having a great time. I tell her what's been happening.

'You must be careful, Louise. The family is a criminal family, and they want their children back.'

'But they can't get them back, can they?' I say, in desperation.

Surely someone is investigating the sexual abuse that has been reported across multiple siblings now.

'These children have certainly been exploited,' Dara says. 'One of my other foster carers has a boy who is a year older than Billy. He has revealed that he has been made to watch pornography at regular intervals. We think from when he was three years old. They have been taught how to touch themselves and others, how to French kiss, how to be alluring and seductive. It is a world of wrongness.'

I can feel the bile building at the back of my throat as Dara speaks. Suddenly our conversation ends. Her voice disappears. I know that she is driving with her phone on speaker; she must be in the famous social work tunnel where they, annoyingly, lose their signal in mid-conversation. I am a bit shaky after having it spelled out like that. No matter how often I hear about these children's lives, I will never get used to it.

It certainly is a world of wrongness.

Chapter Fourteen

The children are back from school.

Billy is not benefitting from any of my 'home learning' efforts. I show him flashcards to help with his alphabet, but he wants to play with them and throw them across the room. I get the boys' old farm animals out of the loft. I suggest we make a farmyard, and name all the animals, making their animal sounds. Billy is not of the same opinion, and sits chewing their heads and laughing. I try drawing and painting. This is an absolute disaster: he stubs all the felt tip ends and rips up the paper.

I have better success with shaving foam play for a little while, until he begins smearing the white foam over his face. It is all good fun until he says, 'I've got cum on my face.'

By this point I feel too uncomfortable and too demoralised to continue. I'm struggling, and I need the support of Dara more than ever; but she, along with all the other social workers, is firefighting in the Blackthorn climate – and anyway, by the end of the week she will be gone.

God, I feel way out of my depth. I need to have a conversation with someone in authority about Billy's schooling. I'm not what he needs at all. School is what he needs. I don't have anything like the skill to deliver an education to someone with his behavioural demands. With the ever-louder messages from the government that cutbacks are hitting hard and fast, I know that home-schooling is the cheapest option for Billy. But it's not sustainable for me: I'm effectively providing all-day every-day childminding services for a child who legally should be in school. Foster carers are being used more and more to soak up the bigger mess. I know full well how much it would cost to educate a child like Billy in the private sector. But foster carers are expected to factor in schooling with all their other responsibilities for less than 30p per hour. I know that Dara said that the system is broken. To me, it feels more than broken: it feels mad.

Right now, Vincent is trying to teach Billy how to catch the soft indoor ball. It's hilarious. They're out in the conservatory. I hear laughter – which is nice – but every so often I feel Billy's energy change. I dash in with my tea towel.

'Chill, babes,' I call out, in my best *EastEnders* accent. Vincent knows me very well and is used to my attempts at spontaneous comedy, but my efforts still provoke a 'Mu-um!'

Vincent, I think, *you are a star for taking time out to play with Billy, but how dare you judge me when you mostly talk in improvised Geezer or Rasta.*

Billy is jumping up and down in excitement. Somebody at least appreciates my efforts. He makes lovely little sounds of joy, and the game resumes.

I'm busy making a tuna pasta bake for dinner, with cheesy flatbread tears. Proper winter children's food. I hope Billy likes it. He's doing okay with trying out some new food. I can't get him to touch a vegetable, or at least nothing beyond the humble baked bean, but he is exploring the potato family. He likes chips, crisps, wedges, waffles and hash browns. He loves ice cream and will sit like a statue to ensure he is striking a 'good boy' pose. He's learned that this is the requirement for sugary treats.

Right, I'm ready. I place the huge baking dish onto the table with as much of a flourish as its weight will allow, steam bellowing. I go to the bottom of the stairs and call out their names one by one, including Lloyd. His comment last night was 'not pasta *again*', so he has been given pasta. That'll teach him to be snotty.

It's the usual chatter and the noise of chairs being pulled out, making scrapes along the kitchen flagstones that make my teeth ache.

All sitting, everything ready to go. Or at least, very nearly. I forgot the water glasses, so I do my usual trick with Lily who is sitting nearest to the glass cupboard.

'Lily, while you're up …'

'But I'm not up!' she complains, in an Emo-whine, before realising that she is defeated. It works every time and it makes us all laugh.

There are cushions on Billy's chair to help him reach the table nicely. Today he takes one off and chucks it on the floor. I walk round to his chair and bend down to pick up the cushion from the flagstones.

He reaches out and thumps me on the head.

'Ow!' I can't help the exclamation from escaping. That hurt, and I've no idea what made him do it. 'Billy, that's unkind. No thank you.'

He is grinning and dribbling at the same time.

I catch Vincent looking at him, not Vincent's happiest face. I think he probably feels protective over his mum.

I move out of the way. Suddenly Billy is up on the table. He is on all fours, like he was when he was being a dog and biting our legs. This is madness. He pushes the bowl of steaming pasta onto the floor. It goes everywhere. It is chaotic in seconds, just like before.

Lily begins to cry and moves over to Lloyd for comfort. She has witnessed, and experienced first-hand, a great deal of violence in her early life. For her, I know that scenes like this may trigger emotions in ways that we can't begin to imagine.

Billy has got himself into a standing position on top of the table and tries to kick Vincent and Jackson in the face.

'Leave the kitchen, boys,' I say, but they don't.

Something primal deep inside them wants to stay and protect their parents and Lily.

From the corner of my eye I see my two little pooches quietly tucking into the tuna pasta on the floor. Ruthless.

'In that case, grab the rest of the crockery,' I shout, anticipating Billy's next move. Vincent and Jackson do move then, to try to reach everything off the table, but it's too late. Billy kicks over the drinking glasses and smashes three plates.

Lily is beside herself.

'Billy, come down from the table. You will hurt yourself,' Lloyd commands lamely.

Billy ignores him and instead starts jumping up and down on the table. He bounces effortlessly, as if the hard pine is a trampoline. I'm surprised he doesn't hit his head on the ceiling.

I make eye signals to Lloyd to take Lily out and keep her calm. I look at my sons, ready to take action and intervene. They're not having any more of it. Jackson is standing on one side, Vincent at the end of the table. I don't bother trying to talk Billy down. He's in la-la land and won't hear me.

I look at the boys and mouth, 'I'm going to grab him.'

They both nod.

'Billy!' I say, firmly and loudly. Then I launch myself towards him, wrapping my arms round as much of him as I can. His legs are still kicking, but Jackson gently holds his feet. To our surprise Billy is calm, but the calm is momentary. As soon as his feet land safely on the ground he is on the run, darting around the kitchen, pulling everything apart. Jackson fills the space by the door as best he can. Billy runs towards him. Jackson holds out his elbows like chicken wings to try and make himself bigger. Billy swerves, evidently thinking better of taking Jackson on.

I have had enough now. My kitchen resembles a disaster zone, with smashed crockery and appliances hurled to the ground. Billy makes another loop round the table. As soon as he is within reach I pull him towards me, wrapping both my arms across his front to make a human straightjacket.

'Ssshh', I say, a hundred and ten times, until he finally calms and becomes limp.

Vincent and Jackson right chairs and pick up broken crockery from the floor. The tuna pasta is long gone, courtesy of Dotty and Doug. They exit the kitchen, leaving me standing with Billy. I remain in that spot for a good 20 minutes more.

I can hear scenes from *Friday Night Dinner* coming from the sitting room, so I guess that Lily must be feeling better.

Lloyd returns to the kitchen. He's not angry, just sad. 'I don't think we can do this, Louise. It's not fair.'

With a slow resigned nod, I agree.

Chapter Fifteen

The morning after the dinner table massacre, the children seem fine. Even Billy seems to be suffering no discernible after-effects. He's in his room playing. I can hear him telling his ugly fluffy teddy about his dinosaur. Nobody who hadn't witnessed last night's behaviour would believe him capable of it. Until you have seen a small child in full-on destructive mode, it's impossible to explain the amount of damage that they can do.

I know I'm tired. It's in my eyes and the aches all over my body. My back aches most of all. I want to have a rest. It's exhausting being poised for Billy's outbursts, that strange rise in energy that builds just before he explodes. It's been happening on and off for weeks. If it was a grown man behaving this way, we'd call it 'domestic abuse'. It's fiendishly hard work, and I'm conscious of my growing concern for Lily in particular, but the boys too. Billy is potentially dangerous, and Lily is still a vulnerable child in the care system. Right now that 'system' for her means our home, and it isn't safe. The exhaustion fuels the helplessness I feel. So far, I have hardly any faith in the support that is meant to be around us. We should have a social worker at the other end of the phone, but we don't. And I don't blame them. It's not their fault. I know that Emma and her colleagues are being pulled in every direction themselves. How did children's social care turn into an under-resourced version of a hospital A&E unit?

It being Friday, I can console myself that at least to-morrow I won't be woken up by my alarm. It's scant relief, though. Like most people I know, my body clock is tuned in to wake up, so I suspect I'll be up and about regardless. I am like the current weather forecast, on amber warning for days. I know that the weather isn't helping, but I feel unsettled, all at sixes and eights. I hate feeling like this. My brain is all over the place. I know this is when I'll miss something or make a mistake. I need to be vigilant with Billy. I don't know when he will make another display like last night's. It's utterly enervating.

I get the bigger children off to school with less drama than usual. The one comfort I have from last night's event is that they will be dining out on it today in the playground and the classrooms. It's ironic that foster carers are repeatedly told about GDPR and confidentiality, but how do you apply that to foster siblings? Especially after last night's hoo-ha. How could they not talk about it? I often wonder how many homes will be discussing a version of Billy's behaviour at dinner tonight once word has got around. Lots of people look at me and say, 'I don't know how you do it.'

Nor do I, after scenes like last night.

I'm still worried about broken glass and crockery. It's those little splinters that concern me. The children tend to run in and out of the kitchen with bare feet, and the animals can easily get hurt too. I move everything and get the broom and vacuum cleaner back out. I start running the tap, because it takes a while for the water to go hot.

Ping ping ping. Here we go: today's Blackthorn stories (the Eleven Amigos are rapidly depleting, but people stay in the group to keep up with the news). There are also lots of 'check the weather' messages from the flood group.

Aaah, here's a new one, someone called Fitzroy Bright. Is that a German name? I wonder. There is a message.

Hi Louise, I will be your new supervising social worker, taking over from Dara. Normally Dara would bring me out to meet you, but that won't be possible as she's too busy. Can you let me know when is a good time?

Well, I think now would be quite good! I turn off the tap and text back, *Today?*

Fitzroy says he will be with me in an hour. Some good news, finally. I like this social worker already. Perhaps Dara's departure won't spell doom and gloom after all.

I let Lloyd know, and we busy ourselves in preparation for his arrival. I grab all Billy's paperwork and finish tidying the kitchen. I check the downstairs loo for any morning rush-wee sprinkles, and feel a bit more confident, a bit more in control.

I check on Billy. 'We're going to have a visitor this morning. Our new social worker is popping in for a coffee soon.'

He looks up and smiles, and there it is: the familiar drool hanging out of his mouth – a probable combo of bad teeth and too much time alone spent blowing bubbles. He is sitting on the floor with his teddies and dinosaurs, playing a game. Unlike many other children I have looked after, Billy is now happy to play, happy to play by himself, happy to lose himself in imaginative play. Some children, sadly, haven't a clue what that means. The downside is that he struggles with sharing, and the other social niceties around playing, but I do marvel at his ability to amuse himself. He loves chatting away to Ugly Ted.

The door goes right on time, and I'm happy to see Fitzroy and his broad, warm smile. He is very tall, and I detect the trace of a Caribbean accent as he says, 'Good morning,

Louise', and reaches out with his hand to shake mine. Not German in the slightest. I'm frequently wrong about names. Straight away he has a presence, and he's a clear departure from my previous supervising social workers. Dara who?

Lloyd comes out of his office, where I know he will have been speed-emailing his clients to make an hour for this. I show Fitzroy into the kitchen. He stops in the little square hallway by the kitchen and is the first person ever to comment on the art on display there. It's my little square of 'social commentary'.

Lloyd is not nearly as outspoken as me, or as naturally rebellious. When I initially said I wanted to hang some posters and paintings of a political nature in that spot he said, 'What will social workers think?'

My reaction was, and still is, 'I don't care what they think.'

But Fitzroy somehow makes me think that I do care. I want his approval. Fitzroy looks at the copy of Charlie Hebdo with the famous cartoon of the man wearing a head scarf that made his face look like a penis. He's holding a sign with *Je suis Charlie* written on it. That cartoon cost the lives of the cartoon creators, who were shot dead in their Paris office in 2015. 12 people were killed and 11 injured by two brothers representing Al-Qaeda.

'Paris, 2015. I was there.'

Of course he was.

'I was based in Germany at the time, serving in the army, but was spending time on leave in Paris, and happened to be staying near the shooting. It was a horrible time.'

He pauses for a moment, then collects himself. 'Forgive me. I didn't expect to be standing in the house of a foster carer who has dedicated four small walls to the worst aspects of global politics. I'm glad, though', he adds.

He looks for a moment at the cartoon of Donald Trump from the front cover of a copy of *Big Issue* and a Russian Revolutionary poster which we got at an antique market years ago.

He gives a nod, which I interpret as acknowledgment that we're on the same page. Lloyd begins talking about the pictures with great gusto. I smile to myself, recalling his reluctance to display them.

Fitzroy sits down in the red bentwood chair in the kitchen. I can't help but wonder, given his impressive stature, if another wouldn't have been more suitable. Lloyd makes coffee and Fitzroy lifts his heavy brown satchel onto his lap. His easy manner almost makes me want to get some wine and glasses out and settle in for the day, but of course we don't.

He shakes his head and smiles. 'Well, Lloyd and Louise, what have we all got ourselves involved in here?'

Just those few words do much to sweep away most of my anxiety and concern. We are in a bad situation, perhaps as bad as we have known, and thank the Lord for Fitzroy, who is happy to declare it as such.

He sits back and makes a wonderful deep chuckle. 'It certainly looks like the LA have got themselves into a fine mess here.'

Not what I was expecting him to say, and it confuses me a little.

'What do you mean, the LA?'

He gives me a look which tells me that he will not be covering anyone's back if he thinks they have been stupid.

'Well, there's a bit of a story behind this Blackthorn mob, but we'll get to that.'

Lloyd delivers our coffees, to a nod of appreciation from Fitzroy.

'But first, a little about me, so you know what you are dealing with.'

I can already detect a little of what I'm dealing with in Fitzroy, and I like it.

'I retrained as a social worker after I left the army, not long after that shooting, actually,' he continues. 'So I have only been doing this job for a few years. My wife and I moved to the area four months ago. She's a nurse and wanted to work back in the NHS, after working for an agency who ran her ragged.'

Yes, that doesn't surprise me. I nod my understanding.

'I joined the team a few months back now. Initially I was doing Life Story work?' He poses the latter as a question to check that we understand. We do, and I'm very supportive of it. It's important that children in care understand why they don't live with their birth parents, and why they've entered the care system. It's important for their emotional wellbeing and self-esteem, for helping them to see themselves in a more positive light. It often begins with celebrating the child's achievements, recognising the resilience they've already shown by overcoming adversity.

'Well, no one else had touched it, and Life Story work was picked up in the last Ofsted report, so I took it over. I've enjoyed getting it established, and it's been fine, but when Dara's role came up I realised I wanted to get back to the chalkface.'

'How well do you know Dara?' I ask.

He does the deep chuckle again. 'Good enough for her to tell me that I would enjoy working with this family.' He pauses. 'And good enough for her to tell me also that you are not a pushover, Louise.' He shakes his head and laughs. 'You would get on just fine with my wife.'

We sit down to business. We spread all our paperwork out on the table and begin to try and make sense of Billy's and the others' lives. My phone keeps pinging with messages from the Blackthorn WhatsApp group. I daren't tell my new supervising social worker that we're running our version of a social work department without the paperwork. Not yet, at least.

I smile and tell a little white lie to Lloyd. 'It's the flood group.'

'I noticed the sandbags,' says Fitzroy.

'Well, it'd be difficult to miss them,' I counter. We all laugh and get back to business. Though we are of course focused on Billy and his most immediate needs, I can't help but keep coming back to the larger issue of the whole Blackthorn situation.

'I mean, who *are* the Blackthorns? What was going on? Why did it take so long for these children, who have clearly been suffering all sorts of abuse, to be pulled out?'

I have to be careful, because one of the foster carers has a policeman for a husband, so we do have some inkling about the nature of this family, but it's too soon to play that particular hand.

'I agree with you, Louise. When I first looked through all the paperwork it was the thing that I couldn't understand. Why had they not all been arrested before, years ago? The answer is that I don't have an answer. Not yet, anyway. The police took computers away and are still going through them. It's not looking good.'

His face changes as he says this, to become full of concern. All trace of his earlier jollity is gone. 'I don't know whether you are aware or not, but several large boxes of sex toys were removed from one of the houses on the estate.

That particular location had been set up as a studio for the making of porn films.'

I feel sick. But it means that I can be completely honest with Fitzroy about everything we have gleaned so far.

He nods, 'I've read your logs, Louise.'

Whenever I hear that word I always want to go into my William Shatner impression: *Captain's log, Stardate 4524.2. Billy's last outburst was worse than an attack from a Klingon warship on Deep Space Station K-7.*

Somehow I resist. Poor Fitzroy probably isn't ready for that version of Louise yet.

We're still poring over the paperwork when Billy comes into the kitchen.

To my absolute horror, he spots Fitzroy and addresses him with a pejorative term beginning with 'n' that I can't even bring myself to write.

I feel myself flush cold with shame.

But Fitzroy looks at Billy and says only, 'Hello, my young friend, how are you?'

I have two thoughts in that instant. The first is that *blimey, this man's cool*. The second is to wonder how a five-year-old boy can be racist. Surely that comes later, after one's fear of life is converted into racism, as human beings seek to blame others for their own insecurities.

I guess that Billy has not met that many people in his short life, and we live in a predominantly white area, with views on Brexit, and particularly on immigration, that make my toes curl.

Billy walks up to Fitzroy with some curiosity. Thankfully he doesn't repeat the earlier word. Instead he responds to Fitzroy's warmth by saying, 'Hello,' in return.

There is a pause, and then Billy adds, rather sadly, 'Are we going to have a party?'

Given the horrible scenarios we've just been discussing, the adults round the table all give each other sharp looks. Easiest to pretend we didn't get that bit.

'No, Billy. No party,' I say wearily. Instead I ask, 'Would you like to play in the conservatory?'

I can keep a keen eye on him from here if he chooses that option. He does, and takes the dogs with him. I get up and fill a small bowl with cheesy cheddar biscuits. He likes those; they extend the list of potato-related items that Billy will eat. He contents himself with the dogs and the toys and occupies himself for another thirty minutes or so, giving Lloyd and me time to cover further ground with Fitzroy. When Billy seems to be getting restless once more, we decide to leave it there. But it has been a very productive first meeting with our new supervising social worker. Not least because I now have Fitzroy on speed dial.

'Call me if you need help, or anything at all.'

This is not an easy offer to make, but I sense that Fitzroy means it. As he stands up he suddenly remembers something else. 'I have found Billy's old social worker.'

Well, this is news. I immediately perform an eyeroll. 'You're telling me that he already had a social worker? That he was on the books?'

'Yes, indeed. And there are plenty of questions I need to ask him.'

While Fitzroy is putting on his coat in the hallway (which, like everything else he does, he seems to manage with effortless ease), I ask him another question.

'Did you like being in the army?'

'Now that's an interesting question.' He thinks for a moment. 'My parents were proud of me. They were the Windrush generation, and it meant a lot to them. They liked it. Did I? I suppose, like all organisations, the army has systemic problems, but on reflection I'm glad I was a soldier before I became a social worker. The training from my first career is paying off.'

His parting shot is something very surprising. 'I've got to say that I felt safer in the army than I do in social work.'

'What does *that* mean?'

He performs the deep chuckle a final time. 'In the army, you mostly know who your enemy is, but not in this system.' He lets out a whistle and then his face opens into a broad smile. 'I am a big grown man with powers. But for these children, their fates are blowing in the wind.'

This accords so closely with my own view that I want to shout out, 'Hallelujah!'

I don't. Maybe Fitzroy is religious and it would offend him.

Nevertheless, here is someone who is really listening to the needs of the children. Experienced enough to know what he is doing (an image of Emma flashes into my mind involuntarily), but new enough to not yet be worn down by the system.

Hallelujah, indeed.

Chapter Sixteen

Fitzroy is better than his word. He calls every morning to see how we are. We are so happy and relieved to feel that we have someone on our side, someone who cares. Really cares. I know it's his job, but we haven't always encountered this level of commitment. I try and imagine Fitzroy as a soldier and can't. He's too, well, *not* like a soldier. But what do I know? I'm not one myself, and I can imagine that actual armed combat is only a small proportion of a soldier's role. I wonder whether Fitzroy was more administration than active service. He's damned efficient, whatever his background, and clearly used to working with all sorts of people. More than that, I feel he is a good man. There is no weird energy coming off Fitzroy, unlike a few others I could mention. My thoughts are drifting, a sure sign that I need more coffee.

Lloyd is in a Zoom meeting with his European team. By all accounts, they're a lovely bunch. I know it's a corporate arrangement, but they manage to make it feel as though they are part of a family, or at least that's how Lloyd describes it. It's very good.

The other thing that's good is that I can't see any flood group messages. A very positive sign, because they're right on it when there's bad weather, which makes me think I can relax on that front, at least for the time being. I do have a missed call from a mobile number I don't recognise. I don't like receiving messages or calls from people I don't know, and it's unusual. Everyone in publishing works via email; only my art agent calls or texts me.

I call the number back. It's Billy's latest social worker. No mention of Emma, or what might have happened to her. She didn't last long. The new one sounds young, but she might be brilliant, let's see. I tell myself to keep an open mind. We've struck lucky with Fitzroy. Who's to say we won't again? She's coming this afternoon.

Billy's new social worker is called Andy, and Andy is a woman. This may be short for Andrea, or someone from the LGBTQI+ community. I am enormously supportive, but at the same time I'm terrified of pronouns, ever since one young person called me a 'transphobic bitch' because I said, without thinking, 'good girl'. Since that incident, I try to pay more attention to how people, particularly some young people, like to be addressed. Blimey. Life itself seems to have become so bureaucratic: a label and drawer for everything, even identity. Can't we just be 'ourselves'? Even saying that to myself makes me feel like an old fart.

Meanwhile, Billy is on the loose. He's in his fleecy pyjamas. He looks cosy and cuddly, and he's even remembered to wear his slippers.

'What a star!' I try to give him lots of praise, whenever I can.

He wraps his arms round my legs. Thankfully, he's not able to reach anywhere else. Oh God, I hate the tarnish that knowing about his sexual abuse brings. I hate what it does to my brain. I find that everything can be sexualised, right now. I'm on the lookout for it. I'm reading signs into all sorts of things, perhaps when they may not be there at all. It distorts everything.

He has taken to making little click noises with his tongue of late. He's thrilled with his new skill. I do the same back to him. If an alien happened to be looking into our lives at this moment in time, they would probably assume that this was our language. We click-sound for a while, until I offer the famous breakfast of Nutella and toast.

Not today. Billy takes a box of cereal from the cupboard of doom. 'These, Louise.'

Well, that's unexpected, but how can I refuse? I get a bowl down from the rack, and even though it only takes a few seconds, it's enough time for Billy to jump up and down and clap his hands. Imagine if all our lives were this joyful because of a box of cereal!

He's tried some before, when he first arrived, but then the Nutella took over. But he hasn't shown much interest since. No doubt he has seen the others tuck into cereal, and he must know that they're allowed to help themselves as a snack. Perhaps he wants in on that action. It's mostly down to Vincent, whose insane growth spurt continues, meaning that he's taken to coming downstairs after we've gone to bed for another bowl. The house is so quiet at night that I can hear the chink sound of the cereal hitting the bottom of the bowl in the kitchen. I don't begrudge it for a second. My adoptive mother was prone to starving my adopted brother and me. I remember her beating the living daylights out of me after she caught me with my finger in the mincemeat jar. I was so hungry I would have eaten carpet ends. Having children has taught me that I wasn't a bad, wicked, greedy child (as I once thought). Instead, I was hungry.

I'm also minded to think that if I try and control the children's eating too much it could create food issues later in life. Nearly everyone I know seems to have a food issue of

236

some sort. It's a weird dichotomy we're in in relation to food marketing, and the push and pull between diets and guilt eating. I don't hear of people in developing countries talking about the latest fad diet. So my philosophy is not to make an issue out of food. Ultimately, the children will, on the whole, regulate themselves.

Notwithstanding that all children will eat to death their latest favourite food.

Lily is the best at this. Because she is a vegetarian who will not eat vegetables, providing a meal that is not vegetable patties made out of sweetcorn and mashed potato is tricky. She did, recently, discover noodles with Quorn chicken bits fried in hoisin sauce. She literally had it every day for a month. Then I gave it to her one day and she looked at me like I had served up a plate of raw liver in blood sauce. She refused to eat it ever again. I guess she had just become bored of it. Not much I can do about that, other than go with the flow. Like most of this parenting lark, as it happens. Unless, of course, the child happens to have a knife in their hand. That example comes to mind because it has happened several times over the years. In that case, well: I guess you still go with the flow, just a lot faster.

I sit down with Billy while he eats his cereal. He tucks in with great gusto and seems to be enjoying it immensely. It's still a chocolate cereal, but at least it's something other than Nutella on toast. We are moving in the right direction.

There are frequent moments where I am impressed with Billy, especially given the picture we are building up of his background. He's a bright spark and, when not in one of his chaotic rages, totally adorable. I continue to see small acts of kindness, and there's definitely care and empathy towards the dogs. They might not be Ant and Dec, the Staffies he has known, but he seems to be gentle with Doug and Dotty.

Nevertheless, I still dread taking him out, especially anywhere where we are likely to encounter other people. We have walked up and down the fields so many times, the dogs' legs have got shorter. I have taken him to the shops a few times. I actually don't think he has been to the shops much before. I'm not sure. I have looked after children who behave appallingly in shops, and it's usually because they always did; no one had ever shown them what to do, or expected them to behave any better. In my view, children come with an inbuilt morality. They instinctively know what's right. But if they live with chaotic or controlling adults, that instinct can get buried. So I know that I need to do more with Billy. He won't learn if I don't get on and push past the burn. After all, I've fished children out of chest freezers in supermarkets, and peeled children off the now-dented roof of a parked car. (That was an interesting insurance argument with his social worker.)

But it's always tricky, because venturing out with Billy means that I have to go into full-on 'Stand aside, foster carer here' mode. I wish it could be more like, 'Please forgive me and this child, we're representatives of the care system.' I wish people would be more understanding. It's actually other people that make it hard. Getting ready to take Billy out can feel like getting ready for a sports event. I need to be fit and alert, ready to dash any time. I need to concentrate hard, to look out for any signs of impending changes in behaviour, to read the child like a book.

But, mission not impossible.

'Let's have an adventure today,' I say. 'We've got the whole morning before we have a visitor this afternoon. Andy is coming.'

'I don't like Andy.'

'You haven't met Andy yet. Andy's a woman.'

'I don't like Andy,' he insists.

I let it go. I'll deal with it later, but I wonder if an 'Andy', whoever he/she is, has something to do with some of the unpleasantness in Billy's past.

I help Billy get dressed, mostly by picking up his debris. He can manage most things himself and is quick to get into his clothes. He doesn't at all mind me asking him to wear two pairs of socks because he's going into wellies.

I shake his bedding out. He chose the bedding from the airing cupboard himself. It's a dark red and dark orange duvet set bought for a teenage girl a while ago. She was an emo and wanted black everything. On the grounds that I needed to have a sense of 2D and 3D so I didn't go flying, we agreed on this set; in the end she actually loved it and leaves it here now for when she visits.

With the laundry under one arm and Billy's hand in mine, we walk down the stairs into the hall where the post has landed on the mat. I ask Billy to gather it up for me. He loves doing little jobs, and, as ever, I make a huge fuss of his achievements.

Washing machine on, back door locked, wellies in bags, and my bag of 'just in case' packed and ready, we head to the car.

I start along the road one way and then change my mind. I think Billy needs to run and be free, then sit at a table outside and have a snack. Let's see if we can do this. I drive in the opposite direction because I remember there is a country house that stays open all through the winter. You can sit outside and the lovely staff there wrap blankets round you. It's a bit further than I intended on driving, but I need Billy to have opportunities to meet people and not freak out.

We motor along. As I drive I check on Billy in the mirror: the thumb is in and he looks happy and relaxed. The sun is low and there is still frost on the trees and hedges. I point all this out to him. I'm convinced that even if children don't ordinarily react to these things, it's my duty as a person to make them aware that the world around them is beautiful, ever changing and theirs. I heard Jackson and Vincent discussing the autumn leaves when I took Jackson to rugby training recently. I was so touched that after the hundreds of times I've talked about trees, light, colour and shapes, it's gone in. I don't know what the future holds for this little fella, but for now I can do my tiny little bit. I know that if we didn't have other children I would keep him, but I also know that this boy needs more, much more, than my household can offer at the moment. We park up and are ready for the off. We have our little routine down to a tee. I have hold of his hand as soon as I am able to, then I do my strange version of Mary Poppins and skip us up to the big gate with gusto.

No one else is here, no one at all.

I can't resist. I look at Billy and give him a wink. 'Billy, let's run!'

I run for about two minutes before deciding that was a mad idea and I have no breath, but watch Billy run and laugh. He's lost his hat somewhere, but never mind. His joy and release is worth it. We walk the entire grounds: up hills, through trees, round a lake.

By the lake we wave to a couple of men clearing some weeds from the water. Billy keeps waving and they wave back. I do one long wave and pull Billy away, or these poor men might be stuck with us for a while. In moments like this he is a delight, finding joy in everything. And now he has a stick. I love watching children carry sticks. They are so proud and excited. Billy is no exception. He wields it exultantly. The fresh air has given him gorgeous rosy cheeks today, and his eyes are shining.

We find the coffee shop in the grounds and it's open, thank goodness. I take hold of Billy's hand before he has a chance to argue and walk slowly towards the door. There are tables outside and I eye them up. I open the door and the heat and smell of homemade soup is welcoming. In fact, I think I'll forgo the coffee and have homemade pea and ham soup; the bread looks delicious.

I lean towards the counter, Billy's hand still firmly in mine.

'What would you like?' I ask.

He crinkles up his nose and shakes his head. There are cakes on display, and packets of mini biscuits, but none is what he is after.

The lady behind the counter, no doubt with the voice of experience, says, 'We can make a bowl of chips?'

'Perfect,' I say as Billy jumps up and down to signal his approval.

I watch his face as the lady chats to him. He's doing well, handling everything that's being thrown at him today. I keep his hand in mine, as an emotional reminder that he's okay, he's safe. We walk outside and sit down. Another member of staff comes out and chats to Billy, and, sure enough, she offers us blankets to put across our laps. We wait for about fifteen minutes for the food to arrive, which gives us time to play I Spy.

He loves it. I have to say that with his tiny vocabulary it can get a little dull from my point of view, but I know how much his language must be developing when we play games like this.

Our snack arrives. I take a quick check of the time, wondering if I can get away with calling it 'early lunch'. Billy's eyes light up, and the waiter chats away amiably to him. He must be enjoying the attention, but I watch his legs flailing about and feel a tad nervous. I'm finely tuned to the early warning signs now. But he's fine, as far as I can tell. I squirt ketchup over his chips, which provokes further delights. It's so nice when simple pleasures can bring such joy. My soup is wonderful. As we're finishing, a couple come across to look at the menu chalked up on a nearby blackboard. I hear her say, 'Let's have the fondue later.'

How lovely. I am so glad we have the National Trust membership that enables us to come to all these beautiful places. I fold the blankets up, but before I can say 'Jack Sprat', Billy has gone.

He is nowhere to be seen.

I scan the horizon. Nearby trees. Where could he have got to in the space of a few short seconds?

My first thought is for his safety. My second is for his new social worker. Andy is coming later and I may not have a child to show her.

But my panic is unnecessary. The couple who were checking out the menu have Billy with them. They have a hand each, and are swinging him along. He looks so much as if he belongs to them that I'm reluctant to break up the picture.

'He ran after us as we were on our walk,' the woman explains.

'Thank you so much,' I say, as they hand over his hand.

The man chuckles. 'We nearly got a party invitation out of it,' he says. 'He ran up to us and asked if we were going to Sharon's party!'

That's odd, I think, wondering who Sharon might be. Then I remember that 'Sharon' is the name he gives to that ugly teddy.

'Oh, right,' I say, with what is probably a slightly bemused smile.

'Enjoy your party!'

It's too complicated to explain that we're not going to a party. Instead I take an even tighter grip on Billy's hand while we head back to the car via a small area of woodland. When there is no one else in view again, I let go and let him run and run.

He has no sense of danger, while being totally scared all the time. It's a strange mix. I'm still trying to work out what his safest types of environments are. He runs wild outside, and at home he's okay now, but for the first few weeks he opened every door and drawer, and he twitched at every sound. I wonder if one of my friends is up for me making a house visit just to see how he does.

When we get back I unpack the bag and get my phone. Flood group has had some developments. They want to set up a campaigning group and oh, what do you know? They think I should lead it. That's great, because obviously I haven't got a lot on, just sitting twiddling my thumbs. I can tell a man thought that one up. There is a saying that 'if you want something done, ask a busy woman.' Or at least I think that's how the saying goes. *If you want something done, sunshine, do it yourself*, I'm tempted to reply. I feel most indignant, but I know I'll end up doing it anyway.

Billy is fine. His cheeks look even rosier now that we have come back into the warm.

'You're a beautiful boy,' I tell him, just about supressing the urge to pinch them. He touches my face and laughs, and there is the dribble flying about, but he *is* a lovely little boy and I feel so sad that whoever has been looking after him hasn't been kind.

I settle Billy down in the conservatory and look for Lloyd. He's not answering, so might be at the gym. I wipe the kitchen table, where there are still toast crumbs from earlier. I can't have Andy getting crumbs on her laptop.

I look through the door towards Billy, playing in the conservatory. He has arranged Lily's old dolls into sex positions.

Oh my.

Andy is going to have an interesting time.

I call to him, 'You alright in there, Billy?'

He sings back to me, 'Yes.' He doesn't know that the way he is playing with the dolls is revealing many more concerns to me. I knew a girl at school called Caroline. Her parents were 'right on' academics and swingers. It was the early eighties. She was the first person who provided me with an awareness that not all adults were like my adoptive parents, who would give out an electric shock if they touched each other. Caroline's parents had parties where the guests looked like the middle-class intelligentsia of Oxford. The men wore coloured sweaters across their shoulders over their laundered shirts and slacks; the women wore floaty dresses or really tight jeans. Joni Mitchell would be blaring, and from Caroline's attic room we could hear people below in the bedroom having sex. I heard *three* voices. Oh, I was blown away. I have never been one for that sort of thing – much prefer a cup of tea and a ginger snap. But it was an eye-opener. I leave Billy to play. I don't feel it's the right time to ask him to play a different game, without the necessary explanation, and that one I may well leave to the social worker. That's if she lasts long enough.

Lloyd is soon back from the gym, and somewhat red in the face.

'Simon pushed me too far, today,' he gasps.

Simon is his coach, and Lloyd is not one of life's natural gladiators. He much prefers sitting down with a book, but I have encouraged him to move about more and preferably get outside in the fresh air. He's like his mum: they can't understand why I enjoy going for walks. Fresh air has never been high on the agenda. When they pull me up on it, I'm tempted to explain that I like getting out of the house to get away from them, but that would be mean, and untrue.

Lloyd's in and out of the shower in minutes. He rushes to his office to check his emails, then moves towards the kitchen. When he puts his head through the door to Billy, he is offered an enormous, dribbly smile in reply.

I remind Billy that Andy is coming.

'I don't like Andy.'

I keep explaining that Andy is a lady (to the best of my knowledge), and Andy is also a social worker.

There is a knock at the door, and Lloyd goes to let Andy in. I hear a light, young female voice. I watch Billy closely. He isn't happy at all. He is standing still, tense, facing in the direction of the kitchen door, knowing that Lloyd and Andy will be coming through to the kitchen any second.

'It's alright, Billy. Andy is not the same Andy you're thinking of. It's a different person called Andy. It's fine, you're okay.'

My words do little. He's still in a state of heightened tension. I want to know who Andy – his Andy – is.

I stand by the sink, next to the coffee machine, in line with Billy. I want to keep him safe. Here is Andy. I reach out to shake her hand and ask, 'Is Andy short for Andrea?' hoping that might reassure Billy, who is listening intently.

'No, it's not, actually.' She smiles. 'My mum named me Andy and my sister Robyn. She wanted us to have unisex names. It's Andi with an "i" rather than a "y".'

Fair enough, I think, although I don't know if it will be enough for Billy.

Lloyd's phone rings. He checks the number. 'I'm so sorry. I've got to take this. I'll be back in a few minutes.' I know his team have a big trade show in Mumbai. It's probably something to do with that. It can't be helped.

I offer Andi-with-an-i a seat. Like Emma, she seems very young; but I am getting older, so everyone looks young. Andi is not confident at all, and reveals that she is only just qualified. I suspect this case, and all the other Blackthorn children – 26, I seem to remember – are taking up all her department's time and staffing.

She clears her throat, nervously. 'So, I'm aware that some of the other Blackthorn children have been challenging,' she begins.

I daren't tell her I already know this, and way more. Instead I smile as reassuringly as I can. She asks about Billy's schooling.

'Not the best day,' I explain. 'He went for one morning and the headteacher asked us never to darken his door again.'

The whole experience has become funnier with the intervening time. I tell her about Max reassuring me as I left Billy with him that they were a trauma-aware school. I hope the story will break the ice. 'I enjoy people who have never experienced trauma trying to tell us what it's like.'

Andi looks confused. 'Oh. I thought he was attending school every day.'

'No, he's not.'

'I didn't know ... ' she trails off.

That sounds to me like a paperwork mishap.

'I sent it all through. He was definitely not welcome back.'

'So what provision have you put in place for him in the interim?'

'Actually, that's your job,' I say, deciding that I don't like the way this is heading. 'I've been looking after him at home because he hasn't been allocated a school.'

She busies herself checking through emails.

'Nope. It's not here. I knew nothing about Billy not attending school.'

She says it in a way that implies that I am very much the one at fault. I feel myself bristle at the injustice of this. I have to remind myself that she is young, and her head will still be ringing with a lot of the text she learnt at college. I must remember that.

'Have you received my notes?' I ask.

I hate calling them logs. I'm not on a ship.

She has, and claims she has read all through them. They also contain details of the school day, and the poor results I've had with flashcards and different types of art and educational play. But never mind.

Next she asks me about Billy's health and lifestyle choices.

I bite my lip. He's five years old and, as far as I can tell, he hasn't had much of a life so far. Not least because he's *five*.

I don't always make the best lifestyle choices, and I've got 50 years on him. Give me strength.

She talks about his behaviour and I inadvertently let out a 'huh' sound. That may have sounded as if I am fed up with his behaviour, but that's not my intention. I'm sad that Billy and all these children end up in this state. I also believe that they shouldn't have to, so something is wrong. I can't help myself. I come out with it, straight between the eyes. 'Why were these children left for so long?'

I expect the usual flannel about cutbacks and lost files; perhaps a hint of a teeny institutional failing?

She doesn't give me any of that. She sighs, and says, 'I don't know.'

She has read the dinner table massacre incident, the charging dog moment, and some of his medical reports.

'Do you have any idea when Billy's appointment is? For the specialist to *look at his rectum*?' I find myself emphasising the words, a little unnecessarily perhaps, but to make a point about what I think is really important here.

She shrugs. 'That could take months.'

Next Andi wants to see his blue book. This is the looked-after-child medical record. It contains recordings of weight, height and milestones, as well as any medical concerns. I get up to get it from the office where I keep foster children's records in an old-fashioned filing cabinet. I got it from a car boot for £10. It's brilliant and has two keys, both hidden. In fact, the spare is so well hidden I have forgotten where it is.

As I turn to walk out of the kitchen, Andi says abruptly, 'You can't leave me alone with Billy.'

I'm taken aback.

It's her bloody job to be near these children, surely?

'Why?' I ask. My patience is really beginning to wear out now.

She lowers her head and pulls up her sleeve. There are red bite marks on her arm and she looks like she is going to cry.

All of a sudden I feel sorry for her.

'I met one of Billy's sisters two days ago and she did this to my arm,' she sniffs. 'I had to go to the hospital and wait five hours to get a tetanus jab.'

'I'm sorry,' I say. 'I'll wait for Lloyd to come back before I get the blue book.' I don't know quite what else to suggest.

Right on cue, Billy chooses that moment to jump up from the conservatory floor and appear at the kitchen table. He is in full heightened-energy mode, all the signs I recognise: tense facial features, loose limbs, pent-up aggression. If he was an adult I'd say he's spoiling for a fight. I want to put my armoured suit on and wait for this to pass.

He flies around the kitchen, pulling things off the side as he goes. He runs up to Andi and calls her a 'hairy c-u-next-Tuesday.' Then, just as Lloyd walks in holding his phone, wanting to know what's going on, what all the noise is about, Billy halts just in front of the nervous social worker and pulls down his trousers, pants and all. He stands there playing with his willy and sucking his fingers.

The whole room changes colour. We all have to pull ourselves back in.

'Would you like a biscuit?' It's lame, but it's all I can think of to try and diffuse the situation.

I give Billy his treat after he pulls up his pants. Then I usher him into the sitting room to watch *Bing*. We've moved on from *Pingu*. He settles down in minutes. Meanwhile I can hear Lloyd making more coffee, and soothing voices. By the time Billy is safe and settled enough for me to leave the sitting room, Andi is packing away her laptop and charger. I look at her to try and gauge how she is. The signs aren't good. Sometimes social workers must feel as downcast as the rest of us about this stuff. It's difficult and never fails to test us. There are no easy answers.

Andi waves to Billy as she passes the doorway to the sitting room on her way down the hall to the door.

'I'll get Billy's file up to date and work on his care plan.'

'We looked forward to seeing it,' I smile.

Once the door is firmly closed behind her, Lloyd and I look at each other. 'Another lamb to the slaughter.'

Back in the kitchen I hear further phone pings. I find my Dame-Edna-style reading glasses. They live permanently in the kitchen, and I note that they're greasy. I must clean them. The messages are from the Blackthorn group. Two more of the carers have called 28-day notice. Bobby and Neal apparently told the social worker that if he didn't take their Blackthorn child away today, they would drive him to the county hall with his bags and leave him there. I know that Bobby would definitely do that. Bobby and Neal are a lovely couple from Scotland. I learnt quickly that Bobby has a heart of gold but does not suffer fools gladly. I'm sure if they called notice it's because of the lack of support. I can't quite count, but I think we're probably down to about Five Amigos left now from the original eleven who took in Blackthorn siblings.

More pings.

Two more Blackthorn children have exposed themselves today.

Must be something in the water.

Chapter Seventeen

It's the weekend, and thank the Lord for that. I get Friday-itis badly myself, let alone the children. The end of the working week means time to kick back. For the junior members of the household, this means I'm not waking them up at 7am on Saturday. Lloyd usually likes a lie-in at the weekend, too. I don't. I never have. Time in bed means me being unwell, or in the early stages of a romance. Once I'm awake in the morning I can't stay in bed. There is always so much to do, and I like to feel that I am getting ahead of the game. The washing machine on, tumble dryer on, dishwasher on, hoover on. Each little accomplishment makes me feel better than lying in bed would. While the rest of the household slumber on, or wonder if they're hungry enough to heave themselves out of bed to forage for breakfast, I whizz around doing all the jobs that my family thinks the fairies do.

It's not too much of an exaggeration to say that I nearly divorced Lloyd after a comment he made when we were in our old house in Portsmouth. It was a four-storey town house, and I worked full time. We had young children, and as far as I was concerned, the house was pretty much together and it was a nice home. One night, while we had friends over for dinner, one commented that it must be hard work keeping a house like that in order.

'Oh, the house seems to run itself,' said Lloyd, nonchalantly.

I have never forgotten that comment. So, when I find a pair of his underpants on the floor, I tend to dust the shelves with them.

Billy is soon up and gunning for breakfast: chocolate cereal followed by Nutella on toast. What with the other children noticing Billy's snack choice and copying it, I have found the jar somewhat depleted of late. Consequently I thought I would be clever and buy a cheaper version. Billy, though, is disgusted by the substitute. He realises immediately and refuses to eat his toast.

'I don't like the taste.'

His words make me smile, and it's a nice thing to write in his log/'notes'.

This morning I have pulled out the old farmyard set from the loft again. It belonged to the boys years ago. They loved playing with it, and I think that Billy has moved on from chewing everything, so it's worth risking it. I look at the array of animals and realise that from an educational perspective, I will need to point out that the farmyard set does have a few zoo animals (a family of giraffes and water buffalo) roaming within it. But I don't think I need to be too much of a stickler for detail today.

Billy enjoys setting it up. After watching plenty of animal-themed children's TV over the last few weeks and looking at some of the picture books we have, including my own childhood encyclopaedia of animals and plants, he is much more familiar with the names of different animals than he was when he first arrived. He has also learnt to make many more animal sounds, and now has quite a versatile repertoire of noises to draw upon. I sit down next to him on the floor and hold up each animal in turn, asking Billy to name them.

He loves this game.

'Duck!'

'Zebra!'

'Moo cow.'

He does call the pig a dog at one point, so that reminds me to take him for a drive to the pig farm. It's a bit of a drive: about an hour away in the car. Vincent was heavily into pigs when he was little, and so when we used to drive past it, near Stonehenge, on the way to Oxford, we would call out, 'Vincent, look, it's Pig Village!'

So, I will take Billy to 'Pig Village', and park on the side of the road so that he can see the pigs. There is also a country restaurant somewhere nearby that has a Tamworth, a Large Black and several Oxford Sandy and Blacks. I remember that they're there because I took another group of foster children to visit a few years ago. What I remember was leaning on the wire fence only to learn it was an electric fence. The zip of my coat caught on the fence and my hair stood up on end. The children thought it was hilarious. It took a while for my body to feel right again, but that didn't seem to detract from the general entertainment value as far as they were concerned.

Billy wriggles over to sit on my lap. My radar is up at any physical contact or proximity, but he does just sit there like a child on an adult's lap; no suggestion that he has experienced sexual abuse. Bizarrely, I find this one of the most moving experiences so far in my career as a foster carer: just the ordinariness of the moment, and his seeking out of non-sexual contact. He sits and plays, chatting all the while, and then leans back into me to begin sucking his thumb contentedly, with his famous dribble coming down his wrist onto my lap. I edge myself back to lean against the sofa. I don't want my own discomfort and bad back to stop him from enjoying the moment.

I find myself stroking his hair and inhaling its aroma, which is mainly strawberry from his shampoo. I want to enjoy this for as long as I can, and for as long as he can, because I know that Billy, and all the other Blackthorns, are going to have a bumpy ride. Every experience of joy and calm contributes in some way to reminding them that there is another way of doing life.

I nod off!

When I come round, I realise that my momentary lapse is probably due to the fact that I didn't have my second cup of coffee earlier. I'm useless without coffee in the morning, but I can't drink it in the afternoon. I become wired, and end up with the dreaded night-time mind chatter. Thoughts along the lines of: *I hate my life; it's not fair; why, why, why?* That sort of rubbish. It took me a while to realise that it was caffeine that was doing it, but now I make sure I avoid caffeine, and sugar for that matter, for several hours before bedtime. I need as good a sleep as I can get. As far as I'm concerned, that is the foster carer's most important requirement.

Billy is being very creative. He has taken most of the logs from the log basket and built an extension onto the fireplace. There is a thick trail of sawdust across the carpet to his slippers. I check my watch and draw a sharp intake of breath. It's 10.30am and I am nowhere near where I should be by this time on a Saturday morning. Mind you, nor are the others. Where are they all? I know that if I cook some bacon the boys' bacon detectors will bring them down, especially if I turn the breakfast into a tasty brunch.

It's horrid weather outside: cold and dank. Proper winter. I think I'll persuade Billy to let me have the logs back to build a fire and heat this old and very cold house up.

'Would you like a brunch, with some bacon?' I ask.

Billy nods his head with excitement. He certainly is enjoying his food these days, even if what he eats mostly stems from the potato or the cocoa plant. I did get him to eat a banana last week. He was most impressed with his own technique of peeling. It was more sort of ripping and squashing, but we've all got to start somewhere.

I get the ingredients ready, and just assume that they will all want brunch, even Lily, who can still enjoy it if I use a vegetarian sausage mix to make her three breakfast sausages. She actually likes those. The only downside to making this sort of brunch is the lingering smells, but, if fully sated, the family are likely to be out of my hair for a few hours. Who knows, I may even get a chance to do some work on my seahorse book illustrations. It's the hope that kills.

Billy loves his brunch, and even dips a piece of toast in his egg. In fairness, he does it while studying Vincent perform the same action, but it's the first egg I've seen him eat. I did give him an egg a little while ago while we were out on a walk. I had a peeled hard-boiled egg as part of our little picnic. He put the egg in his mouth and began pulling it backwards and forwards in what I can only describe as a pornographic way. I offered him a Penguin biscuit and I remember that he dropped the egg. I put his and my own in the bin. When you have a sexualised thought in your head, it's hard not to keep going back to it and for it to pepper ordinary objects and activities. I haven't been able to eat a hard-boiled egg since. I dread to think what a hell it must be to be trapped inside porn addiction. Hell for the addict, and hell for whoever they rein in to act out their fantasies. I know that one way or another, the children in my house will have encountered pornography. It's ubiquitous in our digital, online age. I do wonder how a child can begin to 'unsee' anything like that if they encounter it too early. Still, it doesn't seem to be a political priority. Where there is huge profit, governments seem only to nibble at legislation to protect other's interests. If that sounds dark, it's probably because I have seen the fallout at first hand in cases like Billy's. I'm only guessing, but how would a little boy know how to slide a boiled egg in and out of his mouth like that if he hadn't been shown, asked or told to do it?

Brunch done, I send them all off to get dressed.

'You too, Billy.'

I encourage Billy to follow the crowd in things like this. It will help him learn and feel confident, and I will stop being seen as the bossy adult for a few minutes at least. I know that I will have to fly around their rooms and gather the washing and bins after. The older children have started taking more and more food upstairs, so that I seem to be perpetually short of teaspoons and bowls. Unless you're running a gulag, no matter how often you say 'don't take food upstairs' to a teenage audience, or, when I want to be especially tough, 'the mice will get into your rooms', food will still make its way to their rooms.

I see crisp packets bulging in dressing gown pockets as they depart the kitchen. I resist my own juvenile thought of crushing them as they walk past. It's one of those things that you decide not to pursue, like towels on the bathroom floor. I call each domestic offence out as I find it, and I am routinely ignored. Then, as my grown-up stepdaughters have shown, your words live on. I've seen them have the same battles in their own household. It's going in somehow, that's all I know. I plod on.

I left my phone in the studio last night, to avoid the pings waking me up.

Free advice: never confiscate a child's phone and put it in your own room, even on silent. Their capacity to receive messages makes my own bombardment from the flood group and the Blackthorn group look positively quiet. One Android phone kept talking at me so much I thought I had been visited by spirits. It pinged and beeped until I moved it into the bathroom. I could still hear it. I put it in the bread bin between a loaf of bread and a packet of crumpets. Bad idea: the bread bin vibrated. It kept me awake until I put it in the back garden under an unused upside-down flowerpot.

I pull back the studio curtains to reveal the windy grey day, and realise that I've lost track of what this storm has been named, Bert or Hubert or Cuthbert. I don't know. What I do know is that my phone screen is full of WhatsApp messages. The flood group are keeping an eye on the weather. Wind is forecast, but the wind is preferable to the rain. James, who owns the bakery, has uploaded a small film on how to pack a sandbag. I'll be watching that avidly.

The first Blackthorn message is from a carer called Kristina. She lives with her partner, Will. Kristina, like me, is an artist and, like me, foolishly believed our experience and talents would be swept up to help our young people through art, but, like me, she is long past waiting for the offer and is instead now running art camps from her home. She and Will have a bit of land. I think Will is a retired BBC radio producer. He's a bit older than Kristina; she is his second wife. Saying that, I don't know if they are married; who cares, anyway? I read her message.

Oh my God!

I rush upstairs to show Lloyd. He's still in bed on his iPad, catching up on the sport.

'Look at this. Loooook!'

In the chat there is a picture of an Ugly Teddy, but not Billy's Sharon. This one belongs to Kristina's Blackthorn teenage girl. She has thrown it out of her bedroom window along with a gaming console and clothes. Will gathered it all up and noticed that her teddy was damaged. When he tried to fix it, he discovered something. Other messages are flying in with pictures of ugly teddies. Some on the floor, some on beds. Lloyd sits bolt upright and examines the images. He takes the phone off me.

'Rude!' I say, in my best Miranda Hart impersonation.

He laughs and does not apologise. What he shows me next is no laughing matter, though. He scrolls through and reveals the humdinger.

In each teddy there is a communication device.

Oh my God!

This explains so much. 'Sharon' must be the person Billy talks to.

An actual person.

I think back to when Billy was telling the teddy that he was a 'good boy'. How odd that seemed at the time. I recall him nodding furiously and telling the ugly teddy 'yes' at times, as if he was responding to it. I thought at the time that it sounded very realistic. Well, it's hardly surprising: it was real. I remember how sweet it was that 'Sharon' would make things better during the flood. It all starts to make more sense now.

But at the same time the whole concept is rather mad, and I need to get my head around what has been going on. Lloyd is having the same realisations as me. There are dozens of messages. People are starting to tally up dates. The morning of school at Flatfields Primary, there were a couple of other reports on WhatsApp about other children being sent home and all sorts.

Patterns of behaviour.

I think about the various times that I thought there must be 'something in the water'. Not at all. These children are being told to behave in particular ways at particular times. They are being controlled.

I leave my phone on the bed and walk to Billy's room. The darling boy is dressed in clean clothes from his drawer. I explain that drawers work both ways and that his room will be bigger if the drawers are shut. As I say the words, I'm not sure if Ugly Sharon Teddy is watching me. I don't know if it's a two-way communication device, if it can record, or if it can just 'broadcast' to Billy. Whatever – it makes me feel incredibly self-conscious. I behave like a social worker is hidden in the teddy rather than a criminal. I switch into 'perfect carer' mode, which strikes me as ridiculous after about three minutes of trying to sustain it.

Billy has set up a game with his dinosaurs and cars. He is happily playing, and he has even worked out how to use the CD player and is listening to Winnie the Pooh, narrated by Stephen Fry. He's having a childhood and meanwhile, I'm thinking about taking Ugly Teddy to the cops!

What I actually do is leave Ugly Teddy alone. For now. I busy myself in a fake way by moving things about until I leave his room as I might do on any ordinary day. I don't want to give anything away about our discovery to anyone who might be listening in.

I go back to Lloyd, who is scrolling through the pictures of ugly teddies. They were *all* given one before they came into care. I guess the children weren't loaded onto a lorry all together, so the sight of many brand-new ugly teddies hadn't caught anyone's attention. I guess the children were escorted in small groups to fit in cars and ambulances if needed. But if they arrested everyone there, how did so much go unchallenged? How was this allowed to continue?

Who the hell is this Sharon person, and what does she want with all these children?

Chapter Eighteen

First thing on Monday morning I phone Fitzroy and tell him about Ugly Teddy and how all the Blackthorns have one.

He is running to catch up and explains that he has only just arrived at the office. He hasn't had a chance to get to his desk.

'I walked up the stairs today,' he explains, with his customary chuckle. 'I'm trying to stay as fit as I can in case I have to chase a tiger.'

I know he's joking, but the thing about Fitzroy is that I can imagine him doing just that.

'Well, I don't exactly have a tiger for you, but something of a python's nest instead.'

I try to explain all that I have gleaned this weekend. Will showed us, with the aid of another little video, how to remove the device without damaging the teddy, so we could keep the teddies where they were so as not to upset the children. It meant that I didn't get round to poor James' sandbag video.

Billy's Sharon is still on the windowsill, but without eyes and ears to make mischief. I never quite liked the 'cut' of that teddy's 'jib'. I wonder if Martin's allegation will be dropped now that we know the children are being controlled. They should be, and his union will soon hear about this. I suggest that he tells them and, just in case he's feeling shy, I email the NUPFE and refer to all of us who may require support, with the introduction: 'I understand you are working with one of my colleagues …'

I don't have any way of knowing for sure, but I suspect that Sharon (if indeed that's his or her real name) is controlling the children to cause maximum damage to the placements. I know that one of the social workers (I've lost track, we seem to have dealt with so many in the last few weeks), mentioned that there was a drive to get the Blackthorn siblings reinstated with their birth parents. Given that we know there is also a criminal investigation underway into the Blackthorn family more widely, this will have the dual effect of creating chaos while taking some of the attention away from the criminals and the main criminal activity.

'Right. Here we go,' says Fitzroy, finally at his desk and logged in.

'Well, well, well. What a thing we have going on here, Louise.'

I nod, before remembering that he can't see me. He goes on to tell me about what I need to do with the device.

'Don't worry,' I tell him. 'I've already spoken to the police. They will be round at some point to collect the device and take a statement. The desk policeman told me that they had now all heard of the Blackthorns.'

The police officer also asked me how my fostering of a Blackthorn was going. I couldn't lie, especially to the law. So I said that, on the whole, he is a 'sweet little boy who craves positive love and attention, but there have been some rather interesting moments.' He laughed. I couldn't tell whether it was in solidarity, or perhaps what he saw as my naivety regarding the Blackthorn case. I don't have time to tell Fitzroy how the rest of the weekend was spent. But, from various dealings in the past, I know that the police have a realistic view on children's social care and of the children in it.

Earlier on in my foster carer career, it was a police officer who helped me understand that foster carers, or indeed any adult, don't have to put up with violence or coercion from anyone, even children and young people. His words all that time ago were something that has stood me in good stead for my expectations of social workers, and the children themselves.

Although I'm busy on the phone, I always have one ear and eye out for Billy. He's in sight, playing with Doug on the sofa in the conservatory. I'm not sure what they're playing, but Billy is chatting away happily. Maybe it's because Sharon is now 'unplugged', and he needs another friend to talk to. I am very, very curious to know who this Sharon person is. And whether she is a she, or a he? I don't mean in LGBTQI+ terms: sometimes criminals mix up their gender to put people off the track. Sharon may in fact be Pete or Sid. Billy has approached more than one male figure in anticipation of a 'party'. (It still makes me shudder to think about the implications of that.) Technology has caused an explosion of predatory people coming forward to harm children.

'I have some interesting news of my own,' Fitzroy says.

It transpires that Fitzroy has located Billy's original social worker, a man called Joseph who left the children's social services soon after he worked on Billy's case.

'Now that's interesting. How did you find him, and what's he doing now?'

'I believe he's in the food industry.'

'Well that's quite a move from children's social care.'

Fitzroy chuckles. 'As is the army. Or perhaps not so much. No, I think Joseph runs a restaurant these days.'

'Mmm. That's nice.' I wonder what happened to make him jump ship like that. Whether it was a specific incident, or collective pressure; or indeed whether it was connected to the Blackthorn case in any way. That's enough of my Miss Marple for today. I feel quite tired after that level of thinking.

'Anyway, we'll find out, I hope. I've arranged to meet Joseph at a service station to talk about the Blackthorn case in a little bit more detail.'

I have to say that part of me loves situations like this. I enjoy mystery and suspense. I love detective work and think if I hadn't gone to Art School and scratched that itch, I would have loved to have been a detective. On another, perhaps more realistic level, I understand that I'm probably the last person to fit into the police force, given how much compliance is required to do that level of work. I do admire the police. I know they sometimes get a bad press, but perhaps that also partly corresponds to the amount of money that has stopped going into the police budget. Anyway, another topic on which I probably shouldn't be allowed to get started.

'Ooh, good. When?'

Fitzroy is going to meet Joseph in two days' time, and I can't wait.

'Let me know all about it as soon as you've finished your meeting, won't you?'

'Louise, you are as bad as my wife.'

I smile. I trust that Mrs Bright is a good woman and, like me, does not suffer fools gladly.

The rest of the day passes without incident. The children are soon back from school. The evenings are becoming incrementally lighter. By 4.45pm it doesn't seem quite as dark as it has done of late, so optimism is a natural emotion right now.

I leave Billy with Lloyd for a short while, in order to drop Jackson off at his rugby training. As we get into the car, I realise how much I have missed him. How much I am missing out on with my family. Billy takes up all my time, and having a school-age child not attending school is way more than I signed up for.

Andi, who hasn't been good for much so far, has passed on another piece of information that she thought I'd be 'pleased to know about', because it's 'something they can do to support my particular context'. Other foster carers, who have some time, can apparently take a child out or stay in the home with the child to offer a babysitting service.

I'm afraid I rolled my eyes when I thought of all the stupidity and ignorance that has been ploughed into this latest scheme. So, a foster carer who is calm and sorted in their placement is then asked to step up and help other foster carers. When a foster carer has a secure placement, that is a reflection of their hard work and dedication. The amount of time they have given to the child is probably what allows them to be good at their work. Time to sit down, time to have a bath, time to see your other children in your home. Don't take that away from them to give them 'babysitting' duties. When we went out to dinner a while ago before Billy's arrival – a rare treat indeed – we did what most parents do and spent the evening talking about the children, but hey, such is life. We used the services of an approved babysitter. For three hours we paid £40. So, if a foster carer like me with a few qualifications under my belt and a professional career is asked to step up to help another foster carer by looking after their foster child, I would effectively be working for nothing. That compounds the already messed-up view of who foster carers are and what they are capable of. It simply exploits foster carers further. I know Andi's suggestion is well intentioned, but it has just succeeded in making me cross. In spite of all that extra light in the day.

When I get back from rugby, Lloyd is looking a bit unsettled.

'What's wrong?' I ask.

Lloyd does his weird big eyes; a look that means, 'I want to say, but someone is here.'

I look around to see Billy under the butcher's block in the kitchen. It's a proper butcher's block that I got from a butcher's shop in Portsmouth years ago. I can see Billy's hand poking out, then a knee.

I ask Lloyd, innocently, 'Have you seen Billy?'

'No, not for a while.'

'Aaah, that's a shame,' I say, very deliberately. 'I was going to do sweetie bowls. I'll do one for Lily and Vincent, because they must have finished their homework. I'll have to wait to do Billy's until we find out where he is.'

I know that they haven't even started their homework, and this is partly my fault. I used to sit down with them and help, especially if it was art, English, history or RE. I am very much the humanities department in this house; Lloyd is everything else. With maths he tries his best, but they keep changing the methodology, making his knowledge, and all those other clever clogs who paid attention at school, somewhat out of date.

I knew that if I mentioned either Nutella or the sweetie bowl Billy would wriggle out from his hiding space. He pops up, looking as bright as a new penny. I decide not to ask Lloyd in front of him exactly why he has been under the butcher's block – and anyway, time is snatched away by Billy's enthusiasm to help fill the sweetie bowls. The sacred bowls for sweets are old picnic cups. Each of the children has their preferred colour and, unlike with the car where the eldest sits in the front, with sweetie bowls, it's the youngest who is in charge. It's a big rite of passage in this house, and is seen as a role of respect and maturity, even at five. I haven't previously asked Billy to oversee this ritual, and, if I'm honest, I suggested it as a way to get him out from under the butcher's block with minimal damage or, as they say in the insurance industry, 'risk limitation'. Anyway, it's a good way to test Billy's counting skills.

I almost cry with laughter as I watch him carefully set up three cups. He knows exactly what to do: he has seen this procedure performed by Vincent a number of times. He has a bag of Haribo and puts one in each cup, counting as he goes.

'One for Lily, one for Vincent' – there is a pause long enough for one to go in his mouth – and then, 'one for Billy's cup.' I like his style.

He also loves watching us smile and laugh at his endearing behaviour. He jumps up and down with glee, and dribbles.

'Could you carry Lily's and Vincent's sweetie bowls up to them?'

He's only too delighted to be of further assistance.

Once he has left the kitchen, I look at Lloyd. 'Are you going to talk me through what he was doing under there?'

Lloyd wrinkles his brow. 'Well, I'm not entirely sure. When you left I couldn't find him at all. I've been hunting all over the house. Eventually I discovered him there, but not long before you got back, if I'm honest.'

It dawns on me that Billy only feels safe with me. We have spent all our waking time together, and now he has attached himself to me entirely.

While that's very flattering on the one hand, I also feel a little stab of fear. Not fear for him, but for all of us if I don't think this through.

I clear a space in my studio to do some art with Billy. It has irked me that my usual method of using art as a way to relax the children I work with has failed thus far with Billy. I have only met this challenge in adults before. Those adults who, when they hear that I'm an artist, say, 'I can only draw stick men.' My standard response to that is, 'Yes, and a well-known artist called L.S. Lowry made a good living from doing just that.' It always depresses me that adults have somehow acquired the belief that they are not creative, or that art is how well you draw a bowl of fruit. I believe everyone is creative. I believe it's an instinct the same as eating, drinking and sleeping. I would go so far as to say that it is our education system that has eroded creative instinct, and a lot of that is related to opportunity. Or rather, lack of opportunity.

Billy is generally not encouraged into my studio. None of the children are, frankly; so the fact that I have invited him in is rather exciting. There is a code of conduct that I expect all children to adhere to while in here. I think these boundaries are important and help children learn to respect others' privacy, possessions and work as part of developing the most useful skill of all: emotional intelligence. I think that art can help with all of these. When you are involved in an activity that absorbs you, it is much easier to just be. The brain has a little holiday. I'm hoping that by inviting him into my 'sacred space', Billy will accept that invitation to a little holiday.

I have a pile of white party plates. I give Billy a pair of children's safety scissors and show him how to cut a triangle shape out of the plate. We glue the triangle onto the back of the plate to make a tail, and thus a fish. He gets it straight away, and is excited by his creation.

'Look 'Ouise, look.'

Like other young children, Billy struggles with the 'Lou' part of my name. I don't mind. I quite like being called 'Ouise.'

I have prepared several pots of paint in primary colours. I have, of course, taken the precaution of putting newspaper everywhere. We both colour in our fish, and I'm delighted that he doesn't look at mine to compare. This is the bit I was just referring to. He is not self-conscious; he just gets on with doing what he feels. It is a proper form of self-expression. This is all interesting, because he is often in such a heightened state of tension. I guess he feels safe. Safe in here, and safe with me, Doug, Dotty and Pablo the cat. All the animals are snuggled up in their bed by my other desk.

Because I put the little heater on by Billy, the paint is drying fairly quickly. This is good news for Billy, who is a long way from developing the art of patience. He doesn't have to wait long before he can stick the eyes on. I have a supply of googly eyes. He sticks one where most would put the mouth – but who cares, he has finished his mud-coloured masterpiece and is made up by the results of his artistic endeavour.

So, I have learnt that Master Billy's preferred mediums and methods are paint, cutting, and wonky eyes. That is progress.

When it is completely dry I will put it up in the most important gallery of all: the fridge gallery.

I decide that I can come back later and tidy all this up. I fancy a cup of tea, and this wonderful young artist needs to get his pyjamas on.

Billy is still busy playing with the dogs. Though he loves them, I know that he has no brakes, and if I don't keep him moving then something will be broken or hurt.

'Come along, Billy. Come along, Dotty and Doug.'

Neither he nor the dogs seem to be able to hear me. They are remarkably similar sometimes in their capacity for selective hearing. I resort to the oldest trick in the book. I turn out the light and begin to close the door to leave. The magic works. They are behind me and then out of my studio before two shakes of a cat's tail. Although not this particular cat. Pablo is still stretching, dancing to nobody's tune but his own.

In the light of day the next morning, I stand marvelling at the brown fish on the fridge.

'Come and look at what Billy did!'

The artist is revelling in his audience.

Lily is a bit fed up, though; she puffs out her cheeks. 'When are *we* going to do some art in your studio? We haven't for ages,' she whines.

Then Jackson says the same. Not Vincent, though. Art's a mug's game as far as he is concerned. As a Geezer, he can only talk about Banksy, and since he and his little 'too cool for school' crowd decided that Banksy was a corporation, he has also decided that art is either saddo-therapy or mega expensive street art. I resist the temptation to question his critique. Nevertheless, they are all generous with their enthusiasm for Billy's creation. I can see Billy glowing with pride.

The need for children to be seen and recognised for who they are is immense. If we can't give them that, then who are *we*?

Chapter Nineteen

The children are out at school, and I have enlisted Billy to help with the chores.

'Next job is to pick up the dog bowls from the floor so I can put them in to soak,' I say, indicating to Billy to pick them up. 'Their saliva makes the bowl sticky, so we need to make sure we give them a good wash.'

'Sticky licky, my fat dicky, suck suck, cum cum, in my bum bum.'

Oh no, here we go. Those aren't words that a five-year-old should know, let alone chant in a rhyme. This time I can't let it go. I pursue the conversation.

I may find out something useful for Fitzroy or the police, who still haven't asked to speak to Billy or many of the children yet. They've interviewed a few of the teenagers so far. Once the ugly teddies' communication devices were discovered, it must have been a great relief for them. They were able to talk more freely to the trained and experienced police and social workers.

I remember my adoptive mother told me, on the few days I did go to school, that she had installed a hidden camera in the classroom. She was watching my every move. Imagine how messed up that made me. I sat still, too scared to move. I never asked or answered questions in class in case I embarrassed her and myself with my stupidity. I believed her for years, and I'm not joking when I say that just *thinking* I was being watched made me so unhappy.

How much worse has it been for these Blackthorn children?

These children have not just been watched in their bedrooms, or wherever they were told to take the ugly teddy. They have been manipulated to cause harm and chaos, to break down the placement. What must it be like for little Billy, who is clearly happy and thriving and attached to me, to have to be instructed to hurt me and my family?

The more I think about it, the sicker it makes me.

Poor little boy. I feel rage surging across my body. The pressure they have put these children under is unforgivable, and I suspect this is just the tip of the iceberg. All I glean from Billy is that 'sticky licky, my fat dicky, suck suck, cum cum, in my bum bum' is linked with a game they played at the parties.

'Were these children's parties? Or parties with adults?'

I know the answer, of course, but I learn that not only were adults at these parties, but that they touched the child they wanted to 'play' with, which was the signal to go to a room. That's quite enough information for now. It's about as much as I can take, let alone Billy reliving it.

I know that Fitzroy is on his way to meet Joseph, the ex-social worker. Perhaps that will enlighten us further.

Next chore is the washing. As I pull Jackson's bedding out from the washing machine, Billy tells me that he does the washing at home.

'After a party the children have to wash the sheets.'

I feel sick again. We load up the tumble dryer and I ask Billy if he would like to make some more fish. He jumps up and down, dribble flying everywhere. I am suddenly hit by a bolt of lightning. The drooling, the dribble. I wonder if that is from having men's penises put in his little mouth for

273

sexual pleasure. Dear God, I hope not. I am raging. As soon as I am able, I need to add my hypothesis to Billy's notes, and when we eventually get the appointment for the specialist to look at Billy's rectum, I will tell him about the dribbling.

I cannot describe how I feel in this moment. I can see how children like Billy become demonised by society. I know it has gone on since forever, but it does not make it right, especially when we have so much knowledge about sexual abuse. Why the hell has it taken the police and children's social care so long to help these children?

It's a mystery. How does an adult or older child think it is *ever* okay to exploit the mind, body, innocence and trust of a child? Or, with knowledge of that act, to let it continue and do nothing?

This Joseph bloke has got some answering to do, as far as I am concerned.

I take Billy and the dogs out for the hill walk. He runs around in his usual zigzag, covering twice as much ground as me. The dogs happily follow. Today we see a rabbit.

'Bunny!' Billy points in amazement.

Even better, we see three deer shoot past us. The rabbits and the deer all have the same upright white tails. We talk about them all the way home. I see a missed call from Fitzroy. I make Billy a snack, Nutella toast and a few red grapes, and then I suggest *Toy Story 2* on DVD. We've lost number one, but I'm sure Billy will forgive me. I don't know how successful the grapes will be. He's seen the others eat them, so there's half a chance. Or he'll throw them somewhere, I don't know. But I do know I'm desperate to talk to Fitzroy. Lloyd is in his office chatting to a client. I take myself off into the kitchen, turn on the kettle and make the call.

The chuckle. 'Hello Louise, how are you?'

'I am good but, more importantly, how are you?'

Fitzroy tells me of the very useful meeting he has just had with Joseph.

I sit down at the table with my cup of tea and listen.

'He is a nice guy and, under the circumstances, it was good of him to meet me. He didn't have to, especially after what had happened to him.' He tells me how Joseph was a fairly new social worker when he came into contact with the Blackthorns. 'I remember how that feels: it's terrifying.'

He explains how Joseph had been asked to collect a new mum and take her back to the Blackthorn home. Billy's mum was young, perhaps 15 or 16, and Billy was not her first baby. When Joseph arrived at the house, he told me that he felt like he was carrying a sacrificial lamb into their kitchen. Apparently, the house was full of men. He described them as rough and tough looking.

'His exact words were, "Hillbillies meet Hell's Angels".'

He carries on with the story, how Joseph had been told by his manager to just hand over the paperwork and get out, and under no circumstances to engage in conversation.

'He remembers something very horrible at the end. On his way out of the house, this house of horror where he had left the mother and the baby against all his better instincts, he is convinced that he heard one man say, "When can I have a go?" Joseph was pretty sure that he didn't mean a cuddle.'

'Oh, no. That is truly sinister. If that means what I think it means.'

There is no need to spell it out any further.

'I have a terrible feeling that Billy has experienced a lot of sexual abuse,' I say. I realise that I'm crying. Tears spill down my face and onto my hand as I hold the handle of the teacup and steel myself to listen to whatever else Fitzroy has to say.

'He told me about two men who came to his front door *with guns*, Louise, warning him to back off. Joseph was scared. Well, who wouldn't be? He told his manager, who didn't take it seriously. He found his car burnt out in the car park. He told me that no one wanted to take the Blackthorn case seriously. He reported that a lock had been put on the Blackthorn file both online and physically. No one could access the file apart from his manager.'

I sit in horror as the scale of what has been going on for Billy and all the other children unfolds, and the reality takes hold of me.

'But how? I mean, how could they fit so many people and children in a house? Why were there only men? What about the mother? Where were the women?' I'm full of questions.

I'm not of the old belief that all women are soft and kind and know how to nurture. I had two domineering mothers of my own, so I know full well that isn't true.

'Look, as far as I can tell, the Blackthorns operated like some sort of mafia, and ran a small council estate near a very pretty village,' Fitzroy explains. 'A spurious safeguarding claim was made against him. Joseph's career was over, and the made-up allegation meant that his DBS (Disclosure and Barring Service check) prevented him from working in the industry again.'

'What a nightmare. How does he feel about what happened?'

'He said he'll never work in children's social care again, even if they paid him a fortune. He said he wouldn't trust them to look after a piece of bread.'

Chapter Twenty

We are back from another walk, and, as I am now Billy's teacher, I set him up with a BBC education programme, *Bitesize Daily*. It's very good and we like working our way through, and Billy loves doing well.

A few years ago, I bought some school exercise books from a car boot sale. It seemed an odd thing to be selling and I wondered if they were knock-offs, but I had several colours and kept them in the cupboard to use as notebooks. They have come in very handy as our home learning has evolved. For each subject I have given Billy a different book. I have also bought him a rucksack and drinks bottle to help with the idea of going to school (eventually). A few times we have walked the dogs in the morning at the same time as the school run, so Billy can get a good sense of what a school child does, especially ones about his age and height. He has a pencil case with a few pens and pencils in and a plastic ruler and rubber. I get him to work on the pages. I am trying to teach him the date and how to write his name. The yellow book is for this express purpose. It is called 'Billy Blackthorn', and every page so far has my writing at the top and his version underneath for the whole page. We have spent days crafting B I L L Y. I don't think we're ready for Blackthorn just yet.

But this is our routine.

I think, perhaps, that without the intervention of Sharon the Ugly Teddy, Billy might have managed to stay at Flatfields Primary School. But I can't know that for sure.

After a couple of months, his relationships are improving, and though his biggest bond remains with me, he gets on much better with the others now. Lily can still be a bit curt with him at times, but I think she's curt with all of us. It's her hormones. She is definitely doing brilliant eyerolls and door-slamming and full-on turn-on-the-heel hissy fits. My adoptive mother would have slapped me so hard round the face if I had even whispered under my breath what Lily can freely say to us. She has been back in contact with her birth father and, along with the time and input that Billy requires, her needs take me further and further away from Jackson and Vincent. I know they are safe and well, but it does not stop me from feeling guilty and afraid.

I'm scared of letting them down, and fostering is not easy at the best of times. But I've discovered that when your birth children need you, the foster children can sense it and act up even more, wanting to win in the fight for attention. Jackson likes a drive, so when Billy is in bed I drive him to the next town and back. He is quite easy to talk to, so by the time we get back on the last road he has generally told me what his concern is and how he feels about it. I offer some suggestions as he plugs in his phone, and we listen to his music and sing and have a laugh. When we had our New Year's Eve party, I was dancing away to Pulp's *Common People*, which is now on his playlist. That's sweet. Vincent is the most level-headed of all of them, if a bit eccentric at times, but then I think about who his mother is. It's in the genes. But I try hard to read him, too. I don't take any of their emotions for granted, and neither boy demands much attention.

I love Billy more and more. He's a treasure, but as each day goes by I know he needs more than I have to offer. God, it's hard to divide myself up evenly between them all. I think that's what's bothering me the most.

The window cleaners arrive. They usually come every six weeks or so, but because of the bad weather it's been a good few months since I last saw them. Rainwater is dirty water and would have ruined their good work. I must confess the inside could do with a bit of a clean, judging by those little smears that reveal themselves in a certain light. That will have to be a spring-cleaning job when the evenings are light and I can open the windows without them blowing off.

They appear at the sitting room window, announced by a chorus of cheerful whistles with their long ladders clanking against the brickwork of the house. They are a lovely bunch, always say hello. A mass of beards and beanies and thick lumberjack shirts under waterproofs. I look up and wave.

Billy sits frozen to the spot.

He begins to shake. He leaps up from the sofa and begins to walk in circles.

'Please no party, please no party, I'll be good. Please no party.'

I hold his hand and lead him into the kitchen, but he is too far into his fear and trauma. He runs into the conservatory, picks up Lloyd's Dr Martin boot by the backdoor, and hurls it straight at the glass. A panel of the garden room smashes in an instant. Tiny shards of glass everywhere.

It all happens so quickly.

Lloyd comes tearing out of his office. 'What's wrong? What's happened?'

Billy is beside himself.

Before I have a chance to understand what he's doing, he scoops up several lethal-looking glass shards. In a split second they are in his mouth and he is crunching on glass.

I freeze. Lloyd is as shocked as me. I literally don't know what to do, but two tall adults standing there with faces like theatrical tragedy masks is not going to help.

I usher Lloyd out of the door.

'Grab the kitchen roll, and a dustpan and brush.'

I always try to recall our training, our resilience training. But frankly, that disappears in the heat of the moment and what kicks in is human instinct. What comes to mind is all the films I've ever seen where someone is talked down from jumping off a roof or a bridge. I crouch down and pick up the boot.

'Would you like to give me the glass that's in your mouth?'

He crunches down. A trickle of blood appears at the corner of his mouth.

How did he know how to do this? Why did he even *think* of doing this? Why did he need to do this?

My eyes are watering. I don't know when I've ever felt so impotent.

From behind me, Lloyd appears, not with the kitchen roll and dustpan and brush, but with a jar of Nutella, some chocolate cereal and an ice-lolly. Brilliant.

Billy's face shifts back to the Billy from before. It's a total metamorphosis.

He slowly spits out three pieces of blood-glass.

Before he tucks into all things chocolate and sugary, I get him to swish his mouth out with water, cross my fingers and hope for the best.

Peace is restored.

An uneasy peace, but it will do for now. I settle Billy down with a film and a blanket, hoping to restore some of that energy he lost earlier. I know that we should probably take him straight to casualty, but I don't think he could cope with a wait of several hours, and I certainly don't want to be doing that with Billy Blackthorn. Imagine.

He tucks into the entrée for the worst sugar rush in history and begins humming, with his eyes closed. He can't be in too much pain or he wouldn't be able to do that. When the ice-lolly has been reduced to a mere dripping trail of syrup across the sofa, he finally lets me look into his mouth. I feel ill and I'm still shaking from the horror of watching him eat glass, but I try to steady my hands for the job.

The blood evidently looked worse than it was. I can only see a small cut. Still, poor child. I wonder what horrible memories those window cleaners dredged up for him. It must have been their appearance that caused his behaviour. It can't be anything else. His behavioural change was like an allergic reaction. I think for a minute. In the dark recesses of my brain, back in the time of BB, Before Billy, when I still had time to listen to such things, I'm sure I heard someone discussing allergic reactions on *Woman's Hour* or the *The Food Programme* on Radio 4. The common ones I remember being discussed were almonds and avocado, I'm sure. He's clearly not allergic to nuts, judging by his love of Nutella. I do remember him eyeing up Lily's crushed avocado on posh toast with a swish of lemon, a flick of sea salt and shake of pepper this morning. Lily's nod to her dream future life, though I know if I had given her that she would have turned up her nose, but because she made it it's the best thing ever. Even so, that can't have been what caused him to react like that. It must have been the window cleaners. Something triggering about their appearance. When he's properly settled later I'll explain who the window cleaners are and what they do. I don't want to make him think about them again yet.

I see a missed call from Fitzroy.

I leave Billy for a moment, leaving Lloyd to hover nearby, but I'm certain the storm has passed. I sit down at the kitchen table to call Fitzroy back, but he beats me to it. I slide the green button across.

'Hello Louise, and how are you today?'

I give him a quick summary of the window cleaner event and we debate possible triggers, working our way back round the circle to the beginning with heavy hearts. Fitzroy's army background has put him in good stead for a case like the Blackthorns. He is strategic and manages expectations brilliantly. I continue to find his manner impressive. He is reassuring and in control, while being totally kind and human at the same time. It's a winning formula.

'I have done a little bit more digging around,' he tells me. He explains that, in spite of the restrictions, he managed to get into the Blackthorn file via another tech root. I have no doubt that when we met, he must quickly have realised my limitations with technology in terms of both skill and interest, so he skips the detail.

'But I managed to make a copy and study it at home. It's an astonishing collection of documents. Pages and pages of records of concern. Claims of sexual abuse. Neglect. Copies of emails, notes from telephone calls: it goes on and on.'

'So why the hell wasn't anything done about it?'

'The problem was that hardly any met the apparent benchmark, and those that did rise above the bar were all "unsubstantiated".'

'But how could that be?'

'It really is just like talking to my wife. Hold your horses,' he chuckles.

I do my best to wait patiently without interrupting as he explains.

'I spoke to the police and they were just as confused, and it raised suspicion. Had they arrested the right Blackthorns, for example? It turns out that Joseph's manager from five years ago is now the Area Coordinator. She is, or I should say she was, until a few hours ago, my boss.'

'But, no more?' I ask, intrigued and butting in, in spite of myself.

'No more. She was arrested, along with a police officer from Child Protection.'

'Why?' None of this makes any sense.

'Because they are both Blackthorn family members who were protecting the clan.'

I stare at the phone in a state of disbelief.

I'm desperate to tell Lloyd.

He must have heard my gasps from the sitting room and has stepped away from his supervisory post. He pulls out a chair, sits down and makes a questioning face.

'Fitzroy,' I mouth back. My face must be registering the shock I feel at his revelations.

'Can I put you on speaker, Fitzroy? Lloyd's here.'

'No. No. I wouldn't recommend that. You'll see why in a minute.'

I shake my head at Lloyd, and so he's left trying to deduce what's going on from my reactions. And it gets worse. So much worse. So much scarier and darker than we dared to let ourselves think. Fitzroy carries on explaining about the Blackthorn setup.

'The community was divided up into different areas. One area was the children's. They lived in two or three of the houses, which appear to have been set up like dormitories. The men operated various criminal activities, mainly protecting the enterprise of four of the Blackthorn women. The women brought the children up to be in porn films, some extremely hardcore. They had exclusive parties for those who could afford it, to spend an evening with a child.'

'Hence Billy's references to, and fear of, parties.'

The next bit is truly horrible. Fitzroy tells me how the main event, and the most expensive, involved babies. Films of adults doing unmentionable things with babies who appeared to be just days old.

The bile comes up from my stomach into my mouth.

I run to the sink, just in time to move the washing up bowl out of the way before I'm sick.

When I get back to Fitzroy, he apologises. 'That's why I was trying to tell you slowly.'

I have turned completely white, and I stay that colour for the rest of the day. Lloyd still doesn't know what I heard, but he knows it was bad. I know that I am going to be ill all over again when I tell him later.

'So, it turns out that it was the Blackthorn women who were at the top of the tree,' he continues, checking first that I'm ready to hear more. 'The women were breeding children to use them for these *evil* purposes. Ultimately as a money-making enterprise.'

I feel sick again.

I take the phone with me to the sink and pour a glass of water. It makes me feel worse. I vomit again. I take several deep breaths and pick up the conversation.

'Who the hell are these bitches?' I demand to know.

Fitzroy assures me that when this comes out, the whole

world will know. 'But at the moment the investigation is ongoing. Believe it or not, it may be that Billy is one of the lucky ones.'

'Lucky? What do you mean, "lucky"?' An image of a five-year-old boy crunching down on glass flashes unbidden back into my mind.

'There is grave concern for the whereabouts of some children. The files were re-examined and the descriptions and dates don't all match the children now in care. We are missing some children.'

'What do you think has happened to them?'

Fitzroy sighs. It's with despair. 'We don't know. Because they were tipped off, because they knew that the police were coming, there are more children somewhere. There are back routes from their homes onto the main roads.'

There is still so much to piece together, but it's unbelievable to think that there are still children out there who are going through what Billy and his siblings did. And I am having some lightbulb moments as I think about 'Sharon' and the antics of the Blackthorn children controlled through communication devices in the teddies.

'So, they wanted those children back, yes. Not because they were to be reunited with their birth mothers, but because they were business. Those children were making them very rich.'

Fitzroy sighs again.

I still have so many questions, but our main priority is the children. The ones we know about, and the ones we don't know the whereabouts of.

I sit down and feel a little better, breathing slowly to steady myself.

Lloyd still doesn't know, so I ask Fitzroy if he can bring Lloyd up to speed. 'I don't think I can say some of the things you just told me.'

Fitzroy understands, so I disappear to check on Billy while I leave them to it. As I walk into the sitting room I feel my ribs expanding, filled with love for this little boy and all he has had to endure. What a child. I look at him, and think back to all our times together. All the times I have not wanted to take him out in public. Even this morning, not wanting to take him to casualty because of how hard it is to be with him when there are other people around. And no wonder. He has existed in a parallel universe to mine for most of his life.

I am overwhelmed by all the complicated emotions I feel, but I'm fired up to fight for everything he now needs in order to reclaim his life.

Meanwhile, the beautiful curly-haired child is lying on a blanket on the floor. He has his chin in his hands, elbows on the blanket, engrossed in his film, chilled out. I want to wrap him up in that blanket and never let him go.

For now, I leave him watching his film.

Back in the kitchen, Lloyd is looking a bit peaky. He hands the phone back to me.

'How far did you get?' I say into the receiver.

'Lloyd is level with you now, so I'll tell you what we think and I'm sure you will agree it is the best plan. Given the explicit nature of the footage the police have seen, we have appointed a team of psychologists and other experts to an emergency multi-agency meeting. The sexual and emotional abuse of all the children is so severe that they will all require deep therapeutic support. That's twenty-four hours a day.'

'Thank God,' I say. They will get what they need. Finally.

'The group also decided that, for now, they all need to be placed separately rather than being reunited. So far, they have all been okay with being separated, it seems. Some are even thriving, like Billy. It's going to be hard, but we have to prepare all the children for the next stage.'

I feel bereft.

I don't know what to think or do.

Like me, Lloyd is still pale, and so sad-looking. I don't think I've seen Lloyd affected like this before. I know that I have never been affected like this before. All that pain, all that misery. And for what? Some sick, evil, perverted fantasies. It's a cruel world.

I'm in two places, two minds. I'm relieved because the decision for the next stage with Billy has been taken out of our hands. And it's the right thing. But we've all fallen for Billy, especially me. I want to keep hold of him, continue the good that I know we're doing for him. But having Billy here as a long-term placement would not be in the best interests of the other children. It's all for the best. It's just hard.

I've been impressed with Fitzroy all along. He's a marvel. But I now have renewed respect for the local authority and the police. They all had the wool skilfully pulled over their eyes for years because their institutions were infiltrated by criminals. Joseph questioned it and, even though he had to leave because of it, he had had the courage to begin to challenge it.

It takes a long, long time for the dust to settle back around our lives after they have been touched by Billy and his story.

Epilogue

In the end, Billy stayed with us for another three months, and then all the Blackthorn children left as swiftly as they arrived. It wasn't dramatic, or even too emotionally challenging. It was calm and gracious. After knowing what had happened to these children, no one was parenting them according to the rules and training. Instead, there was so much love for them. They were special. What we were doing for them was special. The Blackthorn Amigos were special. The foster carers were dazed and confused by these children's circumstances and, if it hadn't been for our WhatsApp group, I think we would all have struggled even more than we did.

The plan for all the children to be looked after by a team of trained professionals around the clock came to fruition. Their education was geared to try and get the children on the rungs of the ladder to a better life. Billy spent three years in his unit. I went to visit in the early days. I'm still not sure if it was a good idea. His key worker reported back that he was upset when I left. I was upset too. I had to pull the car over and cry. I so desperately wanted to keep on being in Billy's life, but I knew I had to look at the bigger picture.

He did well, as I knew he would. Over time, he was able to build attachments and have his skewed view of the world straightened out enough for him to go back into foster care. He was given a long-term placement with a couple whose children had long since flown the nest. One of the foster carers had professional experience of working with sexually exploited children.

Billy eventually got his hospital appointments. The medical treatments he underwent added to the severity of his need for therapeutic support. How does a child deal with all that? How does a child grow up to become an adult, knowing that adults abused them as a child?

Billy's story helped me further understand my own relationship with the abuse I experienced as a child. My childhood abuses were severe, but nothing that compares with the scale of the Blackthorn operation. Evil profiteering from the flesh of innocent children. I remember being concerned by how highly sexualised some of Billy's behaviour was. Because of what was done to him and the way he was groomed to behave, I maintain now that no matter what he was forced to do, he remains innocent.

Billy began to do well academically. He grew to love art (no doubt it was that muddy fish!), it eventually became an area in which he was able to let go. He was also very good at maths, and ended up in the top set for lots of subjects. I don't know exactly what they did for Billy in those three years at the unit, but whatever it was, it certainly helped.

Sadly, it didn't work out the same way for all the Blackthorns. A few of the teenagers ran away, found their previous abusers, and went back to that life. It's distressing how many teenagers do this. It's the hard part of fostering and adoption. Children boomerang, often when they reach the mid-teenage point in their development, at around 14 or 15 years of age. Perhaps it happens at the moment that they begin to see just how much hard work is needed to create a life, and heal from their past. Perhaps it all seems too much.

I think that some bottle it. They opt to lie on the sofa and avoid life. Some, like Billy, thrive in care. His care plan was brilliant and well thought through in the end. He benefitted greatly from his care experience.

It took us a while to move on from Billy. We had a break from fostering for a few months, and it was a good idea. There was a lot to 'process', I suppose. We had never before, and hopefully never will, experience anything like that again.

To the best of my knowledge, Billy is thriving still.

Afterword

I'm so glad that Billy got the support that he needed, but I remain aggrieved that there is no therapy or support for foster carers. Even in situations as diabolical as this one was, we just have to get on with it, performing like robots. Luckily, in this instance, we had that Blackthorn WhatsApp group. It was a lifeline. We needed each other. I remember sitting up for hours with Martin after the allegation against him was finally dropped. It took six months. I find that unforgivable, and it has left a dark shadow over his life.

I'm still fighting flood issues. Myself and some of my community have set up our own flood resilience group and we are determined to bring to account the individuals and organisations responsible for repeatedly flooding a community.

More horrors were eventually exposed from the Blackthorn setup. Even though 'Sharon' was giving commands to the children through the ugly teddies, there was no kind of gender equality within the hierarchy of the Blackthorn family. In many ways, girls in the Blackthorn family might be compared with girls within the Taliban. During its five-year rule in Afghanistan between 1996 and 2001, the Taliban became synonymous with misogyny and violence against women. They claimed that this was born of the desire to create a secure environment to protect the chasteness and dignity of women. This translates into women not being granted autonomy over their own lives. The same was true of the Blackthorn women, like Jade and her siblings. Except that there was no claim to chasteness and dignity for them.

Far from it, in fact.

Their bodies were not their own; instead, they were owned by the men in the Blackthorn family. The older women and mothers in the family had a strong sense of obedience and compliance to the men, even to their teenage sons – which translated into disloyalty towards the children. Incest was an accepted part of their way of life, and outsiders' views on that were not welcome. Actually, outsiders' views were held with hostile contempt.

It was never quite worked out who Billy's father was. The question of paternal responsibility was an alien idea to the Blackthorn family. The fathers generally went without the knowledge of whether or not they were fathers of the many children. Given the strange setup, it was often impossible to know exactly when children were conceived. Jade never wanted any of her babies. It was simply her 'turn'. The younger Blackthorn girls served the male sexual appetites, while the older women ran the businesses. The younger girls had no status. And no future. Boys, though, were celebrated as men when they became teenagers and turned 13. Part of the rite of passage was for them to have sex in front of the other men with one of the women. It didn't matter which. Familial relationships were mostly ignored, so it might be an aunt or a sister who was chosen. No ceremony involved. The men gathered round to offer their 'encouragement', usually in the form of cheering or a running commentary. Sometimes that encouragement was physical: a grope or a slap to help out. If you didn't know what was happening, you might mistake the scene for a crowd of fans at a WWE wrestling match. And of course, a 13-year-old hasn't much idea of what he's doing, moving to the jeers and cries of the crowd. It doesn't bear thinking about.

Jade probably began her life just as her own babies did, trapped in a horrible cycle of abuse that was allowed to go on for years. Jade's life was shit, utterly shit, but in many ways she had very little idea quite how awful it was. Human beings are quite adaptable. She had learned, like the other women around her, to accept what appeared to be 'normal'. She was an innocent child among wolves. And nobody did anything about it.

We must perhaps ask quite how Billy's family became such an enigma within the community in the first place. One of the consequences, of course, being that the estate became off-limits for the local authority and even the police.

I wish that, in the twenty-first century, things like this no longer happened. But abuse like the Blackthorns inflicted comes as the result of supply and demand. The realist in me knows that there always has been, and always will be, a taste for sexually abusing children, and the unregulated porn industry has a huge part to play. All we can do is be vigilant and absolute in our views that pornography is exploitation, no matter how you look at it.

Let us not be fooled into thinking that Billy's family are the only ones to blame in this tale. They are the perpetrators, no doubt. Yet we should apportion some of the blame to those in positions of trust and authority who choose the path of least resistance, even when they can see that wrongs are being done. Specifically, blame should fall on those who undertake unscrupulous practices instead of doing right by those in their care.

Children's social care should be about early intervention and prevention. Instead, we have a system that contains children until they're old enough to go to youth offending units and then prison. A system that involves private companies profiteering from the misery that these ruptures cause. I am convinced it's a form of child farming for profits, because the youth offending units are also run by private companies, the same companies who offer 'solutions' for children earlier in the system, often with a different name. Children's social care should never have been allowed to be privatised. These people's Bentleys and Aston Martins are bought with the money that should be helping children to have a good chance at life. That simply doesn't happen, no matter what their websites say. That's what I mean by child farming: keep them unhappy, keep them in care.

I have it on good authority that the local social workers have been warned to keep away from me because I write books about children in the care system, and that makes me dangerous. Still, I remain good friends with Dara. I'm delighted that she wanted to continue our friendship once her professional responsibilities were dispensed with.

And I meant what I said about having newfound respect for the local authority after the final decisions about the Blackthorn care plan were implemented. I love that people like Joseph and Fitzroy and Dara operate in the profession. I just hope that there is one Fitzroy for every corrupt Amber. Between us, we'll do our very best to continue to shine light into the lives of as many children as we can.

Louise Allen

Acknowledgements

These books are never easy to write – my heart is broken again with each one. Sometimes I need a laugh or a reminder of why I do it. I want to thank Theresa Gooda who has become a great ally offering good advice and the occasional silly text that makes me smile. I would not be able to write my books without the support and commitment from my publisher Welbeck and my editor Beth Bishop. Jane Graham-Maw is my agent who always has my back.

My family who, as you know, are as much a part of each story as the foster children who we welcome into our home as I am: Lloyd, Jackson, Lily, C, Millie Mitchell and wee little Maeve.

I am incredibly grateful to our trio of alpha readers: Catherine Lloyd, Alexandra Plowman and Karen Furse, for all their insights into early drafts of the manuscript. I would also like to thank Annamarie Smith who has joined our reader team.